THE UNKNOWN CIVIL WAR

THE UNKNOWN CIVIL WAR

ODD,
PECULIAR,
AND UNUSUAL
STORIES OF THE
WAR BETWEEN
THE STATES

WEBB GARRISON

CUMBERLAND HOUSE
NASHVILLE, TENNESSEE

Published by
CUMBERLAND HOUSE PUBLISHING, INC.
431 Harding Industrial Drive
Nashville, Tennessee 37211
www.cumberlandhouse.com

Cover design by Gore Studio, Nashville, Tennessee

Library of Congress Cataloging-in-Publication Data

Garrison, Webb B.
    The unknown Civil War : odd, peculiar, and unusual stories from the War between the States / Webb Garrison.
        p.   cm.
    Includes bibliographical references (p.) and index.
    ISBN 1-58182-122-0 (alk. paper)
       1. United States—History—Civil War, 1861–1865—Anecdotes. I. Title.
E655.G38 2000
973.7—dc21   00-043085

Printed in the United States of America
  2 3 4 5 6 7 8—04 03 02

to my children
Carol, Bill, and Webb
and their spouses
Mary and Cheryl

INTRODUCTION

THOUSANDS OF WELL-ACCEPTED bits of information stem from the approximately fourteen hundred days during which the North and the South devoted all their available manpower and resources to attain military victory. A comparatively small percentage of these facts, however, is generally acknowledged to be incomplete. Likewise, much is known about the leaders of this war, but there is also much that is not known. For example, it's well known that Abraham Lincoln's mother, Nancy Hanks, was herself illegitimate. Little is known of her parents, and we have no little information on how Lincoln reacted to this gap in his knowledge of his heritage. We do know that the sixteenth president believed that he might somehow be a descendant of Thomas Jefferson in more ways than political (see pages 60–64).

The realization that Lincoln had unanswered questions about his lineage leads us toward the perception that there are a great many instances in which our general and common knowledge of the people and events of this war can become avenues for new lines of inquiry. Thus this book has taken shape out of a fresh evaluation of many assumptions about the war and generally accepted notions of the personalities involved.

One of the most famous documents of the war is Robert E. Lee's Lost Order, which was found wrapped around three cigars prior to the battle of Antietam and delivered into the hands of the Federal commander, George B. McClellan. The identity of the subordinate who misplaced the orders is unknown, other than his penchant for tobacco (and there are some intriguing

articles lately that try to identify this person). That the commander of the Army of Northern Virginia modified his battle plans
when he discovered that the enemy knew them in detail is generally assumed. Yet nothing in Lee's correspondence or reports
indicates when he learned of the loss, McClellan's discovery, or
what he did about it and when.

Although not as strategic to the war effort as Lee's Lost
Order, Jesse D. Bright is an interesting footnote to the history of
the war. Bright was a U.S. Senator from Indiana and was the only
Union senator to be expelled from Congress during the war.
Many leave the matter at that, but a search for the reasons behind
Bright's expulsion leads one down some interesting alleys.

There are many matters that have not been scrutinized
beyond a simple glimpse, many facts that have been accepted
unquestioningly, perhaps because they are easily eclipsed by
the overarcing story of the sectional war between countrymen.
In virtually every field—and perhaps one of the reasons why
the Civil War continues to captivate the imagination of suc-
ceeding generations—new eyes discover new instances in
which long-held interpretations have overlooked some aspect
of the war experience.

That was the case when a young woman asked how we know
that the fatal wounding of Stonewall Jackson at Chancellorsville
was accidental. This simple question gave a hard yank to the
chain of many scholars of the Civil War. Although the accidental
"friendly fire" by Tar Heel troops has rarely, if ever, been questioned, when the matter was investigated, it was found that the
earliest first-person account of the fatal incident did not treat it
as accidental.

To deal effectively with the apparently ridiculous question
posed by this relatively new student of the war, it was necessary
to scrutinize several variables in the account of Jackson's wounding. The vast majority of Civil War scholars never considered the
possibility that Lee's losing his "Right Arm" stemmed from an act
that a century later become known as "fragging," or killing an
officer during combat in such a way that the casualty is assumed
to be a result of war. This unusual perspective on Jackson's

wounding might not have been considered had it not been for an interested and untainted new scholar of the war.

Few of the novel viewpoints discussed here are as complex as the matter of Jackson's wounding. Several, however, may serve to provoke new thought and reevaluate the assumptions that many make about the war. We are far from having all the answers.

This volume offers some—but far from all—results of one lifelong Civil War devotee's inquiries into a variety of events. Hopefully, it will stimulate more questions than answers.

CHAPTER ONE

SHENANIGANS & SNAFUS

LOTS OF MARYLANDERS DIDN'T HAVE A CHOICE

As SOON as the war began in Charleston Harbor, strategists on both sides took a hard look at Maryland. Although slavery was legal there, nine people out of ten in the state were free. Most of those who lived in western Maryland were intent on saving the Union, but it was a different story in Baltimore and the eastern precincts of the state. Shiploads of dry goods made in the North flowed to the South through the port of Baltimore, and ties with the Cotton Belt were so strong that a Secessionist might be behind any stump. Maryland could go either way—and the political leaders of both North and South knew it.

Maybe Confederate president Jefferson Davis didn't want to stir up any more trouble than he already had on his hands. Maybe he just couldn't devise a workable scheme for bringing

Northern cartoonists who ridiculed Lincoln said his great height caused his body to need frequent oiling to supplement poor circulation of his blood.

Maryland into the fold of the Confederacy, right behind North Carolina, making a round dozen Rebel states. For whatever reason, he did very little as precious weeks passed in April and May 1861.

Less than a hundred miles away, there was a fellow whom several Yankee newspapers joked about when they were not criticizing his every move. It would be a little while before anyone caught on to the fact that the Northern president—referred to disparagingly by some as "the Original Gorilla"—was not cut from the same bolt of cloth as his Confederate counterpart.

As he reviewed the situation and concluded that Maryland must stay in the Union, Abraham Lincoln's actions left thousands of Marylanders with no choice.

Lincoln dispatched Gen. Benjamin F. Butler to Baltimore and said nothing when Butler seized Federal Hill and turned its guns toward the city.

That was only the beginning of a series of actions designed to prevent the North from having to drag another state back into the fold. To this day, no one knows for certain who suggested that the Maryland legislature be knocked out of action for a while. If Lincoln didn't hatch the plot, he sure didn't do anything to halt its execution. Soldiers in blue began knocking on doors and detaining quite a few prominent Baltimoreans. Among their prisoners were nineteen Maryland legislators, the mayor of Baltimore, and police chief George P. Kane—all of whom were imprisoned (and isolated) at Fort McHenry.

Union Gen. Benjamin F. Butler seized Federal Hill in Baltimore and put the city under its guns.

HARPER'S PICTORIAL HISTORY OF THE GREAT REBELLION

Ordinarily, a writ of habeas corpus would have facilitated a prisoner's release after an overnight detention. Such was not the case in Baltimore. Lincoln suspended the writ of habeas corpus "on a line between Washington and Baltimore." That meant that those officials who were behind bars stayed there without being charged. These Secessionists and their sympathizers were never tried and eventually were released. But by the time they were back on the streets, it was too late for the legislature to act. Strong Unionists had been installed in many key positions. On Federal Hill, Butler's guns were still trained upon the city, double-shotted and ready for action.

For the duration of the war, for every two Marylanders who signed up to fight for the Union, one of their neighbors slipped across the border into Virginia and fought beneath the Confederate banner. That reality didn't change the political power structure a bit, though. Maryland might have stayed in the Union if Lincoln hadn't acted. Since he did, the Border State was guaranteed to remain in the Union as a result of a cunning series of masterstrokes so powerful, there was no way they could be reversed.

NEW ENGLAND GRANITE WILL BOTTLE 'EM UP!

THE DEPARTURE of the strangest fleet ever assembled at Hampton Roads, Virginia, took place in September 1861. The *Albarado, South Wind, Friendship,* and twenty-three other decrepit whaling

Part of the granite-laden vessels that made up the Great Stone Fleet.

vessels embarked and charted a southern course. All were loaded to the gunwales with scrap granite from the quarries of New England. Those who knew what cargo the vessels carried might have wondered if Washington had decided to build another artificial island like the one on which Fort Sumter sat.

Such was not the case, however. There was nary a gun aboard, but in the eyes of the Federal secretary of the navy, Gideon Welles, the fleet of old tubs was an armada of warships that would bottle up several Rebel ports. Some of these odd vessels foundered at sea, and others fell behind schedule. Still, on November 15, 1861, three of the schooners arrived at their destination and assumed their posts in Ocracoke Sound, North Carolina—squarely on the bottom. The goal of the little stone fleet was to block the main channels of strategic Southern ports.

By that time purchasing agents were scouring North Atlantic ports for more hulks. They were under orders to buy twenty-five "of not less than 250 tons each." This time the target was Savannah. Twenty more were acquired for use at Charleston. Long before these vessels came close to their destinations in Georgia and South Carolina, however, fast-moving currents had scoured much of the bottom sand in the North Carolina sounds so that, despite the sunken obstacles, Southern shipping resumed and carried on as usual.

Federal plans hit another snag at Savannah, where it was found that two rivers instead of one would have to be blocked. By the time the men on the spot decided the plan would not work in Georgia waters, several of the granite-bearers had sunk under their own weight.

Sixteen of the remaining were picked to launch the operation against Charleston, and fifteen of them made it to the harbor. Their masts were cut off, and then they were sunk along a thirty-five-hundred-foot pathway in the main channel. Fourteen more were towed into position and sunk on January 20, 1862.

The obstruction at Charleston was complete, exultant naval officers reported. In Washington, Welles calculated that "better than [twenty million] pounds of granite had put an end to blockade running at the port where the war began."

Welles was a first-rate newspaper editor before the war, but he'd never heard of *toredos*—little marine worms that gorge on a

Although some vessels failed to go down at the first attempt, all of them eventually took their cargoes of stone to the bottom.

ship's rotting wood beneath the water line. An untold number of these voracious little creatures had a feast at Charleston. By the time the worms and the tides got through with the Great Stone Fleet, Charleston's channel had moved a few feet northward and was deeper than ever. Blockade-runners scooted in and out with no deterrent except the Federal fleet that had to be moved into position around the harbor.

SOME FIGURED A FINGER WAS A SMALL PRICE TO PAY

WHEN LINCOLN first called for seventy-five thousand men, many Yankees responded enthusiastically. They didn't believe the war would last very long, and they all wanted a piece of the action. Down south, fellows had been hoping for years to get a chance to take a shot at a few Yankees. So both sides had all the men they could use and more for the first few months of the conflict.

The urge to fight for God and country began to quiet down when both sides started telling their people that the men were going to get into uniform whether they liked it or not. Not much if anything was said about draft dodgers, but there were plenty of them. Many a man picked in a draft lottery thought things over and decided that a finger was a small price to pay for saving his hide. So, in an effort to evade the draft, several potential soldiers whacked off a pinkie rather than fight.

That dodge didn't always work, though, when the need for men became acute. Cutting off a little finger might not do the job if the state was behind on its quota of men. Long before it was over, Johnny Reb and Billy Yank both understood that they had to chop off a trigger finger or shoot off a big toe if they didn't want to fight. Even when recruiting officers were scraping the bottom of the barrel, they wouldn't sign up a man who couldn't use a gun or couldn't keep his balance when he marched. North and south, a heap of fellows played "doctor" long enough to do a little amputation job and were still hale and hearty when the corpses began arriving with every train or wagon that rolled into town.

JOHNNY REB'S BATTLE FLAG JUST AIN'T RIGHT

THE CONFEDERATE Congress adopted the Stars and Bars flag on March 4, 1861. It was made up of two red stripes separated by a white stripe and seven white stars in a circle on a blue field in the upper corner. Prof. Nicolla Marschall designed it, and he knew what he was doing. Each star represented one of the states that had seceded: South Carolina, Mississippi, Florida, Alabama, Georgia, Louisiana, and Texas.

In the heat of battle at First Manassas (also known as Bull Run), several soldiers confused this flag with the Stars and Stripes. Gen. Pierre Gustave Toutant Beauregard—often called Old

When the Confederates charged Cemetery Hill at Gettysburg on the evening of July 2, 1863, Kentucky and Missouri were symbolically present on the battle flag although neither of them ever belonged to the Confederacy.

THE SOLDIER IN OUR CIVIL WAR

Bory—who led the Confederate army to victory there on July 21, 1861, set out to clear up the confusion and wound up with a dandy new emblem. A blue Saint Andrew's cross shaped like a big *X* on his flag was festooned with thirteen stars, since the Confederacy had grown with the addition of a few more seceded states by then. It's Old Bory's flag that has caused such a ruckus recently in South Carolina, Mississippi, and Georgia.

One of the questions about the flag, however, is that the Confederacy had only eleven states. Why, then, were there thirteen stars on Beauregard's banner?

After the first seven states left the Union and formed the Provisional Confederate States, only four more followed: Virginia, Arkansas, Tennessee, and North Carolina. A grand total of eleven, not thirteen.

The answer lies in the Border States. For a while in 1861 it looked as if the Rebels would take over Kentucky and Missouri, even though the Blue Grass legislature voted for neutrality. Secessionists in these states, however, soon found that they were outnumbered. In Kentucky the Secessionists elected a governor of their own, but he only lasted a few months.

West of the Mississippi was a different patch of corn. Gov. Claiborne F. Jackson tried to steer Missouri into the Southern fold and even claimed to have reestablished the state capital at Neosho. His legislators passed an ordinance of secession, but it was a case of too little too late. Backed by fighting men in blue, a new legislature met in Jefferson City and voted to stay in the Union and get rid of Jackson.

About 25,000 Blue Grass Rebels did fight for the South, but the blue uniforms worn by fellow Kentuckians outnumbered them by three to one. Missouri claimed to send 40,000 men into Rebel outfits, but 110,000 fought in blue.

When Beauregard designed his flag, apparently Old Bory counted his chickens before they hatched. He included stars for Kentucky and Missouri. In all the time that has passed since then, no one has ever removed the stars from Beauregard's battle flag. Old Bory's two extra stars are still there on the flag flapping above a few state buildings in the South.

A PREWAR MEMO COST A SENATE VETERAN HIS SEAT

IN FEBRUARY 1862 Morton W. Wilkinson of Minnesota took the floor of the U.S. Senate and delivered a powerful speech. The political analysts of the day, however, knew that this was only the first part of an intricate plan to free up a seat in the Senate for a good ole Hoosier buddy of the senator's.

According to Wilkinson, a member of this august body was a traitor and ought to be made to pack up his bags and return to Indiana. The focal point of this treason was New York native Jesse D. Bright. To ensure his removal, Wilkinson introduced a resolution calling for Bright's expulsion.

The matter was referred to the Committee on the Judiciary, which examined the resolution and eventually submitted a recommendation that Wilkinson's resolution be turned down. When their report came up for debate, the plan moved on to its next stage.

Sen. Charles Sumner of Massachusetts limped to the front of the Senate chamber. Six years earlier Sumner, an outspoken abolitionist, had been beaten severely on the floor of the Senate by Rep. Preston Brooks of South Carolina. Now he exaggerated his limp as he made his way to the dais. During his address to the Senate he occasionally paused to massage his leg, emphasizing the assault he had endured earlier and playing on the sympathies of the senators in the chamber.

To pass, Wilkinson's resolution required a two-thirds vote. It went over the top on February 5, 1862, thirty-two to fourteen, and that meant Bright had been expelled. According to the *Ohio Statesman,* the former Hoosier senator "bundled up the portable property in his desk, turned his back upon the court which had tried him, drew [his] pay to the last cent, and with a defiant stride passed into the public land committee-room, where his wife awaited him."

What treason had Bright committed against the country that required his removal from office?

The U.S. Senate chamber, from which Indiana Sen. Jesse D. Bright was expelled for an indiscretion in communicating with Jefferson Davis.

Apparently the only Northern member of Congress to be expelled from the Senate during the four years of civil war had addressed a letter of recommendation to Confederate President Jefferson Davis on March 1, 1861—six weeks before the shooting started in Charleston. It read:

> MY DEAR SIR: Allow me to introduce, to your acquaintance, my friend Thomas B. Lincoln of Texas. He visits your capital mainly to dispose of what he regards a great improvement in firearms. I recommend him to your favorable consideration, as a gentlemen of the first respectability, and reliable in every respect.
>   To His Excellency JEFFERSON DAVIS,
>   president of the Confederation of States

Though Bright's friend had a weapon to peddle to the Confederacy, no one seemed bothered by that. It was instead the address on the letter that Wilkinson objected to. Bright had dared address Davis as the head of a nation—though the Confederate States of America had a constitution, a congress, its own currency and postal system, not to mention an army.

Senator Bright, a seventeen-year-veteran of Washington, was expelled for addressing Davis as "president." He might have kept his seat had his letter identified the same man as "the honorable former secretary of war of the United States."

COMRADES KILLED AND WOUNDED

ANY TIME small arms bark and guns begin to speak, there's plenty of opportunity for mistakes. Smoke, fog, and darkness can make it hard for a soldier to be sure who's in his sights. The color of a uniform is supposed to say which side a man's on, but that's not always the case. In the case of artillery, gunners cut a tremendous number of fuses by hand, and a fraction of an inch can make a big difference.

Until recently, very little has been said about friendly fire in the Civil War, but it started at Big Bethel in 1861 and did not end until Palmito Ranch in 1865. A twentieth-century term, friendly fire was a tragedy without a name during the war

Near the Virginia hamlet known as Big Bethel, Union soldiers mistook their comrades for Rebels and shot more than a dozen of them in one of the war's first instances of friendly fire.

THE SOLDIER IN OUR CIVIL WAR

between the states. Nobody had a handy name for this battlefield error, so it was frequently described but never named. Union Gen. Fitz John Porter called it "fire in the rear," but the phrase failed to find a following. In general, such occurrences were masked with phrases such as "the wildest disorder," "misadventure," and "wild confusion."

Confederate Gen. Thomas J. "Stonewall" Jackson was wounded by small-arms fire from North Carolina troops who could not see well and believed Jackson and his companions were wearing blue. Confederate Gen. Micah Jenkins, whose unifiorm was blue, went down from friendly fire and never got up. Confederate Gen. Albert S. Johnston bled to death at Shiloh after being hit by a single ball. Since it struck him in the back of his leg, the shot could have come from the Rebel ranks he was leading. Confederate Gen. James Longstreet was severely wounded by his own men as he returned from a reconnaissance (Jenkins was in Longstreet's party and was killed). The number of ordinary soldiers on both sides who fell to friendly fire will never be known.

It was bad enough when friendly fire came from gunners shooting too low over the heads of their troops or because spotters failed to direct the gunners accurately. The powder smoke that masked the field during combat was often so thick that no one could see.

In addition to these hazards of the battlefield, many a man would have thrown off his gear and abandoned the cause had he known that he might fall under the sights of

J. C. BUTTRE ENGRAVING

U.S. naval officer Louis Goldsborough ordered his gunners to fire into the hand-to-hand fighting in which Federal soldiers were involved.

Louis Goldsborough's naval guns during the March 14, 1862, assault on New Berne, North Carolina. Aware of the risk of firing on a mixed body of men, he reasoned in his report on the action, "I know the persuasive effect of a 9-inch, and thought it better to kill a Union man or two than to lose the effect of my moral suasion."

NO RIGHT TO BE AN AMERICAN

WHEN THE shooting was over, the surrender terms drafted at Appomattox included provisos that Southern officers could keep their side arms and those who owned their horses could keep them as well. With the exception of general officers, all soldiers were free to go home after they pledged not to take up arms against the United States. In addition, general officers and civilian officials of high rank were stripped of their citizenship. With only a few exceptions, former soldiers were allowed to return to the fold politically by going before a notary public to sign an amnesty oath that read:

> I _____ of _____, _____, do solemnly swear in the presence of Almighty God, that I will henceforth faithfully support, protect, and defend the Constitution of the United States, and the Union of the States thereunder, and that I will in like manner, abide by and faithfully support all laws and proclamations which have been made during the existing rebellion with reference to the emancipation of slaves, so help me God.

Confederate President Jefferson Davis was imprisoned and even placed in irons, awaiting a trial that never came. Many soldiers and some civilians, however, rejected the opportunity to restore their citizenship. A small number went to Mexico. Others started a settlement in Brazil that is still filled with their descendants. A few others hightailed it to England, where Judah P. Benjamin, who had been both Confederate secretary of war and secretary of state, found employment as a barrister.

Lots of Rebels, however, swallowed their pride and put their names on the voting rolls just as soon as they could. Some of them who were under suspicion didn't get that chance for quite a while, though.

The former commander of the Army of Northern Virginia had to wait more than five months for his opportunity to reclaim his citizenship. On October 2, 1865, the brand-new president of Washington College in Lexington, Virginia, signed his amnesty oath and waited for word about when he could resume paying taxes and see his name on a voter roll.

Months passed and that word didn't come, but Robert E. Lee told his son Rooney not to fret as there would be a lot of foot-dragging, he was sure. He didn't know that a party or parties unknown in the federal bureaucracy decided to withhold that piece of paper from processing. Lee spent the rest of his life waiting for word from Washington, not knowing that his amnesty oath had been intentionally "lost."

Exactly one hundred years after Lee's death, a clerk began sorting some papers that had been awaiting filing in the National Archives longer than anybody could remember. Some of these records belonged to the Department of State and dated from the 1860s. Lee's 1865 amnesty oath surfaced, and when it did, his citizenship was restored by an Act of Congress on July 22, 1975.

Some accuse Secretary of State William H. Seward for the shenanigans that made the former commander a man without a country for 110 years, but there's no proof of Seward's involvement. Instead, some long-forgotten employee of the Department of State may have "misplaced" Lee's amnesty oath because he didn't believe that Lee deserved to be an American.

BULLETPROOF VESTS

ON JULY 4, 1861, Lincoln's war message to the special session of Congress suggested that the war would be short-lived. He was

A few shops along Broadway offered bulletproof vests to the men who responded to the call for soldiers and marched through New York before embarking for Washington and the war.

not alone in that opinion. Yet war being war, regardless of length, would put a lot of lives in danger.

Around the time of the battle of First Manassas (Bull Run), several Northerners considered that something could be done to protect the fighting men on the battlefield—and to give some workmen and salesmen nice profits, to boot. By the time the leaves began turning in the fall, some Billy Yanks anxious for action could obtain some insurance of a sort in the larger Northern cities. Significant numbers of troops departed from or passed through Boston, New York, and Philadelphia, and volunteers with plenty of money could get fitted out with steel body armor on the way to the front.

Nothing, however, could be done to protect arms and legs or to evade a bullet or ball coming straight toward one's head. Since the chest and abdomen comprised the biggest target area, they were the most likely places a man might be hit. Shaped plates about one-sixteenth-inch thick and fixed so they could be pulled together like corsets were touted as guaranteed lifesavers. They were so popular for a while that a good many sutlers that followed the armies stocked them.

Before long the "vests" were found to be more of a hindrance than a help. Some of them could deflect a glancing blow from a musket ball, but they were no good against rifles. They were also infernally heavy, and many men with armor were likely to toss them aside before they would march a dozen miles under a hot sun.

Confederate veteran J. V. Harris was a postwar physician in South Carolina, and he recalled having handled quite a few pieces of armor at Shiloh. He remembered finding them scattered around the battlefield near the Federal camps. One set had a bullet hole in the left plate, "just over the position of the heart," he recollected.

At least two Yankees wore steel at Antietam. Lt. James Baldwin's metal vest didn't help him when a shell burst nearby and a

At Antietam at least two Federal soldiers are known to have worn armor, and probably numerous other "steel vests" were used by the men there.

FRANK LESLIE'S ILLUSTRATED WEEKLY

fragment nearly tore off his leg. By the time he reached a field hospital, he had shucked his armor. Adj. Nathaniel Wales of the Thirty-fifth Massachusetts borrowed Baldwin's steel when he headed into the thick of the fighting close to John Otto's farm. This time, the wearer of the heavy stuff was glad he had it on when a bullet hit him in the chest area. It dented the armor and knocked the wind out of Wales, but he lived to tell the story.

Body armor is not mentioned in the *Official Records* of the war, a good indicator that it was practically useless, regardless of the claims made by its makers and vendors.

MAKE FEDERAL WARSHIPS VISIBLE FROM A DISTANCE

AN UNKNOWN clerk in the Navy Department at Richmond is believed to have hatched a seemingly brilliant scheme. The Confederates were losing warships and raiders because they failed to detect the approach of the Federal navy, specifically because the smoke generated by their engines was almost impossible to see.

"Federal warships have a tremendous advantage," the man reasoned. "They burn hard coal that makes very little smoke, while our poor lads advertise their whereabouts by columns of black smoke from soft coal. We can change the odds of the war on water by the simple step of setting the best coal fields of the North on fire. A few bands of intrepid raiders ought to be able to accomplish the trick in a matter of weeks."

Lots of Northern mines that produced anthracite—or hard coal—shipped the product to Philadelphia, where a quarter of a million tons of it passed through during the war years. If the Confederates could ignite fires in the Schuylkill and Wyoming mines of the Keystone State, along with a few in Pike County, Kentucky, the Federal navy would have to revert to bituminous—or soft—coal. As soon as they did, the Yankee ships would be detectable from great distances, and neither side would have an advantage in the-hunter-and-the-hound game being played on the oceans.

As interesting as the plan appeared to many war planners in the South, it was never carried out. The best incendiary stuff available was a combustible liquid commonly referred to as "Greek fire," but it was not very reliable. Confederate operatives had attempted to use it in an attempt to set New York City aflame, but they failed in no small part due to the unpredictable nature of the Greek fire.

No Rebel commander was willing to risk his reputation and the lives of his men in a venture into the heart of the Union's coal country so heavily dependent on Greek fire. Thus invisible smoke continued to mask the movements of the Union navy, and dense smoke continued to mark Confederate vessels as easy prey.

FOREIGN WAR OUGHT TO DO THE TRICK

MAYBE THE wildest of all Civil War shenanigans was suggested by no less than William H. Seward of New York. Like most who had been in the running for the 1860 Republican nomination for presidency, he did not want the North to go to war with the South.

When Lincoln chose him to be secretary of state, Seward believed the bumpkin from Illinois would turn to him for all of the major decisions. By the time he found out that the country lawyer in the White House had a mind of his own, the war wagon was rolling and was nearly out of control.

The first crisis of the Lincoln administration was centered in Fort Sumter in Charleston Harbor. The daily dispatches from the fort's commander, Maj. Robert Anderson, continually requested help and direction.

Seward lay awake at night worrying what might happen if Anderson failed to surrender the fort. If the major was as stubborn as he seemed, it would be disastrous for the country. Unless, he reasoned, Lincoln's attention could be turned to something else.

To keep Southerners and Northerners from slaughtering each other, Seward hatched a plot of his own. On the sly, he tried

U.S. Secretary of State William H. Seward (left) attempted to communicate to Gov. Francis Pickens of South Carolina (right) that Washington would give up Fort Sumter without a fight. Furthermore, Seward advocated starting a foreign war in order to avoid civil war.

to calm things down by letting Gov. Francis Pickens of South Carolina know that he favored relinquishing the harbor fort to the Southerners.

Then he approached Lincoln with the idea of uniting the country by antagonizing old enemies. Spain and England could be embarrassed easily. Agents could infiltrate Canada to stir up a revolt against the British crown. And the Monroe Doctrine might be used to warn France to dismiss any idea of controlling Mexico.

Seward was sure that an indignant United States would be able to declare war on at least one European power. Of course Lincoln would have to take charge of foreign policy, or entrust it to somebody with the skill to evoke the desired response. In the latter capacity, Seward modestly offered to guide the ship of state through the stormy waters ahead.

Sumter was lost, Seward contended, and would have to be surrendered eventually. Besides, once American fighting men focused their ire on England or France or Spain, no one would

PAINTING BY SETH EASTMAN, ARCHITECT OF THE U.S. CAPITOL

Fort Sumter was unoccupied until the day after Christmas 1860 when the people of Charleston awoke to see the U.S. banner fluttering from the flagstaff.

notice other matters—like the one in Charleston Harbor—and there would be no reason for civil war.

To some the notion looked pretty good, but nobody knows whether it would have worked had it been implemented. Lincoln chose to ignore Seward's plan. Instead plans were made to reinforce the Sumter garrison, and in the end the fort was lost and the country was at war with itself.

SECESSION NEVER MADE IT TO THE HIGH COURT

WHEN THE Secession movement climaxed with the formal withdrawal of eleven states from the Union, the constitutionality of this move was never pondered or ruled upon by the Supreme Court. One of the reasons for this was that the justices themselves were not above the sectional issue that had torn the country in two. Chief Justice Roger B. Taney, a native of Maryland and a strong supporter of slavery, had been the chief author of the Dred Scott decision, the most notorious slavery case to be brought to the Court. According to Taney, the slaves were not citizens of the United States.

Similar injunctions across the North followed Taney's Dred Scott decision. In Illinois, future Union Gen. John A. Logan was largely responsible for legislation that denied African Americans the status of residents of what was later to be called "The Land of Lincoln."

The earliest significant secession movement occurred, not in the South, but in New England. At least four towns—Enfield, Somers, Suffield, and Woodstock—tried unsuccessfully to gain permission to secede from the Massachusetts Colony to become part of Connecticut. When it was denied, the four towns withdrew anyway and were annexed by Connecticut in 1749. No action was taken to reclaim the towns for Massachusetts.

One of the issues discussed during the ratification of the Constitution focused on state sovereignty, including the right to withdraw if they should so choose. At one time New York City threatened to secede from the United States, and in 1794 the Whiskey Rebellion in Pennsylvania was a localized attempt to reject and repudiate the excise laws of the United States. The union of states was so fragile during the 1790s that the chief emphasis of Washington's famous Farewell Address was a plea for its preservation.

In 1832 South Carolina, under the leadership of John C. Calhoun, passed a nullification ordinance, which contended that the state had the power to ignore any measures passed in Washington, notably tariff acts, that were contrary to the well-being of the state. President

Marylander Roger B. Taney, chief justice of the U.S. Supreme Court, was among prominent officials who strongly supported slavery.

NATIONAL CYCLOPEDIA OF AMERICAN BIOGRAPHY

Andrew Jackson's threat of military action quelled the nullification movement, but its basic principles were treasured by many southerners for decades afterward.

In 1860 the election of a Republican president, whose party platform restricted the expansion of slavery, was perceived in the South to be the first step toward abolition of the peculiar institution. Lincoln's electoral victory led South Carolina to adopt an act of secession, founding the independent Republic of South Carolina. Thus a series of Secession conventions were convened in Mississippi, Florida, Alabama, Georgia, Louisiana, and Texas. On February 8, 1861, the Confederate States of America was founded with the adoption of a constitution in Montgomery, Alabama.

The constitutionality of secession was effectively denied by Union might—military, industrial, and economic. Once settled, the Supreme Court has never seen the need to rule on the issue.

WAR WAS NEVER DECLARED IN WASHINGTON

ALTHOUGH THE Confederacy declared war upon the United States, the North never declared war on the South. Having issued his 1861 call for seventy-five thousand troops on the authority of legislation enacted to quell Pennsylvania's 1794 Whiskey Rebellion, Lincoln insisted upon treating the ensuing military action as an insurrection rather than a war. He consistently refused to acknowledge that secession had occurred and referred to the Confederate States of America as "the so-called seceded states." Thus Lincoln refused to sanction the exchange of prisoners because he felt that would imply recognition of the Confederacy as a sovereign state.

In the 1863 *Prize Cases* decision, the U.S. Supreme Court rejected arguments that only Congress could declare war and at the same time repudiated Lincoln's doctrine of using troops to quell insurrection rather than to wage war. Despite the fact that war had not been declared by the U.S. Congress, the justices ruled that a state of war was initiated when Lincoln made his first proclamation of a blockade of Southern ports.

SECOND AMERICAN REVOLUTION

IT DIDN'T take much encouragement to evoke some criticism from Lincoln for George B. McClellan's mistakes, but the president pulled some monumental boners of his own. One of these stemmed from his conviction that he was directing the Second American Revolution. Many Secessionists claimed they were fighting such a war themselves, but that made no difference to the man in the White House. He intended to stress that he alone was following in the footsteps of George Washington.

That's why he picked Washington's birthday for the start of a coordinated offensive designed to send Johnny Reb back home with neither musket nor uniform. The Union commander in chief's plan went out nearly a month ahead of time, so his generals would have plenty of time to get ready. On January 27, 1862, Lincoln issued the following directive:

> Ordered that the 22nd day of February, 1862, be the day for a general movement of the Land and Naval Forces of the United States against the insurgent forces.
> That especially—
> The Army at & about Fortress Monroe.
> The Army of the Potomac.
> The Army of Western Virginia.
> The Army near Munfordsville, Ky.
> The Army and flotilla at Cairo [Illinois].
> And a Naval force in the Gulf of Mexico, be ready for a movement on that day.
> That the Heads of Departments, and especially the Secretaries of War and of the Navy, with all their subordinates; and the General-in-Chief, with all other commanders and subordinates, of Land and Naval forces, will severally be held to their strict and full responsibilities, for the prompt execution of this order.

The president knew that the dead of winter wasn't the best time to initiate action in the field, but it would be another year before Washington's birthday would roll around again, and he wanted to make the most of it.

Exactly what did the Union forces do on that momentous day?

In Florida, which Lincoln's order did not mention, Brig. Gen. Lewis G. Arnold relieved Col. Harvey Brown to take command of that military department. There was action of no importance at Independence, Missouri; Vienna and Flint Hill, Virginia; and in Arkansas Bay, Texas. That is all that was recorded in the military record for that symbolic day.

About a hundred miles south of Lincoln and the Federal capital there was plenty of action going on. Richmond, Virginia, was celebrating in the grandest style it knew—whooping, hollering, and fussing about the inauguration of Jefferson Davis for a full six-year term as president of the Confederate States of America.

Cairo, Illinois, was specifically mentioned in Lincoln's directive because of its strategic location at the confluence of the Ohio and Mississippi Rivers.

J. C. BUTTRE ENGRAVING

Jefferson Davis, former U.S. secretary of war and senator, was inaugurated as president of the Confederate States in Richmond ceremonies on the same day that Lincoln ordered his generals to launch an all-out offensive.

One of the first things the new chief executive did was to try out the new nation's brand-new seal of state. As leader of the Second American Revolution he wanted to demonstrate to the world what he already knew—that George Washington's likeness on that official seal would show up very well every time the Great Seal of the Confederacy was used.

FORMER CONGRESSMAN BANISHED TWICE

CLEMENT L. VALLANDIGHAM, a native of New Lisbon, Ohio, was a successful attorney and editor before winning his first term in the U.S. House of Representatives in 1858. While he was a brigadier general of Ohio militia, he met with John Brown and other abolitionists but publicly repudiated their views. When he was living in Dayton in 1862, he launched a gubernatorial campaign with a platform that included condemnation of the war.

At the time, Gen. Ambrose E. Burnside was the commander of the Department of the Ohio. He may have had the outspoken Vallandigham in mind when he drafted his famous General Order No. 38 in which he forbade citizens within the department from expressing sympathy for the enemy. If the Federal order of April 13, 1863, constituted bait, the editor-politician swallowed it hook, line, and sinker.

Ambrose E. Burnside (left) interpreted the law very closely when he ordered the arrest of Dayton, Ohio, resident Clement L. Vallandigham (right). In the year that followed, Vallandigham was the only notable to be banished from both the United States and the Confederacy.

Vallandigham addressed a Columbus audience two weeks later and criticized both the president and the war, probably hoping to be arrested and thereby gain public sympathy. He was right in expecting punitive action. On May 5 he was arrested in the middle of the night and was promptly tried by a military court that imposed a two-year prison sentence.

Vallandigham's prominence in Ohio and among antiwar groups throughout the North had made him a national figure, so the Federal government entered the fracas. His case was discussed at length in a May 19 meeting of the president's cabinet, after which Lincoln took action for which there was no legal basis. Vallandigham's prison sentence was commuted to banishment from the Union, and he was shipped to Confederate soil near Murfreesboro, Tennessee.

Yet Jefferson Davis and his advisers seem to have been wary of the true sentiments of the man whom Democrats had just nominated in absentia for the governorship of Ohio. They wanted nothing to do with Vallandigham, so he was again banished—this time from Confederate soil. Sent to Wilmington, North Carolina, under military escort, he went to Canada by way of Bermuda. From both Niagara Falls and Windsor, Vallandigham conducted his unsuccessful campaign for governorship of Ohio.

Heavily disguised, the man who had been forbidden to set foot in any loyal or seceded state slipped across the border on June 14, 1864, and returned to Dayton. Possibly because Lincoln didn't want to annoy the voters in the upcoming presidential election, the presence in Ohio of the banished political leader was ignored in Washington. Defiantly, however, Vallandigham went to Chicago and attended the Democratic

Arrested by soldiers in the middle of the night and expelled from the North and then from the South, Vallandigham took refuge in Canada before trying to help put George B. McClellan in the White House.

National Convention. There he helped to frame the peace plank that was central to the unsuccessful presidential campaign of George B. McClellan.

DOWN CHESAPEAKE BAY THEN OVERLAND TO RICHMOND

GEN. GEORGE B. MCCLELLAN was convinced that to defeat the Rebels he'd have to seize their capital; however, he didn't cotton to the idea of fighting from Washington to Richmond through the huge body of Confederates he believed was waiting for him near Manassas Junction. To get around the Southerners, he developed a complex plan of action that eventually came to be called the Urbanna campaign.

Initially he would have to find a way to break the stranglehold the Confederates had on the Potomac River. A picked task force set out on February 27, 1862, headed for the river by way of the Chesapeake and Ohio Canal. The men had more than enough boats for passage of the canal, but they never had a chance to use them. The boats were about six inches too wide, and so the expedition returned to base.

Lincoln was not amused when he learned of the reason for the failure. He allegedly commented that although he was no engineer, he had enough common sense to measure a hole before trying to put something through it—especially before spending a million dollars to haul some too-wide boats into some too-narrow locks.

CHAPTER TWO

THE RAILSPLITTER AND HIS CLAN

SUPPORTERS OF the very young Republican Party of Illinois came together at Danville on May 8, 1860, to elect delegates to the national convention that was scheduled to meet in Chicago a week later. In addition to the election of delegates, they wanted to air their views for the record as well. Many knew that Judge David Davis of the eighth judicial circuit had more to do with bringing the national convention to Chicago than anyone else.

Davis wangled that plum by promising that Illinois would not field a favorite-son candidate for the presidency. So the fellows who gathered in Danville planned to listen to some oratory and swap a few votes. They did not expect to do much more than that before they went home. Since much of the business was handled the first day, it looked as if the second day of their session would be pretty dull.

31

Nobody seemed to know what was going on the next morning when Richard J. Oglesby gained the floor. Saying that a long-time Democrat had come to Danville to make a contribution to the Republicans, he received permission from the chair for the presentation to be made.

Then a dirt farmer, who appeared to have just come out of his fields, was escorted through the door. John Hanks looked like he'd been around a lot longer than fifty-eight years. Bent over from long days with hoes and plows, he was described as being "as gnarled as a century-old oak with a whole lot of lightning scars."

Nevertheless, all eyes turned from him to the load he was carrying: two short lengths of fence rail that were misshappened and partly covered with lichen. A big hand-scrawled sign attached to the rails read:

ABRAHAM LINCOLN
The Rail Candidate
FOR PRESIDENT IN 1860
Two rails from a lot of 3,000
made in 1830 by Hanks and Abe Lincoln
whose father was the first pioneer
of Macon County.

As the farmer made his way toward the platform, somebody hollered at the top of his voice, "Yeah, Lincoln! Yeah, Lincoln!" That set the whole place in commotion, and then a very tall and awkward-looking fellow dressed in black was escorted to the front of the room.

When things began to quiet down, the second cousin of attorney Abraham Lincoln shook hands with him and called in a loud voice, "Identify your work, sir!"

With everybody in the house grinning from ear to ear and leaning forward so as not to miss a word, the lawyer from Springfield gave what some considered "a courtroom answer." Speaking to the members of the convention by addressing Cousin John, he said: "I cannot say for sure that I split these rails. Where did you get them?"

The Republican Party was started at Ripon, Wisconsin, in February 1854. From its inception the party was strongly opposed to slavery.

"Got 'em off that farm you improved down on the Sangamon River."

"That must have been all of thirty years ago," Lincoln responded in the high-pitched voice that newspaper reporters in the East would say a lot about later. "I could have split these rails, but I have no way to identify them. What kind of tree did they come from?"

"One's a black walnut, and the other's from a honey locust."

Lincoln turned aside from his rail-bearing cousin to address directly the delegates who were bubbling with delight. "Well, boys," he intoned, "about all I can say is that I'm sure I split a lot of better-looking rails in my time!"

That brought an end to the acceptance of a special contribution to the Republicans from a lifelong Democrat. It also brought practically unanimous support to a hastily framed motion by which Lincoln became the candidate for the presidential nomination from the state of Illinois.

No known document sheds light upon a question that grew more and more important as the weeks passed following the conventions: Who cooked up the railsplitter drama that altered the course of the state's Republican convention in an election year?

Cousin John possibly might have hatched the scheme on his own. It's a lot more probable, though, that his cousin Abraham or Judge Davis or Richard Oglesby was behind the drama.

Whatever the case, the railsplitter image had a powerful appeal to voters living on the frontier or only a generation removed from it. John Hanks, whose name rarely appears in chronicles of the era, started the ball rolling in a grass-roots move to send to Washington a man who would be consumed with the goal of saving the Union.

THE 1860 ELECTION

IN 1860 the thirty-four states comprising the Union sprawled over 2.9 million square miles. The population density, having jumped by one-third during a single decade, stood at 10.6 persons per square mile. A 35.6 percent rise in the number of Americans during the same period brought the total population to 31.4 million.

For the presidential election of 1860, Democrats had a choice between two nationally known men whose views could not be farther apart: Stephen A. Douglas, "the Little Giant," and John C. Breckinridge, who had served as vice president under the outgoing James Buchanan.

Short, pudgy Stephen A. Douglas was known as "the Little Giant."

VANITY FAIR

DICTIONARY OF AMERICAN PORTRAITS

John A. Bell, called "the spoiler,"
pulled half a million votes from
Douglas and his running mate.

John A. Bell was the nominee of the youthful Constitutional Union Party, but he was not considered a major contender. Abraham Lincoln of Illinois, the second Republican nominee for the nation's highest office, was thought to be the sure winner since the long-dominant Democratic Party was split into rival factions.

In November, as expected, Bell came in last with 592,902 votes, Breckinridge third with 848,356 votes, and Douglas was second with 1,382,713 votes. Lincoln topped the field with 1,865,593 votes.

Mathematically, Lincoln was voted into the White House with the support of one out of seventeen Americans, because the right to vote was limited to white males, aged twenty-one or older, who owned property or had seen military service.

OFFICIAL, AT LAST

THE HIGHEST elective office Lincoln had held prior to 1860 was a seat in the U.S. House of Representatives, where he served just one term. Since then he had not occupied any public office for a dozen years.

When the Founding Fathers designed the electoral process, they created the electoral college and gave its members the final word. Electors, whose number was equal to that of congressmen and senators combined, were to vote at four-year intervals "by ballot for two persons." In the 1790s it had been

Vice President John C. Breckinridge presided over the electoral college in 1860, whose verdict was much more pronounced than that of the general election results.

expected that no man would gain the required majority, thereby throwing the election into the House of Representatives where each state would have a single vote.

At first the members of the electoral college were chosen by the state legislatures, but by 1836 only South Carolina still clung to this practice. In other states the tiny fraction of the population constituting qualified voters chose the members of the electoral college on the general ticket with the presidential candidates.

By the time the members of the electoral college gathered to cast their votes on February 13, 1861, the District of Columbia was under guard. Soldiers and marines were stationed at the Capitol, the White House, the Treasury, the Post Office, the Patent Office, and the chief bridges across the Potomac River.

Some observers of the political scene expressed concern that a defeated presidential candidate, John C. Breckinridge, by virtue of his role as the country's vice president, was to preside over the electoral college and announce the results of the balloting. Any fears concerning Breckinridge, however, proved groundless. Breckinridge announced that he had drawn only 72 electoral votes. Bell received only a dozen. And Lincoln garnered a stunning 68 percent of the total—180 votes.

The room in which the electors met was already charged by the issue of secession, and indeed some considered that the tension might affect the voting in a way that would possibly deny Lincoln the election. That tension might have been raised even more, however, had it been foreseen that in less than nine months after he announced Lincoln's election, the former vice president would be a Confederate general.

NEVER RESIDENTS OF THE WHITE HOUSE

JUDGING BY their private and official correspondence, the members of the Lincoln family were never residents of the White House. Though they moved into the structure in early 1861, the documents issued during the administration of the sixteenth president do not use that name for the place in which Lincoln and his family lived for four years.

When George and Martha Washington first danced the presidential quadrille, they did so at 3 Cherry Street in New York City. A few who knew the house's occupants referred to it as "the Palace," but the vast majority of Americans called it "the President's House." The first president to take up residence in the presidential mansion in the District of Columbia was the second president, John Adams.

When the British overran the federal capital during the War of 1812, they put the presidential mansion to the torch. Rebuilt,

Half a century before the Lincolns moved in, the President's House was at what later became 1600 Pennsylvania Avenue.

NICHOLAS KING WATERCOLOR, ABOUT 1800

NATIONAL ARCHIVES

The White House as it appeared in the 1860s. Not visible is the statue of Thomas Jefferson in the area immediately in front of the building.

refurbished, and given a glistening coat of white paint, it became widely but not universally known as the White House.

Lincoln could not have failed to be aware of this usage; the name was in print in an 1811 volume about federalism in New England. There's also evidence that Congress took action to officially name the building the "Executive Mansion." Ordinary citizens may have thought that sounded a little pretentious and generally preferred to speak and write about the White House. The sixteenth president, although he had been born in a log cabin in Kentucky, was not ordinary in any sense. Anyone skimming his letters, memoranda, dispatches, and orders finds "Executive Mansion" jumping out from nearly every page.

DRINKING WATER—FRESH FROM THE RIVER

WHATEVER NAME one might assign to the big house at 1600 Pennsylvania Avenue, the house was not an ideal place to live. On February 20, 1862, eleven-year-old Willie Lincoln died there. His doctors said that he was a victim of "bilious fever," but indications are that he died of typhoid fever, which may have been contracted from the untreated drinking water that was piped into the mansion from the Potomac River.

AN OPEN DOOR

NEARLY EVERY American who arrived at the front door of the Executive Mansion acted as if he believed he was a part owner of the place. Hordes of office seekers, clerks, and one-time visitors to the capital crowded into the house day after day. Until a few months before the assassination of Lincoln, no attempt was made to provide any security for the president or his family. Once a fellow managed to get inside, he was free to wander about at will. Though it was the place where the chief executive worked and lived, the Executive Mansion didn't come within a country mile of being a quiet and comfortable home.

Office seekers who thronged Washington were intent upon seeing the president.

HARPER'S WEEKLY

POOR LITTLE TAD

BORN IN 1853, the youngest son of Abraham and Mary Todd Lincoln, little Thomas had a head that seemed too large for his body. His father took a close look, called him Tad because his bodily shape seemed to resemble that of a tadpole, and the nickname stuck so that his baptismal name was seldom used.

Along with his parents, Tad grieved when his brother Willie died in 1862. The Lincolns, however, were not the only first family to lose a child during the war. Jefferson and Varina Davis also lost a son in the Confederate White House. On the last day of April 1864, little Joseph Davis fell from a second-story balcony to the pavement and was instantly killed. Of the many things the wartime chief executives had in common, none was more poignant than the deaths of two bright, cheerful little boys.

Tad Lincoln was fun-loving to the point of mischievousness, but he was not particularly bright and had a noticeable speech impediment. Nevertheless, he delighted in bursting into his father's office when military officers or cabinet members were assembled and playing pranks on them.

DICTIONARY OF AMERICAN PORTRAITS

Though he did not have his father's mind, Tad took a strong interest in his father's war. He was very pleased when a uniform was tailored to his size, and he took special pleasure at being addressed as Captain Tad. One of his favorite dolls, which he had named Jack, also received a soldier's uniform. Not given to pardon-

Tad Lincoln wore a uniform specially made for him and led his playmates on charges throughout the White House and into cabinet meetings.

ing soldiers as often as his father did, Tad claimed that he had caught Jack deserting or sleeping on duty and saw to it that the doll was executed frequently.

After his father's assassination, Tad was rarely far from his mother's side. In 1867 he was called as a witness at the trial of accused conspirator John H. Surrat (he was acquitted of having participated in the assassination). At age thirteen, while a student at a special Chicago school, Tad managed to learn his letters. Five years later he died, probably of tuberculosis.

THE DRAFT DODGER AT 1600 PENNSYLVANIA AVENUE

ROBERT TODD LINCOLN, the first-born son of the Lincolns, was never a full-time resident at 1600 Pennsylvania Avenue. Seventeen years old at the time of his father's election as chief executive, he'd been away from Springfield for almost a year but returned to accompany the family to Washington.

Unlike his father, Robert was considered handsome. He also had educational opportunities that were poles apart from the few months his father spent in one-room "blab" schools. Robert, however, did not make the most of his schooling and failed the entrance examination at Harvard University in 1859. Instead, he spent most of 1860 at a New Hampshire preparatory school. His parents wanted nothing but the best for their firstborn, so they insisted that he reapply to

DICTIONARY OF AMERICAN PORTRAITS

Robert Todd Lincoln, who later became U.S. secretary of war, began his military career under coercion.

Harvard. This time he made a passing grade and managed to stay in the top half of his class while he was there.

Well before he was graduated in 1864, the Lincolns were criticized for Robert's attending college rather than joining the army. Initially, no eyebrows had been raised that Robert pursued his studies during the early years of the war when so many men volunteered that numbers of them were turned down. Things took a radical turn, however, soon after the first Federal conscription act was passed in early 1863.

Robert was considered a resident of the Executive Mansion, but his citizenship was in Illinois. When the state began to feel the manpower pinch, it became increasingly hard to meet its draft quota, and folk began questioning if "that Lincoln boy" had the makings of a soldier.

Mary Lincoln was willing to move heaven and earth to keep her firstborn out of uniform, so she pleaded with her husband to keep Robert out of uniform. Pushed on the one side by his wife and on the other by public opinion, the president wavered briefly before endorsing Robert's application to the Harvard law school. Robert had been there only briefly before his absence from the army placed his father in an untenable position.

Eventually President Lincoln reached a solution whereby he hoped to satisfy his wife, the public officials in Illinois, and the Northern public at large. His idea was expressed in a letter to Ulysses S. Grant on January 19, 1865:

> Please read and answer this letter as though I was not President, but only a friend. My son, now in his twenty-second year, having graduated at Harvard, wishes to see something of the war before it ends. I do not wish to put him in the ranks, nor yet to give him a commission, to which those who have already served long, are better entitled and better qualified to hold. Could he, without embarrassment to you, or detriment to the service, go into your Military family with some nominal rank, I, and not the public furnishing his necessary means? If no, say so without the least hesitation, because I am as anxious, and as deeply interested, that you shall not be encumbered as you can be yourself.

City Point, Virginia, where Capt. Robert Todd Lincoln helped to make his mother, father, and brother welcome.

Grant replied two days later:

> Your favor of this date in relation to your son serving in some Military capacity is received. I will be most happy to have him in my Military family in the manner you propose. The nominal rank given him is immaterial, but I would suggest that of Capt. as I have three staff officers now, of considerable service, in higher grade. Indeed I have one officer with only the rank of Lieut. who has been in the service since the beginning of the war. This however will make no difference and I would still say give him the rank of Capt. Please excuse my writing on the half sheet. I had no recourse but to take the blank half of your letter.

Though this exchange was about military business, it did not find its way into the *Official Records.*

Robert Todd Lincoln became a captain on February 11, 1865, and was immediately made an assistant adjutant general of volunteers and attached to the staff of Grant. In that role he was among those who made the Lincoln family welcome when they paid an extended visit to Grant's headquarters at City Point, Virginia, six weeks after Robert had received his uniform.

Captain Lincoln held his commission until June 10, never came close to a battlefield, but as a veteran he was eligible to join the Grand Army of the Republic. Many Federal officers and some civilian officials knew that the young man had never spent as much as a half-hour in a drill or any other military exercise and had been shielded from the dangers of the war his father directed.

A "SNEAKING, COWARDLY, SAVAGE SCOUNDREL"

LINCOLN'S WIFE, Mary, had been born and reared in Lexington, Kentucky, and had five siblings plus five half siblings from the second marriage of her father. So many of her relatives were prominent Confederates that her family connections were a source of embarrassment to the first family and caused her own loyalty to the Union to be questioned.

Since her half brother David was fourteen years old when Mary was born, she had no long-term relationship with him and her husband had never met him. Considered in Lexington to be "a born troublemaker," David had run afoul of the authorities more than once while Mary was a toddler. He ran away from home and returned months later with a prominent tattoo. It depicted the flag of Chile, then in turmoil and striving to win its independence from Spain.

David settled down after a fashion as an overseer of a plantation worked by slaves. When the war broke out, he rushed to join the Confederate army. At the time of the battle of First Manassas, he was a lieutenant of infantry and had been placed in charge of the prisons on Richmond's Twenty-fifth Street.

When his ties with the wife of the Union president were discovered, the *New York Times* used stinging adjectives to label him as a scoundrel who found amusement in kicking "helpless, crippled and wounded prisoners." An inmate of one of the prisons supervised by Todd described him as "seething with malignity and bitterness."

In the fall of 1861 David H. Todd was promoted to captain and assigned to the western theater. Hours before the July 4, 1863, surrender of Vicksburg, Mary Lincoln's half brother was mortally wounded. The Executive Mansion in Washington displayed no symbols of mourning, but Northern political enemies of the president, who were numerous and powerful, made the most of the allegation that Lincoln had close ties to a brutal officer under whose care many captured Federal fighting men had been committed.

THE MANSION DRAPED IN BLACK

THE FIRST news about the battle of Chickamauga, Tennessee, reached the Union capital on the evening of Monday, September 20, 1863. As usual, the president was in and out of the military telegraph office several times that night. He showed his secretary John Hay a dispatch from Gen. William S. Rosecrans that

The fall of Vicksburg, which split the Confederacy in two, occurred shortly after a Confederate brother-in-law of Mary Todd Lincoln was mortally wounded.

THE SOLDIER IN OUR CIVIL WAR

Confederate Gen. Ben Hardin Helm, in whose memory the White House was draped in black crepe, was married to Mary Todd Lincoln's sister.

described the fighting and expressed concern that the spot he considered vital might fall to the Rebels. On the following morning, Lincoln talked with Secretary of the Navy Gideon Welles about the action in Georgia. That evening the chief executive sent a telegram to his wife, who was in New York: "The air is so clear and cool, and apparently healthy, that I would be glad for you to come. Nothing very particular, but I would be glad to see you and Tad."

Then the president received a dispatch informing him that Confederate Gen. Ben Hardin Helm, his brother-in-law, had

Helm was mortally wounded at "Bloody Chickamauga," a Southern victory that also cost Confederate Gen. John B. Hood (mounted) a leg.

been mortally wounded at Chickamauga and was to be buried in Atlanta.

In April 1861 Lincoln had tried to persuade Helm, who was married to Mary Todd Lincoln's half sister Emily, to accept a major's commission in the U.S. Army and serve as a paymaster. Instead Helm joined the First Kentucky Cavalry, a Confederate unit, and became its colonel. Within a year he was a brigadier in the Army of Tennessee and at times led a division. During the first assault on the Federal breastworks at Chickamauga, he took a direct hit that surgeons knew he would not survive. Lincoln had always liked Helm and was greatly saddened by the news, and he delayed sending word to Mary as long as he could.

As soon as Mary returned to Washington, she ordered the Executive Mansion to be draped in black crepe, the usual sign of mourning at that time. When it became known that such tribute was being paid to a Confederate general, some of Lincoln's political foes tried to exploit the situation. A persistent rumor alleged that the president was called before a congressional committee and quizzed about his wife's strong Southern ties, but there is no documentary evidence to support this tale.

A FIELD HOSPITAL AT GETTYSBURG

SGT. WILLIAM M. JONES was among the many Southerners who received less than mortal wounds at Gettysburg. His right foot was so badly mangled, however, that the regimental surgeon of the Fiftieth Georgia regiment told the young soldier that it would have to come off immediately to prevent the development of gangrene.

Jones was willing to lose his foot to save his life, but he had little confidence in his regimental surgeon. He requested and received permission for the operation to be performed by the brigade surgeon, G. R. C. Todd. A younger full brother of Mary Lincoln, Todd took one look at the Georgian and saw that complicated procedures would be involved. He sent for surgeon

Henry Parramore to assist him and together they removed the foot and saved the life of Jones.

Given the baptismal name of George Rogers Clark, Todd had practiced medicine in Kentucky until he became a Confederate surgeon when the war had gone on for a little over a year. Initially he had been assigned to the Fifteenth Virginia regiment, but he entered Pennsylvania as one of Gen. Paul Semmes's brigade surgeons. After the Army of Northern Virginia retreated from Gettysburg into Virginia, Todd was sent to Charleston as a medical examiner.

In the city where the war began, both newspapers took notice of the fact that Mary Lincoln's brother was there as a Confederate officer. Word again reached Washington, and the Committee on the Conduct of the War again tried and failed to exploit the Southern ties of the mistress of the Executive Mansion.

A WORTHLESS SCRAP OF PAPER

EAGER FOR a firsthand look at the devastated Confederate capital, the president of the United States departed from City Point, Virginia, for Richmond at 8 A.M. on April 4, 1865. Traveling aboard the steamer *River Queen* and escorted by the USS *Malvern*, Lincoln and his party—which included his son Tad—landed close to infamous Libby Prison.

Guarded only by a dozen sailors, the visitors walked to the headquarters of Gen. Godfrey Weitzel in the mansion that had been called the White House of the Confederacy. Guided to the former office of Jefferson Davis, Lincoln sat briefly in his rival's chair.

After a hasty lunch, the president rode through the streets of Richmond in an army ambulance. Crowds were so great that the vehicle was frequently halted, and newly freed slaves pressed forward to try to touch the hand of the man they hailed as their liberator. That night Lincoln slept aboard the *Malvern* and on the morning of April 5 again roamed through some of the streets still

THE REBELLION RECORD

U.S. Gen. Godfrey Weitzel established his headquarters in "the White House of the Confederacy" after the fall of Richmond and following Lincoln's visit to the Confederate capital.

bustling with admirers but also lined with burned-out business and residential structures.

Eight days later, shortly before midnight, aides went through the pockets of the mortally wounded chief executive. At 10:13 P.M. on April 14, Lincoln had been shot by John Wilkes Booth during the play *Our American Cousin*. One of the men looked into the president's wallet and found only a worthless piece of Confederate currency that some well-wisher in Richmond had thrust into his hand as a souvenir.

"NAY, NAY, WE WON'T PAY!"

ON THE way to Washington in 1861, the train bearing the president-elect and his party stopped several times. There were always large crowds at the stations along the route to greet the man who towered a head above all of his companions. Folk who had voted for him were anxious about the future and wanted to hear what he had to say about the impending national crisis. Lincoln solemnly assured his listeners that there was no crisis. Even though Jefferson Davis had taken office as the provisional head of the Confederate States of America, Lincoln told his audiences that the politicians in Washington were the only persons to be dreaded.

Lincoln, however, knew that he would have to face the Secession issue head-on, and in his inaugural address he made it

Alexander Hamilton was the first secretary of the treasury of the United States. His tax on whiskey led to an uprising and a precedent.

DICTIONARY OF AMERICAN PORTRAITS

clear he was ready to do so. He planned to retake the forts and other Federal installations that had been seized, he said. And he intended to continue collecting the revenue derived chiefly from very high tariffs on imported goods purchased largely by the South. He did not say so, but he had a plan of action. For that plan he was indebted to George Washington and the rye farmers of western Pennsylvania.

During Washington's first term, the country was desperate for new sources of revenue. Secretary of the Treasury Alexander Hamilton suggested that an excise tax on distilled spirits might fill the shortfall. He had not, however, reckoned with the farmers of western Pennsylvania.

These pioneers produced a good quantity of top-grade rye, and for years they hauled it long distances over rough terrain to the eastern part of the state to sell it. Then someone pointed out that whiskey made from grain could go east much easier at a fraction of the shipping cost. Little distilleries soon dotted much of western Pennsylvania. When these whiskey distillers heard about Hamilton's new tax, their rallying cry became, "Nay! Nay! We won't pay!"

Told that they'd pay or go to jail, the western Pennsylvanians gathered all the pitchforks and squirrel guns they could find, along with a few muskets, and started to march on the state capital at Harrisburg. Before they had gone halfway their number had swelled to about sixteen thousand. These hardy individualists living on the far side of the mountains were putting the new central government of the United States to a test.

Washington saw that the farmers meant business, but so did he. At his request, Congress passed legislation permitting him to call out troops from the adjoining states to quell the so-called Whiskey Rebellion. With vast numbers of Revolutionary War veterans behind him, Washington himself marched into Pennsylvania and put a quick end to the insurrection. Two leaders were tried and convicted of treason, but the president commuted their sentences and quiet returned to the countryside.

Years later, President James Buchanan was reminded of the Whiskey Rebellion legislation when South Carolina batteries fired on a supply vessel en route to Fort Sumter in Charleston Harbor and the garrison troops isolated there. Buchanan was a Pennsylvanian, and so the old rebellion was not unknown to him, but as he pondered the language of the legislation, he decided that it did not address the issue of secession. Nor was he anxious to start a war in the waning months of his administration. The next president would have to decide what to do.

It is likely that Lincoln reviewed the Whiskey Rebellion legislation long before he left Springfield. He did not like some of

James Buchanan was reminded of the Whiskey Rebellion legislation shortly after Robert Anderson and his officers (below) relocated the command to Fort Sumter in Charleston Harbor.

H. B. HALL ENGRAVING

its features, but he could not find anything that suited his needs better. So he relied on it after Fort Sumter was surrendered, and he called for seventy-five thousand men to put down the insurrection in the South. Few men who fought in the Civil War knew it, but it would not have taken the shape it had if the rye farmers of western Pennsylvania had been willing to accept the tax that came out of the nation's capital.

The Whiskey Rebellion legislation gave the president the power to call for volunteers to serve no more than ninety days and who would be free to return home thirty days after the start of the next session of Congress. Many anxious New Englanders wanted Lincoln to call a special session of Congress soon after his inauguration. He knew that to do so would limit the volunteers' time of service unnecessarily, for the troops could hardly get to the capital before the special session would be over and then they would have to turn around and go home. So Lincoln delayed calling the special session until July 4, calculating that he would have plenty of time to gather a large army and get it in shape to overcome any resistance it might encounter in the South.

The seventy-five thousand arrived in Washington, making a force five times as large as the standing U.S. Army. There was

Enabling legislation made it necessary to fight before the Northern commanders were ready, so First Bull Run was a disaster.

CURRIER AND IVES

only one problem: the volunteers who flocked to the colors were inexperienced men who barely knew a musket from a bayonet. Lincoln's highest-raking officer and chief military advisor, General in Chief Winfield Scott, did not understate the situation when he assessed these men as wholly unable to fight.

Many had joined the cause in April, and so their ninety days would expire before August 1. Congress had begun its work on July 4, so anyone who was late in enrolling would be free to return home at the end of the month. Therefore those raw troops had to fight immediately or not at all.

Thus the congressional act designed to quell the rebellion of a few thousand rye farmers of the Monongahela Valley forced the Union army to fight at Manassas before either side was ready for combat. The day of the battle, Washingtonians ventured out to watch the action as a Sunday diversion. What they witnessed instead was a rout that spelled the beginning of a long and bloody war. Everything Lincoln had said on the way to his inauguration evaporated with the powder smoke that enveloped the Virginia countryside on July 21, 1861.

SIGNED IN BLIND OBEDIENCE

EXCEPT FOR Simon Cameron, Lincoln's first secretary of war, who was dispatched in January 1862 as minister to Russia to get rid of him, the president kept most of his cabinet members throughout his administration. Very early in his presidency, the cabinet learned that he would not tolerate insubordination. Faced with the Fort Sumter dilemma, he called a cabinet meeting shortly after the conclusion of the inauguration on March 4, 1861, and asked for each man's written opinion concerning the issue of resupplying the beleaguered installation.

All six men knew Lincoln's position on the basis of his inaugural address, in which he vowed to regain the Federal property seized by the Secessionists—with Fort Sumter being the most prominent installation on the list. Yet despite knowing the president's views beforehand, many believed that Lincoln would eventually defer to the secretary of state, William H. Seward, on such major issues, and so most of the cabinet members advised against the course of action Lincoln had indicated he would follow.

A few days after that cabinet session, the cabinet members were convened to poll their opinions again. Having discovered who was in charge—and that Seward would not be making such momentous decisions—they voted in favor of holding and resupplying the Charleston Harbor fort.

By August 23, 1864, every member of Lincoln's cabinet did as he was told and asked few questions. As they arrived separately at the Executive Mansion that morning, each man was given a document that had been folded so it could not be read. The president instructed each of them to sign the document. Without comment the chief executive placed the endorsed paper on his desk and launched into a discussion of a demonstration of Morse signaling that was scheduled for the following day. Though everyone present knew that the Republican National Convention was due to convene in Chicago a few days later, no one mentioned it. If any cabinet member had any qualms about what he had signed in ignorance, he said nothing.

Almost three months later, at a cabinet meeting on November 11, Lincoln signaled for secretary John Hay to display the paper that had been signed in August. Lincoln read it aloud: "This morning, as for some days past, it seems exceedingly probable that this administration will not be re-elected. Then it will be my duty to so cooperate with the president-elect, as to save the Union between the election and the inauguration: as he will have secured his election on such ground that he can not possibly save it afterwards."

Back in August, a series of Federal defeats on the battlefield plus mounting pressure for a negotiated peace forced Lincoln to consider that the war might be lost in late autumn. Determined that the Union must be preserved regardless of any other issue, he demanded and secured the solemn pledges of his cabinet members to press for a military victory prior to the inauguration

News that Atlanta had fallen, as evidenced in this image of railroad debris, gave a tremendous boost to Lincoln's chances in the election of 1864.

of his anticipated successor. Subsequently, however, Gen. William T. Sherman had taken Atlanta and Democratic candidate George B. McClellan had bungled his campaign so badly that Lincoln was able to score an overwhelming victory in his bid for a second term.

In the aftermath of the electoral triumph he did not expect in August, Lincoln declined an invitation to speak at New York's Union League Club. "I don't believe it would look well for me to go around blowing my own horn," he confided to his secretary. Two days later, however, he came close to grinning when he revealed the pledge to his cabinet members that they had earlier signed in blind obedience.

A Seamstress . . . and More

THOUGH SHE was not related to the chief executive or his wife, Elizabeth Keckley was an important member of the Lincoln household. Born in Virginia as a slave of mixed heritage, she was an expert seamstress by the age of eighteen. Still a slave but living in Saint Louis, she attracted prosperous clients and accumulated twelve hundred dollars to buy her freedom. Established as a "modiste" in Washington, she was introduced by a client to Mary Lincoln. Instantly liking Keckley, Mrs. Lincoln made extensive use of her services, and over a period of time the former slave became the chief confidante of the president's wife.

After her son Willie died in 1862, Mary Lincoln turned more and more toward the occult. Keckley possibly may have been a major influence in persuading her to consult spiritualists. According to the seamstress, seances were held in the Executive Mansion and the president, a disbeliever himself, attended at least one of them.

Following Lincoln's assassination, his widow became visibly dependent upon Keckley. Mary had run up substantial debts for clothing, much of which she never wore, and Keckley helped her when she tried to sell some of the wardrobe in New York. Unfortunately, few people were interested in buying Mary Todd Lincoln's "old clothes."

While Keckley was in New York, the seamstress told the story of her life to a writer who put it into a narrative that was published in 1868 by G. W. Carlton and Company. The book was entitled *Behind the Scenes, or Thirty Years a Slave and Four Years in the White House*. Though it included letters from Mary Lincoln that were used without her permission, it did not sell well.

After teaching for a time at Ohio's Wilberforce University, the first woman other than a relative to give an insider's look at life inside 1600 Pennsylvania Avenue returned to Washington. She found shelter at the Home for Destitute Colored Women and Children.

One aspect of Elizabeth Keckley's colorful career was not revealed during the 1860s. After working for a time as a seamstress for Varina Davis before the war, she had spent a brief time in the home of the future president of the Confederacy. Keckley was thus the only person known to have had firsthand knowledge of the two households headed by the rival heads of state.

CHAPTER THREE ⌁

SLAVERY

THOMAS JEFFERSON, EXEMPLAR?

A VERY old oral tradition, not taken seriously until recent decades, claimed that Thomas Jefferson had sired a number of children by a mistress with a mixed heritage. The story can neither be proved nor disproved, but it is a window through which one can catch a glimpse of prewar slavery.

Jefferson's wife, the former Martha Wayles, was the daughter of John Wayles, a prominent attorney and planter in Charles County, Virginia. It was widely known that he had also fathered a number of children through his slaves. Thus, when Jefferson married Martha in 1772, he knew that his future wife was a half sister to several slaves.

Although Martha endured seven pregnancies during their ten-year marriage, only a daughter survived. When Martha was

Thomas Jefferson owned one of the most gifted minds in American history as well vast lands and a host of slaves.

on her deathbed in 1782, soon after giving birth to a daughter, she supposedly exacted from Jefferson a solemn promise that he would never marry again. Whether he made the vow or not, he never took another woman to the altar.

That does not mean, however, that he refrained from taking one or more to bed. Sally Hemings, a household slave, was said to have resembled Martha and was taken to Paris in 1787 when Jefferson served as minister to France.

Recently DNA tests made upon known descendants of Thomas Jefferson and of slaves who bore children to his father-in-law proved indecisive. Several men with the Jefferson DNA were in and out of Monticello over a fairly long period. One or more of these relatives could have been intimate with Sally—who was described as both charming and lovely—without Jefferson's knowledge.

It is impossible to refrain from speculating on the circumstantial evidence. Hemmings's long association with Jefferson cannot be denied by the stoutest defenders of the man's honor. At a time when it was rare for a man of high position to take a slave with him to another nation, Hemmings spent the better part of three years as a member of Jefferson's Paris household and was at Monticello for the remainder of her life.

Sexual relations between masters and slaves were not that unusual and even tacitly accepted throughout the Old South. Diarist Mary Boykin Chesnut made more than one reference to this practice in her famous record. Once she wrote with biting sarcasm about a plantation owner who had worn a path to the

VIRGINIA STATE ARCHIVES AND HISTORY

Monticello, Jefferson's plantation manor, was romanticized by an admirer as an ideal setting for a man of learning and husbandry.

slave quarters. Everybody knew exactly what was going on, she noted, but absolutely no one—least of all members of the landowner's family—ever said a word about it.

It is therefore reasonable to believe that Thomas Jefferson, who may have promised his dying wife never to marry again, kept his word but did not remain celibate. The probability is also high that a slave gave solace to the second president for nearly forty years.

Abraham Lincoln may never have heard of Sally Hemings, but he was curious about the progeny of Jefferson. This inquisitiveness stemmed from two questions he had about his own life.

The brilliant self-taught attorney took no offense when someone called him "the fellow from Knob Creek who don't know what blood runs through his veins." That was true since Lincoln died probably believing himself to be illegitimate. Illegitimacy raises few eyebrows today, but it was a different matter in the 1800s.

Lincoln once sent an inquiry to circuit clerk Samuel Haycraft of Elizabethtown, Kentucky, requesting a copy of the marriage record of his parents, Thomas Lincoln and Nancy Hanks. Hay-craft made a diligent search of the courthouse records and replied that there was no such record. Lincoln scholars, however, believe that he had nothing to worry about. They insist that a marriage certificate that surfaced in a pile of loose papers in another county a dozen years after the president's death is genu-ine and that his birth was legitimate.

Lincoln was also interested in his mother's family history; Nancy Hanks died when young Abe was nine years old. She was an illegitimate child, and as an adolescent Lincoln imagined that she was related to a Virginia landowner. Subtle clues suggest that young Lincoln brooded over the identity of his Virginia ancestor and decided that he was Thomas Jefferson.

Lincoln may have credited his own unusual height to the second president, who was six feet two inches tall and also lean

Lincoln's birthplace is a far cry from Monticello, but the sixteenth president allegedly believed that he was related by blood in some way to Jefferson.

and lanky. He certainly put Jefferson at the top of his personal list of great Americans. Repeatedly, Lincoln stressed that the Jefferson-prepared Declaration of Independence—not the U.S. Constitution—was the central document of American democracy.

If he heard any portion of the Hemings saga, that would not have bothered the Civil War president. To him it made all the difference in the world, however, that Jefferson's blood might be coursing through his veins.

NATIVE AMERICANS ON BOTH SIDES OF THE FENCE

SLAVERY IN North America is automatically linked with African Americans. Yet these men and women were not the continent's first slaves. Several tribal groups of Native Americans enslaved those they captured in war, and these tribes were here well before the first Africans arrived in 1619.

One of the earliest newspaper advertisements for a runaway slave appeared in the *Pennsylvania Gazette* by John England in March 1731. He offered a reward of five pounds "and reasonable charges" to any person who would find and return to him a slave known only as Jack. Described as being "generally pretty Sawcey" and no longer young, Jack was valuable because he was a skilled carpenter.

New Hampshire, seldom considered when slavery is discussed, held 379 male and 295 female slaves in 1773. During the previous year 6,638 slaves were imported from Africa to the British colonies in North America and another 3,146 were brought from the West Indies. Early records vary widely from colony to colony, and only Maryland had a category for persons of mixed blood. No mulattos were reported until 1755, when Maryland listed 1,460 as free and 2,148 as slaves.

Specific records about the number of Native Americans who were held as slaves at the beginning of the Civil War do not exist. It is certain, however, that though they were far less numerous than black slaves, some could be found in most states.

Affluent tribesmen often owned other tribesmen as well as African slaves.

Especially among the Cherokees, a man's prestige was measured by the number of slaves he owned, but most Native Americans who were prosperous enough to be slaveholders had only one or a few of them. A handful of wealthy tribesmen such as John Ross owned two dozen or more slaves, however. Since their total number was small by comparison with the number owned by whites, these slaves played no significant role in the North-South split or in the war that resulted from it.

ORGANIZED RELIGION LED THE WAY

ONE OF the first North-South splits occurred sixteen years prior to the Civil War and divided the largest religious body in the nation into northern and southern segments.

High on the agenda when the Methodists gathered in New York on May 1, 1844, was the issue of slavery. The delegates represented 985,598 white members of the denomination, 145,409 blacks, and 4,129 Indians. At the same time, a few blocks away, the Anti-Slavery Society led by William Lloyd Garrison was conducting its annual meeting. Probably at the instigation of Garrison and clearly with his knowledge that the Methodists might be influenced by their actions, the society passed a resolution urging the "immediate dissolution of the existing union between Northern Freedom (such as it is) and Southern Slavery."

For their part, the Methodists then decreed that any slave-owning church official was subject to investigation. James O. Andrew of Oxford, Georgia, was hastily examined and duly reported as "being connected with slavery." His dismissal from the office of bishop was recommended.

In response, the representatives from thirteen southern states registered their strong protest. The result was a formal Plan of Separation that brought about the founding of the Methodist Episcopal Church, South.

The Southern Baptist Convention, destined to become the largest religious body of the nation, was established immediately afterward. Seven years earlier, a northern contingent withdrew from the Presbyterian Church in the U.S.A. over sectional differences, which included the issue of slavery.

More than a decade before the outbreak of Civil War, about 80 percent of the nation's churchgoers held membership in a body with a clear northern or southern bias. Roman Catholics and Episcopalians were not included in this number. Both bodies were then much smaller than the mainline Protestant churches, and Roman Catholics maintained a national identity during the years of bitter fighting when civil war finally did break out.

Such was not the case with the Episcopal Church. Initially barely present on the frontier, this body placed Leonidas Polk at the head of its diocese in Louisiana in 1835, and some growth was achieved. On June 25, 1861, Polk, a West Point graduate, accepted a major general's commission in the Confederate army. Soon the bishop-general launched a campaign that resulted in the organization of a separate southern church. It maintained its independence throughout the war years then mended fences and rejoined the national body. Methodists, Baptists, and Presbyterians did not make similar postwar moves until generations later.

FUGITIVES WANTED—COST NO OBJECT

THOMAS SIMS was a slave in Georgia, and little is known about him. No history of the state published before 1960 so much as mentions his name, possibly because his ties with the Ivory Coast were close and short. He attracted the attention of the nation when he was only seventeen years old, and what he lacked in maturity he more than made up for in courage and intelligence.

No one knows how long Sims had planned to shake the red clay of Georgia's upland cotton fields from his feet. It is apparent that he did not leave the state and his owner on impulse, because he waited to make his getaway on a special day—February 22, 1851. To Sims, George Washington's birthday had more than a symbolic significance; it possessed a special charm that was calculated to bring good fortune to those who embarked on great ventures that day.

Jubilant to the point of being jaunty, he boldly walked off his master's plantation in broad daylight, but less than sixty days later he returned in handcuffs and leg irons. He had not been ironed in Savannah or Augusta or Richmond, but in Boston, "the Cradle of American Liberty."

In 1793 Congress had passed a fugitive slave act that criminalized any assistance rendered to runaway slaves or any failure to assist slave owners in recovering their chattel. The penalty was a fine of as much as five hundred dollars, but the maximum impost was seldom demanded.

In response, many northern states passed personal liberty laws to protect the rights of free blacks. Over time this legislation blunted the federal fugitive slave act. Also the federal statute was unenforceable beyond the nation's borders, and so Canada became a refuge for runaways. In 1826 this neighbor to the north flatly refused to return fugitive slaves and in 1829 enacted legislation that conferred instant freedom on any slaves entering the country.

The issue of slavery continued to heighten sectional tensions within the United States until the country appeared to be on the verge of war in 1850. The conflict was averted only after southerners received legislative guarantees concern-

Handbills offering rewards for the return of runaway slaves used art such as this to depict the fugitives.

NATIONAL ARCHIVES

Harriet Beecher Stowe wrote an all-time best-selling classic about the lives of slaves.

ing personal property rights—a grand euphemism for slavery—through the strict enforcement of fugitive slave laws. While the Civil War was delayed for another decade, slave catchers were given greater latitude in pursuing runaways. Under the law, officials in the North were enjoined to assist slave catchers in capturing fugitive slaves and returning them to their owners. In many ways slave owners were allowed to bypass the legal system—since the law specifically denied fugitive slaves a jury trial—by taking their cases to any U.S. commissioner for quick action.

Violators of the fugitive slave law were liable to six months' imprisonment, a fine of one thousand dollars, and reimbursement of the owner for the market value of the slave. Any officials who failed to execute a warrant for the arrest of a runaway could face the thousand-dollar fine and pay compensatory damages to the owner for the value of the escaped slave.

With the horizon of freedom lifted from the line between free and slave states, runaway slaves now were forced to find freedom beyond the Canadian border. In the meantime, slave catchers were doing a booming business.

That notoriety also emboldened the antislavery and abolitionist societies in the North. Many violated the law who might not have previously. More personal liberty laws were enacted. And a book shook the country to its core.

Harriet Beecher Stowe called her novel *Uncle Tom's Cabin* and fervently hoped that it might somehow aid a few runaways. She had no idea that it would become one of the most influential volumes of modern times. It enraged and enlightened people by

Because he was a fugitive slave, Thomas Sims was wanted by bounty hunters and slave catchers.

AFRICAN-AMERICAN ALMANAC

making them aware of the atrocities slavery was capable of perpetuating on the enslaved, including the mistreatment of runaways. More than seven million copies were sold prior to the Civil War.

When the Boston police seized Thomas Sims under the provisions of the Fugitive Slave Act of 1850, he had been in the city for a month and was adjusting well to the life he thought he had found. He made no attempt to hide. The cotton fields of Georgia were far away from the first battlegrounds on which Americans had offered their lives for freedom.

That's what Sims thought.

Seized by an officer who was eager to be rewarded, Sims was taken to the courthouse as a prisoner about six weeks after Washington's birthday. Within twenty-four hours he was taken before a U.S. commissioner who heard the brief evidence.

Yes, Sims belonged to Georgia planter James Potter, who had come to Boston to retrieve his property. Yes, the officer who took him into custody had acted according to the law. Yes, the runaway would have to return to Georgia and to slavery by the first available vessel.

Attorneys Richard H. Dana Jr. and Samuel E. Sewall appeared on behalf of the prisoner. So had Charles Sumner, who was still smarting from failing in his bid for a seat in the U.S. House of Representatives and who was considering campaigning for the Senate.

Sims's high-powered defense team had been of no help, however. Instead they stirred up public opinion. Posters were printed to warn the "colored people of Boston" to stay out of sight of the police. Noted orator Wendell Phillips and editor William Lloyd Garrison threw their tremendous influence behind an effort to prevent Sims's return to Georgia.

Public opinion reached such a fever pitch that soldiers were brought in to guard the courthouse where Sims was being held while his owner waited for the right ship to come along. Numerous Boston churches held special meetings on behalf of the fugitive, and street-corner orators harangued already excited crowds.

The authorities placed a heavy chain at a spot calculated to prevent troublemakers from getting too close to the courthouse. Bloodhounds were brought in as well as three hundred special policemen to guard the prisoner at the cost of bloodshed, if necessary.

Lemuel Shaw, chief justice of the Supreme Judicial Court of Massachusetts, consented to review the decision of the U.S. commissioner, but by April 10, the partisans of the runaway realized that their cause was hopeless. "Sims could be dragged away at high noon and not a dog would wag his tongue," Wendell Phillips thundered. That bit of nineteenth-century oratory was considerably shy of the truth.

A shack was being built for Sims on the brig *Acorn*, but the talk on Boston's streets contended that the tiny improvised dungeon would never be occupied. A band of two hundred men from Worcester and another one hundred from Plymouth County were rumored to be en route to Boston, muskets in hand, to rescue Sims.

These armed men never appeared, and the three hundred special police officers assembled at about 4 P.M. on

Orator Wendell Phillips failed in his attempt to keep Sims in Massachusetts, where slavery was illegal.

Saturday, April 13, to hustle the fugitive from his cell and escort him to the ship. Captive and captors marched through Court Square and crossed the site of the Boston Massacre, where Crispus Attucks, a black man, had been among five men who had been shot down by British troops on March 5, 1770. At the head of Long Wharf, they wheeled toward the little *Acorn*.

Escorted aboard the vessel and secured in the hastily built shack, the Georgia slave became the first person to be returned to slavery from Massachusetts. By one account, six days later Sims was publicly whipped in Savannah. If that punishment was actually administered, it ended all news of the plantation worker in Georgia if not in the entire South.

Sumner, Phillips, and Dana repeatedly invoked Sims's name back in Boston. They failed to win the immediate repeal of the Fugitive Slave Act, but collectively the three attorneys—most of all Sumner—aroused multitudes of people. And the Massachusetts legislature paid attention, especially during debate on the selection of the next senator from the Bay State. The seat went to Sumner on April 24 by the margin of a single vote.

Hundreds of Boston policemen surrounded Sims when he was escorted to the ship that would take him back to a Georgia plantation.

MASSACHUSETTS ARCHIVES AND HISTORY

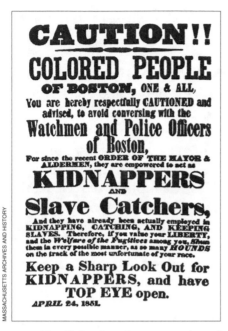

CAUTION!!
COLORED PEOPLE
OF BOSTON, ONE & ALL,
You are hereby respectfully CAUTIONED and
advised, to avoid conversing with the
Watchmen and Police Officers
of Boston,
For since the recent ORDER OF THE MAYOR &
ALDERMEN, they are empowered to act as
KIDNAPPERS
AND
Slave Catchers,
And they have already been actually employed in
KIDNAPPING, CATCHING, AND KEEPING
SLAVES. Therefore, if you value your LIBERTY,
and the Welfare of the Fugitives among you, Shun
them in every possible manner, as so many HOUNDS
on the track of the most unfortunate of your race.
Keep a Sharp Look Out for
KIDNAPPERS, and have
TOP EYE open.
APRIL 24, 1851.

MASSACHUSETTS ARCHIVES AND HISTORY

Thomas Sims's case triggered a panic among the people of color in the North and a rash of warning posters.

Afterward Sumner frequently observed, probably correctly, that he owed his dramatic razor-thin victory to his role in the Sims case. Sumner became an implacable foe not only of slavery but also of virtually everyone and everything southern. His was an unmistakable voice in the cry for the abolition of slavery regardless of the cost.

Abolitionists in general and Sumner in particular were prime movers in shaping northern public opinion in the years preceding the war. Because abolitionists played an important part in the election of 1860, they played a significant role in the drama that elevated Lincoln, a nonabolitionist Republican, to the presidency of a bitterly divided nation. That association, however, dramatically influenced the fragmentation of the Union which followed, and the compromise that had been sealed with the Fugitive Slave Act of 1850 was no more.

THE ONE INSOLUBLE ISSUE

SINCE CENSUS data are only as good as those who gather and compile them, there is no way to know exactly how many persons of African descent lived in the thirty-three states that made up the Union prior to the January 1861 admission of Kansas. According to the census of 1860, there were 2.21 million black men in the nation just before Secessionists fired upon Fort

Sumter. At that time black women (2.22 million) slightly outnumbered the men.

The monetary value of slaves varied widely. A child not old
enough to work in the fields might not bring $50 if sold at auc-
tion. The worth of adult field hands had appreciated at a tremendous rate since Eli Whitney's invention of the cotton gin, so a
healthy slave from twenty to forty years old might be valued
from $450 to $1,500. Skilled workmen such as blacksmiths and
carpenters brought even more, as did expert seamstresses, indigo
and silk workers, and good cooks. Nearly a month after the battle
of Gettysburg, Confederate artillerist E. Porter Alexander suggested that $2,000 for a good wet nurse would be a sound
investment. Almost 4.5 million slaves with an average value of
even $300 represented about $1.33 billion in property. That
meant the value of slaves considerably exceeded that of all other
Cotton Belt assets combined.

This aspect of the complex issue was enough to make nearly
everyone in the country realize that it would take a cataclysmic
event to bring slavery to an end. Notions about gradual emancipation, with compensation to owners, sounded good in princi-
ple. In practice even staunch adherents of this process, such as
Lincoln, must have realized that it would throw the nation in
debt to implement it.

States' rights loomed large in the sectional dispute. So did the
tariff upon imported goods, typically the largest single source of
income for the federal government. Cultural differences were
large and distinct enough to make many Secessionists brag that
each of them could easily lick three or four Yankees single-
handedly. At the same time, typical Yankees sneered at run-of-
the-mill southerners as being uncouth, ill bred, illiterate, and
incompetent ne'er-do-wells. Collectively, however, all other
North-South distinctions and divisions shrank to practically
nothing by comparison with the slavery issue.

Many twenty-first-century southerners fervently assert that
slavery was not the cause of the war. This illusion vanishes after a
brief look at the basic economics of slavery. It can evaporate
after scanning some of the pronouncements of significant south-

ern leaders just prior to the war and during the first months of the conflict.

It would have taken time, patience, and money to solve all other sectional issues, but that could have been done. Slavery *was* the insoluble question that served as an insurmountable stumbling block to any and all efforts at sectional conciliation.

LINCOLN WORKED HARD FOR OVERSEAS COLONIZATION

WHEN LINCOLN sent his second annual message to Congress on December 1, 1862, the lawmakers had at least a fuzzy understanding of what was likely to be included in the Emancipation Proclamation that would go into effect on January 1, 1863. Some of them were surprised that the president proposed three amendments to the U.S. Constitution. Collectively, they made up his personal plan for dealing with the slavery issue.

First, Lincoln wanted slavery to be abolished gradually by enactments at the state rather than the national level. Second, he insisted that slave owners be compensated, much as had been done in those countries that had outlawed slavery in the early

nineteenth century. Finally, he was convinced that the country's deep-rooted racial problem required that emancipated slaves should be returned to the continent from which they had come.

Lincoln was very much influenced by three pioneers in

Noted statesman Henry Clay favored requiring free states to return fugitive slaves, but he was also an early advocate of colonization— which influenced Lincoln's thinking on the matter.

HARPER'S PICTORIAL HISTORY OF THE GREAT REBELLION

ILLUSTRATED LONDON NEWS

Lincoln was an advocate of colonizing freed slaves in the African nation of
Liberia, which had been founded for that purpose.

the colonization movement: Thomas Jefferson, Henry Clay,
and John Quincy Adams. Lincoln himself had been a member
of the American Colonization Society since early manhood.
During his eulogy of Henry Clay in 1852, Lincoln assured his
listeners that "there is a natural fitness in the idea of returning
to Africa her children."

Slightly more than a year later Lincoln spoke on the subject
of colonization at the First Presbyterian Church in Springfield.
His speech was so persuasive that he was invited to be the featured speaker at the annual meeting of the Illinois chapter of the
Colonization Society. Later, in 1857, again addressing an audience in Springfield, Lincoln warned that the only way to prevent
the "amalgamation of races" was to separate them by colonizing
the freed slaves.

Soon after he took the oath of office in 1861, the sixteenth
president conferred with Ambrose W. Thompson, discussing at
some length a large tract of land in Panama owned by the not-

for-profit business Thompson headed. The chief executive was pleased to learn that in addition to having potential use of the land for colonization, a large supply of coal suitable for naval use might be available in the region.

Lincoln, Thompson, their colleagues, and their advisers maintained a running dialogue for eighteen months. The long-cherished plans for gradual emancipation and for colonization had not been made public when the Emancipation Proclamation went into effect. On December 31, 1862, however, the president met with Bernard Kock and signed a contract for the establishment of a colony of American blacks on Haiti's Île à Vache. On January 3, key aides of the chief executive were asked to consider the best way to frame new treaties with nations whose leaders had indicated a willingness to accept former slaves and establish them in colonies.

Yet Lincoln made no more public pronouncements in favor of colonization after he signed the Emancipation Proclamation. He nevertheless clung tenaciously to hope that the Île à Vache experiment would succeed, and he did not give up until surviving members of "the colored colony established by the United States" came home late in the winter of 1863–64.

COSTLY MISTAKE

THE SO-CALLED Kilpatrick-Dahlgren Raid has received a lot of attention as of late. Launched against Richmond, the raid was apparently the idea of Union Gen. H. Judson Kilpatrick, a young cavalry commander so reckless in combat that his men dubbed him "Kill-cavalry." Col. Ulric Dahlgren was a young, impetuous, well-connected officer. As a cavalryman he owned an undistinguished record during two years of frequent fighting. The paths of the two men came together in July 1863.

On the third day at Gettysburg, Kilpatrick ordered a cavalry charge that was barely short of murderous. Though not nearly so familiar as Pickett's Charge by infantrymen under the Southern banner, Kilpatrick's assault was very costly to the Union Army of the Potomac. Brooding over the error in judgment that had smeared his reputation, he pondered how he might remove the stain on his record.

Sometime during the early winter of 1863–64, Kilpatrick devised a bold and daring plan for a raid on Richmond. The venture would take his force deep behind the lines, where his men would do all the damage they could and free thousands of Federal prisoners from the notorious camps in which they were held. The most ambitious aspects of the raid were to be relegated to Dahlgren, who had lost a leg in street fighting at Hagerstown, Maryland, during the pursuit of the Confederate army following the battle of Gettysburg.

If possible, Dahlgren was even more daring and adventurous than Kilpatrick. The twenty-one-year-old officer was the son of John Dahlgren, a distinguished naval officer with a background in ordnance design. The older Dahlgren had been the commander of the Washington Navy Yard and chief of the Bureau of Ordnance during the first two years of the war; in July 1863 he was given command of the South Atlantic Blockading Squadron. The younger Dahlgren had a lot to live up to.

Together Kilpatrick and Dahlgren considered the best ways to inflict the most damage on Richmond and sought and received permission to undertake the mission. Though documentary evidence is lacking, the nature of the raid and its objectives were such that it had to have been approved at the very highest level— meaning that Lincoln had to have known of the plan.

After dark on February 28, 1864, around four thousand men saddled up and headed toward Richmond. Kilpatrick was scheduled to hit the Rebel capital from the north as soon after dawn as possible. Dahlgren, who had only five hundred men, planned to separate from the main force and go halfway around their objective to hit the city from the south.

Things began to unravel before Washington was out of sight. Heavy rain, which had been expected, suddenly turned to sleet that slowed the horses just enough to mean it would be very hard to stay on schedule. Following their detailed plan, Dahlgren and his men left the main column somewhere in the vicinity of Spotsylvania Court House. By riding through Goochland Court House and subsequently crossing the James River, Dahlgren calculated he ought to be near Richmond by the time Kilpatrick reached its northern edge.

Rain, however, had caused the James River to begin to rise by the time the Federal riders reached its banks. Unable to get a good look at the raging stream to judge its depth, Dahlgren decided to proceed cautiously and elected to approach the city from the west instead of the south, confident that nearly simultaneous attacks from any two points would throw the defenders into confusion.

Way behind schedule and forced to go through a region he had not studied, the daring Dahlgren and his men became lost when they reached another river and could not identify it. A scout encountered an adolescent slave who informed the Federal horsemen that the river was the Rapidan. He claimed to know a way to Richmond that would not arouse the countryside, and he volunteered to lead Dahlgren's column to the capital.

The youngster was known only as Martin, and he belonged to David Meems of Goochland. He assured Dahlgren there was a crossing place at Jude's Ferry, a couple of miles from Dover Mills. Once across the river, it would be a straight ride to the outskirts of Richmond. Satisfied with the proposed route, Dahlgren and his rain-soaked weary men followed Martin's direction.

Because there was little moon to light the night, Dahlgren's men took longer to get to Jude's Ferry than anyone expected. Far more important, by the time the Federal raiders arrived, the river had flooded its banks. The time expending in getting to the ferry had been wasted; the strike force would have to retrace its path and send out scouts to find a place where the column could ford the river.

Dahlgren was not pleased with Martin and interrogated him again. The boy vowed that he had led the Yankee horsemen to the right place, but he had no idea that the river would rise so rapidly. Dahlgren was convinced, however, that the young guide had deliberately misled him and ordered that Martin be hanged.

Martin's fate was described in a story in the March 5 *Richmond Daily Dispatch*. "For no other offense than the imaginary one of misleading the enemy," the newspaper reported, "the negro was hung to a tree, where his dead body was found a few hours after life was extinct."

Soon after hanging the young slave, Dahlgren's column fell into a trap set by a handful of Confederate civilians. Dahlgren died on the spot, but his death marked only the beginning of a trail of mysteries and controversies that still swirl about the admiral's son and the infamous raid.

The *Official Records* includes hundreds of brief accounts in which slaves aided Federal forces. It may be a commentary of sorts upon the attitudes of the 1860s that Martin, whose mistake cost him his life, got his name into print. Whereas the *OR* includes scores of names of Native Americans who are identified as such, there are less than a dozen names of persons identified as slaves.

ONLY SLAVER TO DIE

ABOUT 6 percent of the estimated ten to twelve million Africans who were brought to the Western Hemisphere as slaves wound up in the United States. Records are not adequate to determine how many American owners and masters of ships were involved in the trade that was launched by the Portuguese during the fifteenth century. It is well established, however, that only one American who was a professional importer and seller of Africans paid for his actions with his life.

Terms of the U.S. Slave Trade Act, which went into effect during the 1820s, echoed the Constitution by branding involvement in the slave trade as piracy—a crime automatically punishable by death. Thousands of men wantonly violated the act. Those who were captured and convicted, however, received much lighter sentences than the law stipulated.

Articles of convention between the United States and Great Britain were signed in London on March 13, 1824, for the purpose of suppressing the slave trade. Any commander or commissioned officer of either nation's navy was empowered to "detain, examine, capture, and deliver over for trial and adjudication" any ship or vessel involved in the now-illicit slave trade. Many vessels, some of which held hundreds of slaves, were stopped in Africa's coastal waters or upon the high seas. No American who was master of such a ship went to the gallows for his crime, however, until after the Civil War was well under way.

In August 1860 the slave ship *Erie* was detained close to the mouth of the Congo River by the USS *Mohican*. About nine hundred men and women were found in chains aboard. Instead of sending them back to their homes, the American officers decided to put them ashore within the boundaries of the new nation of Liberia. Nathaniel Gordon, master of the slave vessel, was sent across the Atlantic for trial.

Maine native George P. Andrews, a graduate of Yale College who had been admitted to the New York bar in the year the *Erie* was captured, was on the staff of the U.S. district attorney whose headquarters were in New York. Andrews was assigned to prosecute Gordon. In a climate that was emotionally charged by war against the slaveholding South, Andrews sought and received a conviction on the charge of piracy.

Numerous influential political leaders, some of them Northerners, suggested or petitioned President Lincoln for a full pardon. Other influential persons pointed out that the law had never been faithfully observed and the president should commute Gordon's sentence. Lincoln refused to intervene. As a result, the slave trader was hanged on February 21, 1862.

NONISSUE FOR AT LEAST A YEAR

DURING THE first months of the war, slavery was a nonissue. Few men responding to the calls for Union volunteers did so to free the Southern slaves. If Lincoln envisioned emancipation as an early war goal, he told no one. His motivation for going to war with the South was the preservation of the Union.

Slavery increasingly became a factor in the Union war aims by the fall of 1862. Indeed, the Emancipation Proclamation placed the abolition of slavery in the forefront of the Union cause. By 1864, when the preservation of the Union was nearly assured, slavery was emphasized as one of the paramount causes of the war.

Years ago, in his landmark volumes on the soldiers of North and South, noted Emory University historian Bell Wiley wrote that he was not sure that any of the Union soldiers of 1861 had the least interest in emancipation. Indeed, to say that the Federal army was fighting to end slavery implied that Southerners were fighting to preserve the peculiar institution. Yet when many Confederate prisoners were questioned as to what they were fighting for, they usually responded that they had taken up arms because the Union army had invaded their homeland.

The U.S. Congress passed the Second Confiscation Act close to a year after the battle of First Manassas. It outlined for the first time the necessary provisions for freeing the slaves in the states then "in rebellion." The act stipulated that Confederates who did not surrender during the sixty days following enactment of the confiscation law would be punished by having their slaves freed. The act also stated that runaway slaves would be considered freed if they sought safety behind the Federal lines. These distinctions did not grant any rights of citizenship to the freed slaves, but it did make provisions for guaranteeing passage for them to any country that would guarantee citizenship rights to the former slaves.

It was not a perfect document of emancipation, for it ordered the return of any runaway slaves to any owner who remained loyal to the United States. Such were the terms of the old Fugitive Slave Act, and Lincoln was not willing to alienate those Border States where slavery was still practiced that had remained in the Union. It was hoped that such a distinction and the promise of compensated emancipation would entice Virginia and Tennessee to return to the fold.

The act did prepare the way for the Emancipation Proclamation in September 1862, and it also clarified the problem for Federal field commanders as to what to do with runaways and refugees. Many understood that every time a slave was freed, the Union war effort was helped, and people in the North and the South began to see slavery in a different light. Once this happened, emancipation began to look like a worthy war aim, and that opened the door to considering the enlistment of black soldiers.

Thus the Emancipation Proclamation of January 1, 1863, authorized the recruitment of black soldiers. By the end of the war, close to two hundred thousand free men and former slaves took up arms for the cause of freeing the remaining black American population. Few if any abolitionists or military strategists who backed this movement realized that black men in uniform would become one of the decisive aspects of the war.

SAVE THE UNION—BUT PRESERVE SLAVERY

WILLIAM GANNAWAY "PARSON" BROWNLOW of Knoxville, Tennessee, was one of the most cantankerous civilians during the war. He was also one of the strangest men of his day. The parson-turned-newspaper publisher would have been willing to do most anything if he thought it would save the Union. He was also an outspoken, articulate, strident, and belligerent defender of slavery, and Brownlow had a forum for his writings through his newspaper, the *Whig*.

"Parson" Brownlow managed to espouse both the Union and the institution of slavery.

FRANK LESLIE'S ILLUSTRATED WEEKLY

Brownlow's tirades against the Confederate leadership led to his expulsion from the South on March 15, 1862. He had been in the North but a few weeks when he began writing a book on the evils of secession. His *Sketches of the Rise, Progress, and Decline of Secession* sold a phenomenal one hundred thousand copies in the first few months following its release.

Although he did not say much about slavery in his book, his views were on the record through his newspaper. To Brownlow, slavery was about as wonderful an institution as could be imagined. He never flatly stated that slavery had been ordered by God, but that was the general idea behind much of his writings.

According to Parson Brownlow, the people who had been forcibly brought to the American South would have lived and died as heathens if they had stayed where they were born. And he argued that despite their contributions to the well-being of white Southern civilization, this was nothing compared to the spiritual benefits slaves received in return.

Nobody knows how many Southerners held views more or less like those of this former Methodist minister. There were substantial numbers of staunch patriots in Eastern Tennessee, Texas, Alabama, and other areas of Union loyalists who wanted the Union and slavery to coexist. They gambled everything for the Union, but no slave owner in his right mind would surrender valuable property without a fight. "The Union and Slavery" was the watchword of many citizens living below the Mason-Dixon Line.

A TAR HEEL STIRRED UP A HORNET'S NEST

IN THE stratified society of the antebellum South, Hinton R. Helper was born not far from the bottom, and the home folks in Davie County, North Carolina, would never have guessed that he would be capable of making much trouble. Some way or other, however, he began to ponder the justness of slavery.

He was not greatly interested in the slaves themselves. As Helper saw it, these newcomers to North America were a source of trouble to the most numerous people of the South—

NORTH CAROLINA ARCHIVES AND HISTORY

FRANK LESLIE'S ILLUSTRATED WEEKLY

Hinton R. Helper (left) stirred up such a hornet's nest that in many Southern towns and cities his book, The Impending Crisis, *was burned. William H. Seward (right), famous as "Mr. Republican," lost the support of many delegates at the 1860 national convention because he had endorsed Helper's book.*

whites who worked with their hands, barely eked out a miserable living, and did not have a chance of ever owning slaves. These people, he argued, were in direct competition with the slaves and were being undercut because the slaves had advantages over poor whites.

In 1857 Helper gave a big title to the little book he called *The Impending Crisis in the South and How to Meet It.* Slavery, he said, was at the heart of the problem. Hardworking whites at the bottom of the economic heap could not advance economically when they were forced to compete with slave labor to produce profitable crops. Helper insisted that the only way to head off the impending crisis was to abolish slavery, not for the sake of the slaves, but for the sake of working-class whites.

Very few copies of Helper's book exist today. Most of them went into public bonfires throughout the Cotton Belt and the rest of the South. Needless to say, the concepts in the book changed few minds in the South.

Up north, the reaction to Helper's book was vastly different. He found a readership among the well educated who owned a lot of property and who had made their marks in law or politics. During the election of 1860 some leaders of the young Republican Party had given their stamp of approval to the *Impending Crisis*.

Even a halfway endorsement of the book that came from cotton country, however, could be costly, as at least two men found out. John Sherman of Ohio, brother of the future Civil War general, was a prime candidate for the post of Speaker of the U.S. House of Representatives. His fellow lawmakers, many of whom represented southern states, discovered that he gave credence to Helper's ideas. That was enough to torpedo Sherman's campaign for the leadership post.

In 1860, when the delegates to the Republican National Convention rolled into Chicago, word circulated that William H. Seward of New York had given a left-handed endorsement to Helper's book. Seward was within a few votes of the nomination before the convention got under way. Several delegates feared that his links with the *Impending Crisis* might cost them votes at the state and local level. That was enough to block the "impending" Seward landslide and to open the door for Lincoln, who had shown enough sense to keep silent on controversial subjects.

Helper probably never realized the full consequences of his saying that slavery was an economic evil. While Lincoln sent him to Argentina as U.S. Consul, he did not last long in the post. That was the biggest reward he received from his literary efforts. In the South, not enough copies were sold to give him any royalties. In the North, Republicans printed sections of it in quantity to try to influence voters—but they pirated portions they liked and did not pay Helper a cent for the use of them.

CHAPTER FOUR

GENERALS
AND
BATTLES

HARDEE'S TACTICS

WILLIAM J. HARDEE undoubtedly knew that he was indirectly responsible for the way battles were fought during the Civil War. Time after time, Southerners swirled toward the flank of a Union line in a do-or-die effort to turn the flank. Simultaneously, almost as though the battlefield were under the influence of a powerful circular storm, Federals raced toward the Confederate flank trying to turn it. These movements, mirror opposites of one another, stemmed from the fact that most commanders relied heavily upon *Rifle and Light Infantry Tactics*, written by Georgia native Hardee while he was superintendent of cadets at the U.S. Military Academy.

Throughout the nineteenth-century Western world, military leaders had followed the tactics employed by Napoleon Bonaparte.

West Point, as sketched by an artist around the time Jefferson Davis was a cadet.

France's foot soldiers were armed with muskets, and the smooth-bore weapon was basic to much that he did on the battlefield. The introduction of the rifled barrel, however, required radical changes in tactics. Unlike the short-range musket, rifles were easier to load and accurate at greater distances.

A man with an analytical mind and a vivid imagination conceived the idea of placing a manual in the hands of U.S. soldiers and updating combat tactics using rifles. The U.S. secretary of war in the cabinet of President Franklin Pierce was just such an executive. Jefferson Davis had startled the military establishment by bringing camels from the Near East for use in the great deserts of the West—a radical innovation that had many practical aspects. Davis's own years as a cadet at West Point were undistinguished, but he is widely considered to have been one of the most capable men to have ever held the office of secretary of war.

At Davis's urging, Maj. William J. Hardee agreed to take on the job of updating the manual. During most of 1853 he devoted the bulk of his time to the demanding project, and his manual was published by the U.S. government two years later. By 1860 it was familiar to all U.S. infantry officers.

Hardee, however, was among the first U.S. Army officers who resigned their commissions to join the Confederate army, and at the battle of First Manassas he was a Confederate brigadier. Naturally he took his manual with him and special editions went to the Southern army's infantry commanders during the first weeks of the war.

In the North a new edition of the book was known simply as *Hardee's Tactics*, and Federal officers relied upon it heavily. Consequently, fighting men on both sides were frequently given orders derived from the same book. This led to numerous instances in which battlefield observers wondered why so many engagements were characterized by a cyclical movement along the line.

Union Gen. Irvin McDowell also contributed to this phenomenon, though not so heavily as did Hardee by means of his published treatise. McDowell's early education was largely in France. There he received the training that was then standard for all Frenchmen. Though the school he attended was not a

At the time of the battle of First Bull Run, Hardee was a brigadier and both sides styled their strategies after his book on tactics.

ALFRED R. WAUD, MANASSAS NATIONAL BATTLEFIELD PARK

military academy, he learned a great deal about tactics. He returned to the United States at the age of sixteen and became a cadet at West Point.

Just three years after he was graduated in the Class of 1838, McDowell was chosen to teach tactics at the U.S. Military Academy. *Hardee's Tactics* was more than a dozen years away, so during his four-year stint as an instructor, McDowell relied on the Napoleonic models.

When war broke out in 1861, dozens of U.S. Army officers who had studied tactics under McDowell exchanged their uniforms for those of the South. These schooled soldiers, most of whom became general officers, often encountered former classmates in battle. Because both had studied under McDowell, it was difficult for either to break from that pattern. Numerous engagements therefore were marked by a reliance on McDowell's classroom tactics as well as Hardee's teachings.

SIXTEEN CASUALTIES PER SECOND

PICKETT'S CHARGE at Gettysburg is well known. Perhaps because it constituted "the high-water mark of the Confederacy," it is widely considered to have been the most costly charge of the war.

Conventional estimates of the number of men who made up the mile-wide attack line vary around thirteen thousand. Remarkably few authorities venture to estimate the number of casualties, and many simply echo Robert E. Lee's terse comment, "The task was too great." John Michael Priest departs sharply from tradition in his meticulously documented study of the charge that is entitled *Into the Fight*. He calculates that 13,155 men marched toward Cemetery Ridge that afternoon, and that the divisions under George E. Pickett, James Johnson Pettigrew, and Isaac Tremble suffered 8,399 casualties during the hour-long assault. If that estimate is accurate, the brave Southern men who crossed that field fell at the rate of about 2.33 per second.

CURRIER AND IVES

At the apex of Pickett's Charge, Southerners engaged in hand-to-hand fighting with defenders of Cemetery Hill.

Almost exactly one year after Pickett's Charge, at 4:30 in the morning of June 2, 1864, Gen. George Gordon Meade's Army of the Potomac at Cold Harbor, Virginia, launched a charge across a six-mile front. About forty thousand men—three times as many as Lee sent against the center of Meade's line on July 3, 1863— went forward. Many of them had pinned their names and addresses on their uniforms, hoping that their bodies would be identified and sent home after the powder smoke had cleared from the battlefield.

Most of the Union casualties in 1864 at Cold Harbor

LIBRARY OF CONGRESS

Some authorities estimate that Union troops died in the futile charge at Cold Harbor at the rate of about one thousand per minute.

were suffered during a hellish ten minutes of butchery during which 7,000 to 10,000 men were felled by Confederate fire. In sterile mathematical terms that means that as many as 16.6 men fell every second, compared to the 2.33 per second rate of casualties during Pickett's Charge.

George E. Pickett was on the field that June morning, and in some small way he saw his shredded division avenged terribly.

A RELUCTANT SOLDIER WON THE BIGGEST BATTLE

MEASURED BY any standard, the three-day struggle at Gettysburg constituted the largest battle ever fought in North America. And it was won by a Union general who had not wanted to be a soldier.

George Gordon Meade was born in Spain and spent much of his boyhood in near poverty in Philadelphia. He knew that the only place he could get a free education was at West Point. Hence he labored hard to become a cadet despite the fact that he preferred to follow a career in law.

Young Meade was not accepted until his second try. Once he had his education and a commission, he stayed in the U.S. Army's artillery only a year before hanging up his uniform. After six years he found civil engineering more difficult than he had imagined, so he returned to the army because he saw no other way to support his family.

Twenty-one years after becoming a professional soldier by default, Meade was suddenly named to command the Army of the Potomac. It was known that Lee's Army of Northern Virginia was in Maryland and might be on the march into Pennsylvania. Meade moved rapidly northward, but neither he nor Lee knew where their forces would meet. When they came together near the village of Gettysburg, the man who did not want to be a soldier and who had been in command only three days racked up the most impressive victory ever scored on this continent.

MANY RANKS WERE ROLLED BACK

IN BOTH the Union and the Confederate armies, the commissions for general officers were based on the recommendation of the chief executive—Lincoln and Davis—and then confirmed by the respective Senate. Until a commission was confirmed, the rank was considered temporary and was qualified as a brevet promotion, but the officer was authorized to act at the rank prescribed.

Many officers in both armies quarreled bitterly over rank. When a disputant provided evidence that he outranked others on the basis of seniority, they accepted their subordinate roles without additional fuss. During Sherman's March to the Sea, some of the most acrimonious disputes with which he had to deal centered on questions of rank.

In most situations, it was not difficult to determine whether a commander was a brigadier or a major general, but sometimes

The U.S. Senate had to act favorably upon the nomination of a Federal general before his commission was granted.

the documentation was in transit or had been left at a depot or camp. If two brigadiers wanted to command the same body of troops, the man with the earlier commission ranked his rival and commanded accordingly.

Though it could be vexatious to establish seniority when commissions were not at hand, this dilemma was small by comparison with the one created by lawmakers if they should adjourn without acting on the president's promotion nominations. In such instances, an officer slated to become a major general and temporarily serving at that rank was still officially considered a brigadier.

In March 1863 Union Maj. Gens. Charles S. Hamilton and Stephen Hurlbut were embroiled in a violent argument over which of them had seniority and hence commanded the Department of Western Tennessee. Each threatened to have the other arrested. Hurlbut, however, had received his commission two days before Hamilton. When this was demonstrated, it appeared that the quarrel was at an end. Then it came to their attention that Congress had adjourned without acting upon Hurlbut's promotion. As a result, both men were of equal rank as brigadiers; seniority would have to be determined by the dates when their brigadier's commissions were issued.

It was determined that Hamilton's commission was dated May 17—the same day that Hurlbut received his. Thus the question of seniority, which is not clearly resolved in existing military records, could only have been settled by finding out the hour of the day the two commissions had been issued.

DEFEAT BROUGHT OUT INQUISITORS

WHEN SECESSIONISTS fired upon Fort Sumter, Capt. Irvin McDowell of the U.S. Army was serving in the office of the adjutant general. He was a native of Columbus, Ohio, and had gained the respect of the Buckeye State political leader Salmon P. Chase, who had become Lincoln's secretary of the treasury.

At the beginning of the war, general officers in the Union army were in very short supply. Chase pulled a few strings and succeeded in having forty-two-year-old McDowell jumped to the rank of brigadier in May 1861, bypassing three grades. It also helped that McDowell was one of the youngest members of Winfield Scott's staff. He was given command of the still-forming army of volunteers.

The special session of the U.S. Congress called by Lincoln convened on July 4, which started the clock running on the remainder of the enlistment period of McDowell's thirty thousand volunteers. With these special conditions in mind, Lincoln was forced to overrule Scott and his other advisers who reported that the volunteers were not ready for battle. McDowell would have to engage the Confederates immediately.

In spite of the rush to battle, that untrained, poorly equipped army almost carried the day at First Manassas. For his part, as commander of the Federal army, McDowell's orders were not ill-conceived, but they were beyond the abilities of the citizen-soldiers who had hurried to Washington to quell the rebellion. The result was a confused collision on July 21, 1861, that stunned both sides. The rout of the Union army and the "Great Skedaddle" that followed concluded the humiliating defeat.

Many blamed McDowell for the defeat. Two days after the battle, the general met with the president. Lincoln assured him that he still had his confidence. Within the week, however, the president named a new general to command the Division of the Potomac. Gen. George B. McClellan had been lauded in the press and by his superiors for his victories in western Virginia, and his rising star easily eclipsed McDowell's.

McDowell was given command of a corps of the burgeoning Union Army of the Potomac and remained within the circle of the president's advisers. He worked diligently on the elaborate plans for the defense of Washington while more than one hundred thousand volunteers drilled around the capital. Just prior to the beginning of the Peninsula campaign, McDowell was promoted to major general then informed that his corps would remain in Washington to man the capital's defenses while the rest of the army was moved to Fort Monroe on the Virginia Peninsula to begin the campaign to take Richmond.

McClellan was not happy to see his army lose McDowell's thirty-eight-thousand-man corps, not that its presence would have altered the failure of the campaign. Regardless of how many men McClellan had, he always imagined the enemy had twice as many. McDowell's corps, however, did not idly occupy the capital defenses; it marched on Richmond and advanced as far as Fredericksburg. On May 25, 1862, however, McDowell was ordered back to Washington to protect the capital from possible attack by Stonewall Jackson and then ordered into the Shenandoah Valley in pursuit of Jackson.

After the Peninsula campaign unraveled under the hammer blows of the Seven Days' battles of June 25–July 1, which were directed by the newly appointed Confederate commander, Robert E. Lee, McClellan's army was gradually extracted from Virginia and a new commander named to lead the next Union offense against Richmond. The new Federal commander was John Pope, and his march on the Confederate capital began before McClellan abandoned his base on the James River. McDowell's corps was included in Pope's army, and McDowell had Pope's trust.

Pope brashly promised victory and then played the fool for Lee. Stonewall Jackson marched toward the Shenandoah Valley then turned north and attacked the Union supply depot that had been built near the old Manassas battlefield. Pope dispatched troops from his base in Culpeper, and Jackson ambushed them on the old battleground. As Pope poured more men into the area, he was confident that he would destroy Jackson through the sheer weight of numbers. Jackson's corps, however, was reinforced by Longstreet's corps, which had followed his route and joined the battle on August 29, 1862. The Confederates threw themselves on Pope's left flank at just the right time and broke the Federal line. Pope's army fell back and abandoned the field.

The second embarrassment at Manassas released a whirlwind of criticism. Pope claimed that officers loyal to McClellan had sabotaged his plans. Chief among these was Fitz John Porter, whose piecemeal attacks on Jackson's line had failed to break the Confederates. Porter was pilloried publicly, court-martialed, found guilty, and dismissed from the service. But the fury of disappointment did not stop there.

Other accusations were made against McDowell, one of Pope's principal advisers on the battlefield. McDowell had been deeply involved in the decision-making behind Pope's failure on the battlefield, and he contributed to the Union defeat in two ways. First, McDowell was tardy in forwarding a report to Pope that Longstreet's corps was marching toward the battlefield. Second, he ordered the removal of a division from the left flank immediately prior to Longstreet's decisive attack.

Whereas the criticism of Porter came from general officers and politicians, the criticism of McDowell welled up from the ranks of the army, from the common soldiers. There was little doubt after the battle of Second Manassas that McDowell was the most hated corps commander in the Union army.

Soldiers accused the general of treason and threatened to shoot him. Some even suggested that McDowell's hat was a signal to the enemy. They observed that wherever it appeared on the field, the Confederates conserved their ammunition because they were convinced that the general's record of poor command would accomplish more than their fire.

McDowell weathered these criticisms well, but then a letter surfaced in Washington purporting to be the last message from Col. Thornton Brodhead of the First Michigan Cavalry. Brodhead had been mortally wounded during the withdrawal from Manassas. He claimed, "I have fought manfully and now die fearlessly. I am one of the victims of Pope's imbecility and McDowell's treason. Tell the president that to save our country he must not give our flag to such hands." Newspapers across the North soon published Brodhead's letter, portraying it as a dying declaration of a hero of the republic.

With the flames of criticism roaring around him, McDowell wrote to his commander in chief on September 6, 1862, requesting a court of inquiry. Acting on orders from General in

Chief Henry W. Halleck, the court convened in Washington on November 21 with Gens. George Cadwalader, John H. Martindale, and James H. Van Alen constituting the judicial body. When they requested a copy of charges the court was to consider, they were told that the general in chief was not aware of any charges against McDowell. The military justices pondered instead McDowell's letter requesting the inquiry and focused on the accusations of treachery and treason made in the press.

No evidence against McDowell was found by the military court, though some of the testimony was not flattering. Incredibly, the legal review required sixty-seven days. The records of the case fill 305 pages of the *Official Records,* of which 9 pages constitute "Facts and Opinions of the Court." The last two paragraphs of this section read:

> It is to be hoped that the public misfortunes entailed by such calumnies [against McDowell] will in future lead to greater circumspection and secure for patriotic and meritorious soldiers more considerate treatment from the American press and people.
>
> In the opinion of the court the interests of the public service do not require any further investigation into the conduct of Major-General McDowell.

In the end, however, McDowell was a ruined man. The press continued to examine him for weeks after the judgment was announced, focusing specifically on the bits of testimony that were critical of the general. McDowell never held another field command, though. In 1864 he was transferred to the Department of the Pacific, where he never faced a Confederate adversary again.

THEY JUMPED OVER THREE RANKS

AMONG BOTH Northern and Southern fighting forces, the promotion of officers usually took place one grade at a time. Even under war conditions, it took quite some time for an officer to

FRANK LESLIE'S ILLUSTRATED WEEKLY

One of the biggest explosions of the war launched the battle of the Crater in 1864. During the fighting there, Confederate Capt. Victor Girardey received a battlefield promotion to brigadier general—a jump of three grades at one time.

progress through the ranks from lieutenant to captain to major to lieutenant colonel to colonel to brigadier to major general. At least four Federal officers and one Confederate made the gigantic leap in a matter of hours.

At the battle of the Crater at Petersburg in 1864, Confederate Capt. Victor Girardey distinguished himself on July 30, 1864, to the degree that he received a battlefield promotion to the rank of brigadier. Several authorities insist Girardey was the only officer in gray to jump three grades at one time.

Among the Federals, Capt. Irvin McDowell was the first to surmount three grades to became a brigadier in May 1861. His promotion, however, was unique, since it occurred within the ranks of the regular army. George Gordon Meade was a captain in the U.S. Army on August 30, 1861, and was made a brigadier the following day, but his spectacular rise in rank was partly due to the fact that his commission as a brigadier was in the U.S. Volunteers.

The distinction between the regular army and volunteers dates to the early weeks of the war. The standing army of the

United States numbered only sixteen thousand men in 1861. Those ranks were depleted somewhat when soldiers resigned to join the Confederate army. Following the Whiskey Rebellion legislation, Lincoln issued calls for troops to the states, and thousands responded. The U.S. Army did not have the resources to supply the first round of seventy-five thousand men who responded to the president's plea, and so the states were responsible for equipping these volunteers, creating a distinction between the two groups. Likewise, states could also confer ranks. The regular army remained a separate body from the volunteers, but it was not unusual for an officer to request leave from the army to accept a higher rank in the volunteers. At the end of the war, the officer returned to his unit and his previous rank. Service with the volunteers, however, did not preclude advancement in rank in the regular army. Thus during the war Meade was promoted in the regular army at the same time that he advanced as a general of volunteers, although not at corresponding ranks.

Meade was also the only commander to promote three men from captain to brigadier on June 29, 1863, at Fredericksburg—only hours after he was named commander of the Army of the Potomac. These men included George Armstrong Custer and Wesley Merritt.

Custer and Merritt, the latter a member of the famous Second U.S. Cavalry, were promoted to brigadiers of volunteers on June 29. At about the same time, the Union commander of the cavalry, Gen. Alfred Pleasonton, recommended Elon Farnsworth of the Eighth Illinois Cavalry to head a brigade of horse-

A legend was born when George Armstrong Custer was promoted from captain to brigadier general.

men. Both of Farnsworth's commissions were in volunteer forces, and hence were less valuable than corresponding commissions in the U.S. Army.

THE INVISIBLE BLACK FLAG

THE BLACK pirate's flag with its skull and crossbones flew above some vessels whose murderous crews did not hesitate to kill their captives. Although it was not so widely invoked as some references suggest, both Union and Confederate military leaders used the term "black flag" to label any action in which fighting men were either ordered or given permission to take no prisoners.

Surprisingly, given the immense stream of military communications during 1861–65, little is known about these events in which there were to have been no survivors among the vanquished. The term "black flag" occurs only thirty-three times in the approximately 165,000 pages of the *Official Records*.

An unidentified Rebel cavalry unit reportedly rode under a black flag into the battle at Front Royal, Virginia, in May 1862. A Rebel gunboat operating on the James River during the following month flew a black flag at the top of its mast. These literal rather than figurative uses of the pirate emblem were probably adopted because they were thought to strike fear into the hearts of any opponent who saw it.

Most black-flag allusions, however, are symbolic. During the winter of 1862–63 in Louisiana, Federal "outrages" provoked Confederates to unfurl the black flag. Homes were burned or destroyed, private property was seized, and—worst of all— rumors circulated that slaves were being armed and trained for military service. As a result, Confederate Gen. John C. Breckinridge, acting for Gen. Earl Van Dorn, issued an official warning that unless these barbarities ceased, his army would "raise the black flag and neither give nor ask quarter [clemency]."

The short and nearly bloodless war that Abraham Lincoln promised to the special session of Congress in his message of July 4,

The field orders of Union Gen. John Pope gave some Confederates an excuse to resort to the black flag.

HARPER'S WEEKLY

1861, went up in smoke at Bull Run. Still, no one in the North or in the South then anticipated that four years of terrible bloodshed would follow.

In August 1862 civilian Thomas Jordan felt impelled to warn Confederate Gen. P. G. T. Beauregard that "the war is rapidly drifting to the black-flag phase." It was his opinion that Southerners could not escape it "if the new system prescribed in [Union Gen. John] Pope's orders, and already inaugurated in my native county (Page) and village (Luray) is not stopped." Jordan naturally blamed the enemy for the increased inhumanity of the struggle. "We must accept the gauntlet thrown to us," he wrote to Beauregard. "Accept the war as tendered to us, and the sooner the better."

Capt. Joseph G. Peery of Hunter's regiment of Missouri infantry wrote from Little Rock on April 17, 1863, to Confederate Gen. Theophilus Holmes, using metaphorical language about the black flag he alleged was symbolically flown by the enemy. He asserted:

> Old Samuel Cox and his son (fourteen years old), Saul Gatewood, Heal Parker, and Captain Duvall, of Missouri, were a part of those they murdered in Carroll. I will call to mind other names and report them to you. They [Union forces] burned on Osage, in Carroll County, fifteen Southern houses and all of the outhouses, none of those thus being made homeless being permitted to take with them any clothing or subsistence. They seem to have hoisted the black flag, for no Southern man, however old and infirm, or however little he may have assisted our cause, is permitted to escape them alive.

J. C. BUTTRE ENGRAVING

The leadership of Nathaniel P. Banks in Louisiana led his Confederate foes to consider using the black flag.

Two months later, U. S. Grant became involved in a discussion of the black flag policy. In a June 22 dispatch to Confederate Gen. Richard Taylor, he did not employ the phrase, but Grant's meaning is unmistakable. He gave Taylor a scolding about the alleged hanging of some prisoners taken at Milliken's Bend, Louisiana. Then Grant warned: "I feel no inclination to retaliate for the offenses of irresponsible persons, but if it is the policy of any general intrusted with the command of any troops to show 'no quarter,' or to punish with death prisoners taken in battle, I will accept the issue [and do the same]."

In the final month of 1863, Confederate Gen. John Bankhead Magruder expressed extreme distaste for what was taking place. In a thinly veiled threat to Union Gen. Nathaniel P. Banks, he said that he was determined that "the black flag and its horrors" would not be attributed to him. "Should they occur," Magruder warned, "they will result from the views you are said to entertain, and the responsibility will rest with you and your Government alone."

The best-known black-flag incident took place on April 12, 1864, at Fort Pillow, Tennessee. Men commanded by Confederate Gen. Nathan B. Forrest easily subdued the installation then allegedly indulged in a deliberate and wanton slaughter of the black soldiers who had been taken prisoner. By order of Union Gen. William T. Sherman, Gen. Mason Brayman collected depositions from many who claimed to have been eyewitnesses.

James R. Bingham was one of several men whose statements were transcribed at Cairo, Illinois, on April 18, 1864, and he gave a lengthy description of the battle in which he took part.

The seemingly wanton slaughter of black soldiers at Fort Pillow, Tennessee, was attributed to the war's most publicized charge that the black flag was used.

According to him, 500 to 600 Union soldiers resisted "3,500 to 4,000 barbarians." He testified that after 1,500 Rebels rushed inside the fortress, most members of its garrison who were still alive "were killed outside the fort as prisoners."

Bingham owed his life to having hidden in the woods for forty-eight hours before being picked up by a Union gunboat five miles below the fort. Returning to the scene of the horror, he swore that he saw the remains of Lt. John C. Ackerstrom, presumably a white officer of a black regiment. "He had been nailed to a house, and supposed burned alive," according to Bingham.

Of the approximately 550 men who made up the Pillow garrison, 262 were black. Though 58 were taken prisoner, the charge that the rest were murdered created a storm of indignation in Washington. Demands for retaliation were quickly issued by the Committee on the Conduct of the War.

Meanwhile, Forrest issued an emphatic denial that his men fought under the black flag on April 12. He argued that many of the garrison had run for the river with their weapons after the fort had fallen. Although it is indisputable that black forces at

MOUNTAIN CAMPAIGNS IN GEORGIA

At Resaca, Georgia, after the fierce fighting had ended, twenty-three Southerners who had surrendered were reportedly slaughtered.

Fort Pillow suffered unusually high mortality rates, strong evidence to support the black flag charge is scanty.

On the Union side, although there are no records of orders not to take prisoners, many soldiers' letters and diaries give occasional glimpses into barbaric incidents. One of the men in Sherman's March to the Sea wrote to his Wisconsin fiancée after the battle of Resaca, Georgia. He said that twenty-three Southerners were taken prisoner when the little fortress was surrendered. Once they had delivered their weapons, the captives were asked if they remembered Fort Pillow before "the boys killed all of them." In a firsthand account that has to be used as cautiously as Bingham's account of Fort Pillow, this Union soldier said, "When there is no officer with us, we take no prisoners."

NEWSPAPERS WORTH THEIR WEIGHT IN GOLD

ORDINARY NEWSPAPERS often provided helpful information to the commanders in the field. There were numerous instances in which what we today call "leaks" got to the enemy through newspapers sold openly on the streets, and these changed the plans of generals. In the aftermath of Bull Run, Federal forces burned about one-third of Hampton, Virginia, when they withdrew from the town. This piece of news appeared in the *New York Tribune*—along with a summary of the official report of Union Gen. Benjamin F. Butler.

Confederate Gen. John Bankhead Magruder, who saw a copy of the *Tribune,* informed the War Department in Richmond that about four thousand troops had been withdrawn from the environs of Hampton and it was Butler's intention to use these and other forces to strengthen the defenses of Washington. His goal was to make the capital "so strong as to be easily defended by a small number of troops." This clear message that no attack should be launched upon the city any time soon helped to deter Confederate commanders who had their eyes upon it and thereby saved countless lives of their soldiers.

At Shiloh on April 6, 1862, some Federal commanders were caught, literally, with their pants down. The enemy hit so early

The engagement at tiny Shiloh Church, the focal point of the first tremendous land battle of the war, was predicted by a New York newspaper.

When Benjamin F. Butler strengthened the Washington defenses, newspapers inferred that Richmond would not be attacked any time soon.

in the morning that many an officer had not yet donned his uniform. They should have been ready, for a *New York Tribune* editorial of April 2 was entitled "The Expected Blow." In it, readers learned that the Rebels were posed to strike very hard and very soon. Had this information been passed along to Union commanders in the field, some of the thirteen thousand Northern casualties in that battle might have been avoided.

Well ahead of Lee's first move into Maryland, which led to the battle of Antietam, the *Philadelphia Inquirer* noted that he was planning a massive invasion of the North. The vital news was buried in a letter of warning from a Philadelphia resident who had been caring for wounded men. He divulged information that might have changed the outcome of the bloodiest single day of the war and perhaps of the war itself, but it was not noticed and acted upon by Federal commanders.

When the USS *Indianola* was under construction in the fall of 1862, the *Missouri Republican* went to great lengths in describing the size and proposed armament of the warship. By the time she slid down the ways, every Confederate naval officer on the Mississippi River knew what to expect if the splendid new warship should be encountered.

In September 1863 Lincoln and Stanton held what today would be called a press conference. Its purpose was to impress upon newspaper correspondents that no word concerning an impending move should get into print before it was under way. Plans called for the Eleventh and Twelfth Corps of the Army of the Potomac to go to what was then known as the West. This

Plans to reinforce William S. Rosecrans in Chattanooga were revealed to the press—and publicized.

very large body of troops would give new vitality to the command of Gen. William S. Rosecrans after his heavy losses at Chickamauga.

The correspondents of the major newspapers solemnly assured the president and the secretary of war that they'd give no hint of what was about to take place until the troops reached Tennessee. Yet on Saturday night, September 26, some leaders in the capital picked up copies of the *New York Evening Post* and found the story of the troop movement plastered across its columns. Rebels who read the same newspaper knew precisely what was going to take place, so they made preparations to deal with it.

Nearly a year later vital military information was still pouring through cracks in the clumsy censorship programs that had been imposed by Washington and Richmond. The May 15, 1864, issue of the *Atlanta Confederacy* reprinted an article from the *Chicago Times*. It gave a precise report about forces in Louisiana under the command of Union Gen. Frederick Steele. The strength of his army was accurately indicated, along with the distance of his force from his base of supplies.

ONE MAJOR GENERAL EQUALS TWO COLONELS

SOME OF the most complex and time-consuming problems faced by commanders on both sides revolved around the issue of prisoner exchange. In April 1861 the garrison of Fort Sumter was not treated as prisoners of war when it surrendered. Instead,

Anderson's men were given free passage to waiting ships that took them to New York, where they received a public ovation.

A few months later, after the battle of First Manassas, some military leaders wanted to exchange captured Confederates for Union officers and men languishing in the prisons of Richmond, Charleston, and other Southern cities. Initial efforts at devising a program of prisoner exchange failed. At the same time, Lincoln was determined to do nothing that might imply recognition that the Confederacy constituted a nation; to him, they were so-called seceded states that were still part of the Union.

More than any other single factor, the attitude of the president impeded efforts to develop and implement a program by which the two sides could exchange prisoners. Humane considerations aside, both sides would have been relieved of the burden of guarding and caring for prisoners who could be exchanged.

An early attempt at a table of equivalents was based upon the "compensation of men and officers." Had this yardstick been used, the monthly pay of a brigadier would have been divided by the pay of a private to determine the worth of the former. This schedule proved too complicated, and negotiators fell back upon a cartel—or official agreement between governments—that had been developed during the War of 1812.

In February 1862, after months of negotiation, a mutually acceptable program of exchange was adopted and remained in effect throughout the war with only slight variations. The agreement stipulated, "The basis for exchange is man for man and officer for officer, men and officers of lower grades to be exchanged for officers of a higher grade, and men and officers of different services to be exchanged."

According to the cartel, a commanding general was equivalent to sixty privates. A colonel was equal to fifteen men, a major equaled eight privates, a captain six, a lieutenant four, and a sergeant two. These were further clarified according to naval ranks. There were of course disagreements and violations by informal exchanges, but the issue that shattered the cartel and curtailed prisoner exchanges was the enlistment of African Americans by the North.

The South claimed that black Union soldiers were former slaves and runaways and should be treated as such should they fall into Confederate hands. The North, naturally, demanded that captured African Americans in uniform should be exchanged per the cartel.

The matter was decided in brutal terms when Ulysses S. Grant interpreted the exchange of prisoners as a disadvantage to the North. He subsequently ordered an end to the practice in April 1863. Interestingly, the parole of prisoners continued at the discretion of a field commander, and Grant exercised this option after the surrender of Vicksburg in July 1863.

No doubt more than a few officers being exchanged grumbled about the relative value of their ransom as compared to their contributions to the war effort. While some Union major generals doubted that a particular colonel was worth fifteen fighting men, Lincoln may have pondered what he could have gotten for some of his generals.

SHOULD IT BE CALLED THE "ATLANTA CAMPAIGN"?

THE OUTLINE for the Atlanta campaign was developed during a series of conferences between Ulysses S. Grant and William T. Sherman. Having recently been elevated to the rank of lieutenant general, Grant was eager to finalize a plan to bring the war to an end. Thus he and his long-time friend met in Nashville and then in Louisville to decide what each should do in the next few months.

From the beginning Grant made it clear that he was ready to assume overall charge of the eastern theater, where the Army of Northern Virginia would have to be crushed in order to bring an end to the Confederacy.

Like his president and commander in chief—and unlike many Federal commanders—Grant gave priority to crushing Lee's army rather than capturing Richmond. He was confident he could do that, but he needed the help of Sherman in the West to achieve his goal.

HARPER'S PICTORIAL HISTORY OF THE GREAT REBELLION

Nashville, Tennessee, was the site of a lengthy planning session between Ulysses S. Grant and William T. Sherman.

Their conference ended with the plan that Grant would go to Virginia and take the offensive against the Army of Northern Virginia while Sherman attacked the Army of Tennessee, which was led by Joseph E. Johnston. Once Johnston was defeated, Sherman would get to Virginia as rapidly as possible to augment Grant's forces that would presumably still be battling those led by Robert E. Lee. Sherman expected to transport his troops by water, either from Mobile or Savannah. When the two generals parted company, Grant went north and Sherman began planning his operation that would crush the Army of Tennessee— then largely located in the state for which it was named.

When Sherman launched his assault on Johnston from Chattanooga, he was keenly aware that his supply lines would be vulnerable, relying on a single railroad. The greatest danger to the Union advance was the possibility of nagging raids on the railroad by Confederate cavalry wizard Nathan Bedford Forrest, but Forrest never ventured into Georgia to threaten the rail line—although he was never far from Sherman's thoughts.

Sherman led three Union armies into Georgia, always pressing Johnston's army into retreating deeper and deeper into the state. After battles at Resaca, Alatoona Pass, New Hope Church,

Union Gen. William T. Sherman's objective in moving into Georgia was the Confederate Army of Tennessee.

BATTLES AND LEADERS

and Kennesaw Mountain, the Federals began to target the city of Atlanta as the next refuge of their prey. The city is rarely mentioned prior to the arrival of Union troops at the Chattahoochee River. Then and only then does the important railroad center become a significant goal of the long struggle during which the Army of Tennessee was pushed continually southward.

Had Confederate President Jefferson Davis, who had a personal dislike for Johnston, not rashly relieved him and placed John Bell Hood at the head of the Army of Tennessee, it's anybody's guess as to how long the struggle in Georgia would have continued or where it would have led. Once in command not far from Atlanta, Hood rashly launched attacks against Sherman instead of continuing the defensive warfare waged by his predecessor.

Bloody defeats of Confederate forces close to the rail center left Atlanta seemingly vulnerable. Yet defenses erected under the supervision of Lemuel P. Grant, a northern-born railroad engineer, were so strong that Sherman repudiated the idea of a frontal assault upon the city. Deciding to cut off all of its supply lines, he succeeded in doing so and became master of the rail center. His victory came at a time when the war-weary North was hungry for good news, and Lincoln's reelection seemed doubtful.

Although small by comparison with New Orleans, Charleston, Richmond, and Memphis, the surrender of little-known Atlanta on September 2, 1864, was celebrated throughout the North and was a significant factor in Lincoln's victory at the polls. Having won the city, Sherman was not sure what to do with it. Hood abandoned the area and plotted an assault in Tennessee to draw the Federals out of Georgia.

After occupying Atlanta for ten weeks, Sherman dispatched George H. Thomas to Nashville to blunt any assault that the Army of Tennessee might mount. To fulfill his obligation to Grant and convey his men to Virginia promptly, Sherman decided to "march to the sea" and live off the land. His two wings marched 250 miles along a 60-mile-wide corridor in twenty-six days, brushing aside the meager resistance they encountered. The successful execution of the march led the Federal commander to envision marching to Virginia from Savannah rather than moving his army by sea.

By cutting a wide swath through the Carolinas, Sherman believed he could devastate "the cradle of secession" while still moving toward Grant. The opposition, however, was stiffer than what he had experienced in the March to the Sea, but once again he was up against his old foe, Joseph E. Johnston (who hoped to link up with Lee) and an Army of Tennessee that had been decimated by Hood's recklessness at the battles of Franklin and Nashville. Sherman did not link up with Grant—Lee surrendered before that could happen—and Johnston surrendered his army to Sherman on April 26, 1865.

Conventional scholarship treats the Federal move from Chattanooga to Savannah as the Atlanta campaign, despite the fact that the Army of Tennessee rather than the rail center was Sherman's goal when he began his southward move. This term may be so firmly embedded in literature

Lemuel P. Grant, a northerner by birth, fortified Atlanta so strongly that Sherman gave up the idea of making a frontal assault on the railroad center.

GEORGIA ARCHIVES AND HISTORY

and entrenched in thought that it will never be altered. Yet the truth is that Atlanta was seldom mentioned in Sherman's voluminous dispatches, orders, and reports until worries about Forrest were diminished by distance and the spires of the little city were visible from the Federal camp.

NEVER IN BATTLE

THE BATTLE of First Bull Run dispelled the notion that the Union could quickly and easily subdue the rebellious South. Once it became clear that the war would be long and difficult, Union Gen. Winfield Scott's Anaconda plan of "slowly choking the Confederacy to death" affected policies at the highest level. Instead of simply smashing large bodies of foes in uniform, this kind of warfare required guarding one's own transportation and communication lines while disrupting the enemy's as much as possible. As areas of Federal occupation increased in the South, it became necessary to station protective garrisons at more and more points.

Thus huge numbers of men were needed for duties that kept them away from the fields of combat. At least three hundred Federal regiments saw only garrison or guard duty, and these men never heard the whine of a Minié ball. In addition to at least twenty thousand uniformed men who never saw a battlefield, thousands more experienced combat only once or twice.

FRANK LESLIE'S ILLUSTRATED WEEKLY

Union Gen. Winfield Scott offered a plan by which the Confederacy would have been slowly choked to death over a period of many months.

FROM BOTTOM TO TOP

NATHAN BEDFORD FORREST is listed as the only Civil War soldier who launched his military career as a private and ended it as a lieutenant general. That is both true and false. At age forty, the self-made millionaire donned a uniform on June 14, 1861, as a "buck private in the rear rank" of Joshua H. White's cavalry company. On February 28, 1865, he became entitled to wear the insignia of a Confederate lieutenant general, although he seldom displayed symbols of rank.

The fact is that Forrest almost had a rival for this honor. A fellow not well known to most Civil War devotees became a member of the Twelfth Pennsylvania when it was organized at Harrisburg in April 1861. When this ninety-day regiment was mustered out in August, Sam Young stayed in uniform and at Gettysburg was a major in the Fourth Pennsylvania Cavalry. Like the famous Rebel raider, Young rose through the ranks without the benefit of having had formal military training. During the war Young had sixteen horses shot from under him—Forrest had twenty-nine shot from beneath him.

Young, however, did not make it into the pages of *Generals in Blue* since his highest rank in 1865 was brevetted. Unlike the former slave trader from Tennessee, his career as a soldier did not end at Appomattox. He was mustered out of volunteer service in May 1866, but in less than a year Young was back in uniform as a second lieutenant in the Twelfth U.S. Infantry.

As a career soldier he served largely on the frontier, where he fought in many a battle with Indians. More than forty years after the Civil War, Young was made a major general during the Spanish-American War. After two years in the Philippines and a stint as commander of the District of California, he became president of the War College Board and a member of the general staff.

Samuel Baldwin Marks Young's final promotion came in 1903, when he was made a lieutenant general and the first chief of staff of the U.S. Army. Thus two Civil War soldiers began their military careers as privates and ended it in the highest rank that could be reached until recent times.

SECOND TIME AROUND

GEORGIA-BORN Joseph Wheeler had such high standing in his class at West Point that when he graduated in 1859 he received a commission in the mounted dragoons. After "seeing the elephant" or going into battle for the first time against the tribesmen of the plains, Wheeler exchanged his blue uniform for a gray one in April 1861 and became a first lieutenant of artillery. Barely six months later, Colonel Wheeler took command of the Nineteenth Alabama. At Shiloh he led a brigade, and soon afterward he was made the head of cavalry in Braxton Bragg's Army of Mississippi.

At the age of twenty-eight, the now-famous cavalry leader known as "Fightin' Joe" moved into the high timber made up of lieutenant generals at the top of the military mountain. In 1865 he packed his uniform away and became successively a businessman, attorney, cotton farmer, and congressman. As a member of the U.S. House of Representatives, he became chairman of the Ways and Means Committee and was lauded as a symbol of the reunion of North and South.

Upon the outbreak of the Spanish-American War, President William McKinley made Wheeler a major general of volunteers. In that role his subordinates included Theodore Roosevelt and Sam Young, who fought under him in Cuba. After a short stint in the Philippines, Fightin' Joe transferred from volunteers to regular army forces. He ended the second installment of his military career as the one and only former Confederate who became a brigadier general in the U.S. Army.

CHAPTER FIVE

MYTHS, RIDDLES, AND ENIGMAS

THE "GREAT EMANCIPATOR" NOT SO GREAT

THROUGHOUT THE world, Abraham Lincoln is revered as "the Great Emancipator." Many persons who have delved into his life, however, would be less inclined to do so. A casual reading of his debates with Stephen Douglas in 1858 reveal that, by today's standards, Lincoln was a racist.

Incidentally, known far and wide as the Lincoln-Douglas debates, there is something of a riddle within a myth to the matter. Lincoln had a hankering for a seat in the U.S. Senate that was then occupied by Douglas, also known as "the Little Giant."

To unseat Douglas, Lincoln would have to persuade more than half the members of the Illinois legislature to vote for him. At that time, the voting public had no voice in the selection of their senators. The riddle is why Douglas consented to the debates.

Stephen A. Douglas agreed to a series of debates with Lincoln in 1858 when he ran for reelection to the Senate.

PICTORIAL FIELD BOOK OF THE CIVIL WAR

Douglas knew that he had a majority in the Illinois legislature, possibly a slim one but nevertheless a majority. He did not have to debate his opponent, but he yielded to Lincoln's overture and they staged an epochal series of debates that did a great deal to make the name of an otherwise obscure attorney from Springfield known throughout the nation.

Calling them the Lincoln-Douglas Debates may be a reflection of the importance of the public jousting after the Lincoln presidency. At the time the two men sparred verbally, the encounter should have been known as the Douglas-Lincoln Debates, for the contest was between a long-time nationally known leader and a near nobody.

Regardless of what title might be given to the debates, Lincoln's messages reveal much about his racial views. He said not once but several times that he regarded blacks as inferior to whites. Nor was he sure that blacks should be allowed to vote because they did not have the intelligence of whites. The man from Springfield had his own formula for solving the issue of slavery and the racial problem: African colonization.

Lincoln was not, never had been, and never expected to be an abolitionist. One of only a handful of clear positions on the part of the would-be president was that he opposed the westward extension of slavery—but he was not disposed to abolish slavery in the South.

Once Lincoln occupied the White House and found himself embroiled in a war for the Union, he refused to take up the abolitionist banner. Only after more than a year of fighting did he address the twin issues of slavery and race. The preliminary Emancipation Proclamation announced in September 1862 had nothing to do with racial justice. It was a war measure, pure and simple, a way of striking a hard blow at the Confederacy without lifting a sword or pulling a trigger. It's doubtful that Lincoln had any conception how powerful that blow would be when he delivered it. He simply saw it as an opportunity to polarize the war aims of North and South and prevent foreign intervention.

No slave in a state loyal to the Union gained anything from the Emancipation Proclamation. Neither did slaves in Union-governed Tennessee or those in Kentucky, Missouri, and the other Border States within the Union. Thousands of slaves in specified regions of occupied Virginia and Louisiana were likewise given no hope of freedom.

The proclamation promised emancipation to slaves within Confederate territory and to no others. In that respect, it was a hollow gesture of political grandstanding. That it was a lot more is due to the fact that it gained the enthusiastic support of abolitionists for the war effort while firing the minds of slaves who began to hear whispers that Lincoln was going to do away with slavery. That led them to become bolder in trying to help the fighting men in blue and in escaping to Federal lines.

Part of the riddle of the Great Emancipator lies in the fact that he did nothing that had not been done before. Union Gens. John C. Frémont and David Hunter had tried to effect emancipation in the areas occupied by their armies, and both were promptly and firmly squelched by Lincoln. Some of the president's most

While commanding Federal troops in Missouri, Union Gen. John Charles Frémont issued the first proclamation emancipating slaves.

Radical Republican Henry Wilson was among the most sought-after orators in the U.S. Congress, particularly on the matter of slavery in the territories.

implacable foes were abolitionist members of Congress. These Radical Republicans were automatically opposed to nearly everything Lincoln did. What's more, they seized upon every opportunity to frustrate the president. Their leaders were Galusha A. Grow, Thaddeus Stevens, Owen Lovejoy, Joshua Giddings, Charles Sumner, Benjamin F. Wade, Zachariah Chandler, and Henry Wilson.

During the 1861 special session of Congress, these Radical Republicans pushed through legislation they considered damaging to secession. A Confiscation Act was pushed through and declared that a slave "used by a Confederate either in labor or in arms" was free. Of course, the act was meaningless because there was no enforcement mechanism.

In July 1862 the Congress enacted the Second Confiscation Act. Some evidence indicates that Lincoln initially planned to veto it, but he was swayed by the consequences of the measure. Four new actions became legal and permissible. First, military and civil officers were authorized to free slaves in areas under Federal control, regardless of whether or not these persons had been engaged in work for the Confederacy. Second, officials were given a free hand to confiscate any and all Confederate property. Third, recruitment and other military officers were authorized to put "persons of African descent" into uniform. Fourth, the idea of colonizing freed slaves "in some tropical country" was officially approved.

The Lincoln administration did virtually nothing to enforce the Second Confiscation Act. Had it been rigorously observed, there would have been no reason to issue the Emancipation Proclamation. This brings us back to the myth and puzzle with which we started: When and how did the president of the United States become the Great Emancipator?

DID "MARSE ROBERT" ALWAYS MEAN WHAT HE SAID?

ROBERT E. LEE said and wrote so much that—like Abraham Lincoln—his words are often hard to locate. A brief statement widely attributed to the Confederate commander appears in at least a half dozen authoritative volumes, one of which is *War, Terrible War:*

> I have fought against the people of the North because I believed they were seeking to wrest from the South its dearest rights. But I have never cherished toward them bitter or vindictive feelings, and *I have never seen the day when I did not pray for them* [italics added].

Recognizing that Douglas Southall Freeman was very kind and might have allowed a little hero worship to get the better of him, his portrait of Lee depicts an upright, gracious, honorable, and considerate man who is a trifle stern at times. This semi-deified commander of the Army of Northern Virginia who continued to fight long after he must have realized that the Southern cause was lost could not possibly, according to the Freeman image, tell an outright lie. Even exaggeration would be out of character for him.

If Freeman is correct in this depiction of Lee, then we can only read Lee's statement of praying for his adversaries as another side of this enigmatic man. For myself, I find it quite difficult to believe that the general could be this magnanimous.

R. E. Lee may have been the grandest specimen of manhood who ever walked on the continent, but I cannot believe that on the night of May 4, 1863, after having turned back the Army of the Potomac yet again, this time at Chancellorsville, he lifted his eyes to the midnight sky and invoked a blessing upon the people of the North.

Perhaps Lee did pray for Northerners between May and June 1863, but what prayers might he have uttered in early July 1863, specifically on the night of July 3? Even Marse Robert could not have avoided a wee twinge of regret and guilt at having tuned out James Longstreet's warnings of the past three days. Having witnessed Pickett's Charge, he had to have felt responsible for that dreadful carnage. Did he not greet the men who returned from that field with his confession? Did he not say to them, "It is all my fault"? In such a state of mind, could he have prayed for the Lord's blessings on his adversaries that night?

I believe that Lee's memory was not as keen when he claimed "never [to have] seen the day when I did not pray for them." Perhaps he may have had another purpose in mind, something other than a factual recitation of his memories of the battlefield when he wrote this. Rather than recall his every night in a tent on the field, perhaps he chose to look toward the future by downplaying the anguish of the past. Such are the musings of the present when a great man makes such claims.

DID STONEWALL REALLY SUCK LEMONS?

VIRTUALLY EVERY biography of Stonewall Jackson in action insists that he sucked on lemons. In their companion book to Ken Burns's epochal *The Civil War*, Geoffrey Ward and Ric Burns write, "Somehow, the fact that Stonewall Jackson sucked constantly on lemons in the midst of battle adds to the chilling mystery of his military triumphs in the Shenandoah Valley in 1862." In his analysis of the *Confederate Ordeal,* Steven A. Channing credits Jackson's source of the sour fruit to Maj. Wells J. Hawks, the general's commissary officer. He hazards the guess that Stonewall sucked on lemons in order "to relieve his dyspepsia" and says that the troops called Hawks's supply trains "lemon wagons."

How the lemons came to be so available in the field, when food was scarce in the South and its transportation system strained, is a mystery. Lemons had been introduced into Florida and California in the 1850s, but regular commercial shipment of lemons had not started at that time.

In his magnificent biography of Jackson, James I. Robertson suggests that the lemon myth is baseless. Its popularity, he puts forth, is rooted in the fact that great men capture our attention and eccentric myths cement them in our consciousness. How likely was Jackson to have sucked on lemons? Not very. He was an eccentric man for his time; the general was keen on fruit. Robertson suggests that if Jackson did indulge his taste for fruit during his Valley campaign of 1862, most likely it would have been peaches. There are peach orchards galore in the Shenandoah, but nary a lemon tree.

LEE'S LOST ORDER

THE STORY of Robert E. Lee's Special Order No. 191 illustrates the fact that truth is stranger than fiction.

Pvt. Barton W. Mitchell made the find. On Saturday morning, September 13, 1862, Mitchell and a few buddies strolled around their encampment in a clover field at Frederick, Maryland. The Twenty-seventh Indiana had stopped there early the evening before, so these fellows were refreshed the next morning.

Organized at Indianapolis, the Twenty-seventh Indiana did not see much action until March 1862. A great deal of time had been spent in camp at Frederick, so these men were well

Frederick, Maryland, was a small town made important by its location on a railroad line. Both the Confederate and the Union armies camped here, which led to the finding of Lee's Lost Order and the momentous battle of Antietam.

acquainted with the area. They had departed from here to fight in the Shenandoah Valley for a couple of months before first seeing a battlefield shrouded in powder smoke at Cedar Mountain in August. Later attached to John Pope's Army of Virginia, they were quite pleased with the prospect of returning to Maryland when the Rebel invasion in September 1862 caused the Indiana regiment to be dispatched in pursuit north of the Potomac River.

That Saturday morning the small cluster of Hoosiers spotted a rather odd-looking piece of paper, but it was forty-five-year-old Mitchell who picked it up. He emitted a hearty whoop of delight when he discovered that the dew-dampened paper had served as a wrapper for three scarce and precious cigars. Fine Southern tobacco was highly prized north of the Mason-Dixon Line.

Before the cigars could be divvied up, Mitchell noticed the content of the paper that had banded the stogies together. He smoothed out the paper, studied it briefly, and then announced its importance to his companions.

Bucked up the line to the regimental commander, the paper was determined to be either a fake or a copy of a recent order by the commander of the Army of Northern Virginia. Hastily the document was dispatched to the headquarters of Gen. Alpheus Williams, who studied it carefully and sent it to Gen. George B. McClellan.

McClellan, who rarely made any public display of emotion, could not conceal his delight when he scanned that crumpled piece of paper. Specific troop movements of units within the Army of Northern Virginia for the next two or three days were detailed. The discovery of this lost order is frequently characterized as the greatest intelligence find of the war.

This much of the story is so amply documented that it raises only one question that cannot be answered: Who wrapped this important document around the three cigars and dropped them as his unit broke camp and departed Frederick?

Working with a list of officers who almost certainly would have received such orders and following their known movements narrows the list of names to seven or eight at most. For decades after the war D. H. Hill was pilloried for having misplaced the

The Twenty-seventh Indiana fought in the battle of Cedar Mountain.

dispatch (the copy was addressed to him), and various staff officers attached to Lee—Col. Robert H. Chilton, Maj. Charles
Venable, Maj. Walter H. Taylor, and Capt. Charles Marshall—
and Jackson—Maj. Elisha F. Paxton, Capt. Henry Kyd Douglas,
Lt. James P. Smith—have been suspected of the carelessness.

Many believe that McClellan made good use of the intelli-
gence and that he was as ready for Lee as he would ever be when
their forces met at Antietam—or Sharpsburg—four days later.
The truth, however, is that the Lost Order gave little help to the
Army of the Potomac because McClellan moved cautiously and
Lee revised his orders in reaction to McClellan's advance.
Specifically, Lee had sent Jackson's corps to take Harpers Ferry,
Longstreet's corps to attack Hagerstown, and D. H. Hill's com-
mand to serve as a rear guard of the South Mountain passes.
When news came that McClellan was moving west from
Frederick toward the South Mountain passes, Lee recalled
Longstreet's corps to bolster those defenses until Jackson could
link up with the army in the area. Sharpsburg provided the best
ground for a defensive stand, and that was where the Confeder-

*Because McClellan did not act swiftly after he learned Lee's plans, his army
was delayed at South Mountain long enough to allow the Confederate army to
regroup near the town of Sharpsburg and Antietam Creek.*

CENTURY WAR BOOK

ate army reformed when the defenders of the South Mountain passes had to pull back.

When did Lee know that McClellan was aware of the details of Special Orders 191? There are two traditions. The first is that McClellan made a great show of receiving the copy of his counterpart's orders, and at the time he was meeting with a number of civilians from Fredericksburg, one of whom was a Southern sympathizer. This person conveyed the news to Jeb Stuart's cavalry, and Stuart delivered the news to Lee on the night of September 13. The other story is that Lee did not learn of the lost dispatch until reading an account of McClellan's testimony before the Committee on the Conduct of the War or in McClellan's postwar memoirs. Lee himself was not specific in his recollections of the event.

Dispatches reveal that Lee altered Longstreet's orders around midnight on September 13, but that does not necessarily mean this was the result of his learning that the enemy knew what he was planning to do. The assault on Harpers Ferry had begun early that morning.

A significant body of evidence supports the view that the lost order had nothing to do with Lee's change of plans. The story appeared in the *New York Herald* on September 15, two days after the discovery and two days before the battle of Antietam, but there is little chance that Lee was aware of it as his army hunkered down around the creek known as the Antietam.

In his excellent account of the story of military intelligence in the Civil War, *The Secret War for the Union*, Edwin C. Fishel suggests that Lee did not know about the lost dispatch until three or four months after the battle of Antietam. He bases that verdict on the fact that the bare facts of the case were given to readers of the *New York Journal of Commerce* on January 1, 1863. This revelation must have created quite a stir, since McClellan told what he knew about the lost order when he testified before a congressional committee in March 1863. In a recent issue of *Military History Quarterly*, Stephen W. Sears noted that Lee's belated reaction to the news was to regard the incident as simply "a great calamity."

Had McClellan reacted immediately upon receiving the details of Lee's strategy in Maryland, an even greater calamity might have befallen the Army of Northern Virginia. Having information is not the same as acting.

DID PEACE DEMOCRATS DISPLAY COINS?

MANY NORTHERN Democrats opposed the policies of the Lincoln administration, believing that the war was contrived by Republicans to maintain political control of the country and force a racially tinged agenda on the republic. These Peace Democrats, particularly those in the Midwest, became known as Copperheads because they wore an identifying badge made by cutting the profile of the figure of Liberty from a copper penny.

The nineteenth century was a time in which secret societies dotted the country. Private ceremonies and secluded rituals attracted large segments of the population. Freemasonry is probably the most well known of these organizations. Secret handshakes and subtle gestures were not uncommon. Thus the display of something as commonplace as a penny on one's lapel or hatband might be subtle to some and a clarion call to others or a badge of honor.

The Peace Democrats in Ohio, Illinois, and Indiana were especially outspoken in their denunciation of Lincoln and the war. An unofficial leader of the group was Ohio Congressman Clement L. Vallandigham, who was arrested by Ambrose Burnside in 1863

The celebrated case of Clement L. Vallandigham helped catapult the Copperhead movement into the news.

LIBRARY OF CONGRESS

Artists who dealt with the Copperhead movement typically depicted reptiles rather than copper coins.

as a seditionist and eventually banished (although he returned to the country in 1864 and helped to engineer the peace platform for the Democratic presidential candidate in 1864 that all but assured Lincoln's reelection).

The tense debate in these states over the war for the Union led the advocates of the vigorous prosecution of the conflict to label the Peace Democrats as Copperheads, likely a reference to the deadly snake found in the eastern and central United States. In his *Dictionary of Americanisms,* Mitford M. Mathews reported that the earliest printed reference to the Copperheads was in the September 11, 1862, issue of the *Lawrence (Kans.) Republican,* which stated: "That faction of the democracy who sympathize with the rebels are known in Ohio as 'Vallandighammers,' in Illinois as 'guerrillas,' in Missouri as 'butternuts,' in Kansas as 'jayhawkers,' in Kentucky as 'bushwhackers,' and in Indiana as 'copperheads.'"

The comparison of the Peace Democrats to the dreaded serpent and the use of the copper penny may have been interconnected.

Whereas few would relish the calumny of the comparison to a deadly snake, the figure of Liberty was upon the penny. Furthermore, the controversial Vallandigham headed an antiwar group known as the Sons of Liberty. Thus a point of derision may have been transformed into a badge of pride when someone decided to display a copper penny—or its figure of Liberty—as a sign of protest.

DEAR DIARY

WHEN CAPT. James Hope of the Second Vermont surveyed the carnage on the field at Antietam, he recorded several ghastly observations of the Confederate dead around him. One of these was a Rebel gunner who had been struck in his midsection and sliced in two. Along the Sunken Road, Hope estimated that dead Southern soldiers lay three or four deep for about half a mile.

Confiding these scenes to his diary, he also noted with awe that a dead Confederate still kneeled in a firing position as though he were ready to take out the nearest Federal. Hope carefully examined the corpse and found that the kneeling marksman had been hit in the forehead. He concluded that the man must have died instantly because he "remained in perfect equilibrium."

A DEADLY RUSH OF WIND

MANY MEN who made up the Federal task force that Ambrose Burnside led into North Carolina in February 1862 were awestruck by the sudden death of one of their number on Roanoke Island. Half a dozen eyewitnesses were convinced that the wind killed the young soldier when a Confederate cannonball whizzed close to his head without touching him.

Burnside's expedition also experienced an unusual problem of communication. In the first wave of the attack around four hundred soldiers hit the beach at sunset. Early the next morning they found one of the two forts before them had been abandoned. The garrison of Fort Clark had fled to the slightly stronger position of nearby Fort Hatteras during the night. Quickly the soldiers in blue occupied the empty redoubt.

Almost as soon as the four hundred Federals had taken position within Fort Clark they began to receive fire from the Union naval vessels anchored offshore. Rather than move on Fort Hatteras, the Northerners had to seek protection from their comrades at seas. Col. Max Weber later reported that these shells were "bursting right over us and in our midst."

Quick and frantic efforts to bring the naval gunfire to a halt proved futile. No one had considered that the navy had its own system of wigwag flag signaling and the army another. Neither

Federal warships bombarded Forts Clark and Hatteras from a distance—and fired on Union troops in the process.

The men of the U.S. Signal Service made wide use of flags but did not always understand flagged messages from their counterparts in the navy.

tried to learn the other's system, and so, at least for a time, army-navy communication was impossible.

THE REBEL YELL AND OTHER BATTLE CRIES

THERE ARE no recordings of the Rebel yell; thus we must rely on written descriptions. In an issue of *The Confederate Veteran,* an anonymous survivor of the battle of Chickamauga wrote: "[When the Federals came within sixty yards of us, there was a five-second lull in the firing and] then arose that do-or-die expression, that maniacal maelstrom of sound; that penetrating, rasping, shrieking, blood-curling noise that could be heard for miles on earth, and whose volumes reached the heavens; such an expression as never yet came from the throats of sane men, but from men whom the seething blast of an imaginary hell would not check while the sound lasted."

Another participant was content simply to call the Rebel yell "such a shout as will never be heard again." Other Southern soldiers merely termed it "demoniacal" or "a terrific roar." A Confederate diarist said of the sounds produced by the comrades of his company that they "sounded like forty thousand wild cats."

Recently Rod Gragg discovered an account by J. Harvie Dew of the Rebel yell that reverberated across the field at Brandy Station in June 1863. Gragg suggests that the real meaning of the battle cry cannot be grasped unless the printed version includes hyphens, dashes, and exclamation points: "Woh-who-ey! Who-ey! Who-ey! Woh-who-ey! Who-ey!" The *Woh* syllable should be short and low, followed by a high and prolonged *who* that slides into *ey.*

A Federal private who was on a hill at Brandy Station, poised to meet the oncoming assailants, recalled that the Confederates "raised their battle-cry, which, sounding across field and intervening distance, rose to me on the height sharper, shriller, and more like the composite yelping of wolves than I had ever heard it."

At Fredericksburg, Union soldiers of Irish heritage charged the stone wall at Marye's Heights while chanting "Clear the way!" in Gaelic.

No doubt the Rebel yell varied considerably from battle to battle. Its impact, however, was indisputable. The yell is mentioned thousands of times but seldom described. Though it may have intimidated the enemy, the basic function of the yell was to boost the resolve of the soldier producing it to the point where he did not care if he might die within minutes.

In his autobiography, former Confederate soldier Henry M. Stanley tried to analyze the multiple effects of the yell. He concluded: "It drove all sanity and order from among us. It served the double purpose of relieving pent-up feelings, and transmitting encouragement along the attacking line. I rejoiced in the shouting like the rest. Wave after wave of human voices, louder than all other battle-sounds together, penetrated to every sense, and stimulated our energies to the utmost."

Stonewall Jackson understood the impact of the yell. Having ordered a general advance near the Henry house at the battle of First Manassas, he reputedly shouted to his men, "Give 'em the

Soldiers in Zouave units, wearing uniforms such as shown here, allegedly yelled "Zou, zou, zou!" when they charged into battle.

CENTURY WAR BOOK

The wanton slaughter of surrendering soldiers at Fort Pillow caused the name of the battle itself to become a battle cry for those intent on avenging the deed.

bayonet, and when you charge, yell like furies!" Similarly, Union Gen. William Tecumseh Sherman understood the impact of sounds upon those who made them. In May 1864 he sent a dispatch to Gen. George H. Thomas stating, "All cheering of bodies of men, except in battle, should be dispensed with."

Southerners occasionally substituted words for unintelligible yells and found that they lacked the same dynamic. "Death to Wilson's Zouaves!" somehow failed to inspire like those battle cries likened to the howls of wolves.

Battle yells were by no means limited to Rebel yells. What came from the ranks of blue, however, are reported to have been articulated words more often than wordless hollers. As a tribute to fallen Union Gen. Jesse Reno, his men went into battle shouting "Reno! Reno!" On at least one occasion men in blue cried "Chickamauga!" over and over, in unison. Other Federals shouted "Huzzah! Huzzah!"

According to their comrades, colorfully garbed Zouave units tended to shout "Zou, zou, zou!" as their battle cry. Interestingly, reports of this cry are almost invariably punctuated with commas rather than exclamation marks, implying that it might have been more of a chant than a yell. At the December 13, 1862, battle of Fredericksburg, the men of the all-Irish Sixty-ninth New York yelled "Clear the way!" in Gaelic while charging up the killing ground before the stone wall at Marye's Heights. Later in the war, some Union regiments took up the cry of "Hi! Hi! Hi!"— possibly a Yankee imitation of the Rebel yell and more universal than cries such as "Fort Pillow! Fort Pillow!"

One Southern letter writer reported that the Northerners had a "peculiar characteristic yell" that he described as "Hoo-ray! Hoo-ray! Hoo-ray!" He added, however, that it lacked the pitch and resonance of the Rebel yell. This difference he attributed to the fact that great numbers of his comrades had been farmers, hunters, and trappers, but the majority of Union soldiers came from cities and urban areas.

HOOKER NOT THE NAMESAKE

UNION GEN. Joseph "Fighting Joe" Hooker is usually cited as part of the etymology for the introduction of the word *hooker* as a synonym for "prostitute." This is based upon three well-known facts: (1) Washington, D.C., had numerous brothels during the the war; (2) Hooker's departmental commands encompassed the Federal capital at times; and (3) the general had a reputation as a womanizer and a heavy drinker.

While all three factors attributed to the hooker story seem well documented, there is very little evidence to support the derivation of the word solely on Fighting Joe, drunk or sober. The inception of the word actually precedes the war, and its source lies farther to the north than Washington. Sometime in the 1850s every sailor whose ship docked at New York's waterfront was aware that Corlear's Hook in the city abounded with houses of ill repute. On the basis of that locality in which they plied their trade, women of easy virtue were widely known as hookers.

BEARDING THE LEGEND

DURING THE fall of 1860, Republican Norman Bedell of West-field, New York, paid his annual visit to the county fair. When he came home, he brought his eleven-year-old daughter Grace a piece of political campaign literature that featured the faces of Abraham Lincoln and his running mate, Hannibal Hamlin. The young girl then wrote a letter to the Republican presidential candidate on October 15 with the following suggestion: "I have got 4 brothers and part of them will vote for you any way and if you will let your whiskers grow I will try and get the rest of them to vote for you. You would look a great deal better for your face is so thin. All the ladies like whiskers and they would tease their husbands to vote for you and then you would be President."

Interestingly, Lincoln replied quickly to the young girl's letter. In answer to her suggestion, he asked, "As to the whiskers, having never worn any, do you not think people would call it a piece of silly affection if I were to begin it now?"

Four months later, on February 16, 1861, after his election to the White House, the president-elect instructed that his train stop at Westfield. One of Lincoln's aides noted in his journal that the man from Springfield was "greeted by a large crowd of ladies, and several thousand of the sterner sex." Lincoln told his admirers that he had received a letter from one of their townspeople some months earlier and asked to meet the letter writer.

When he engaged in the 1858 debates with Stephen A. Douglas and when he ran for president, Abraham Lincoln was clean-shaven.

In response to his comment, a youngster perched on a post pointed to a small blushing girl. According to a *Philadelphia Inquirer* correspondent who described part of the inaugural trip, Lincoln stepped down from the train and the crowd parted for him as he made his way toward Grace Bedell. When he reached her, the president-elect "gave her several hearty kisses, and amid the yells of delight from the excited crowd, he bade her good-bye, and on we rushed."

This is a great story and a marvelous piece of Lincolniana, but Mark E. Neely Jr. has suggested that little Grace may not have been alone in precipitating the change in Lincoln's appearance. Prior to Grace's letter, a group of "True Republicans of New York" had sent Lincoln an open letter vowing their support of a candidate with whiskers. That letter may have been published in the New York newspapers on or about October 14, and furthermore may have prompted Norman Bedell to suggest that his daughter write a whimsical letter.

The demand for a bewhiskered White House contender was so great that lithographers Currier and Ives had artists add beards on the prints in stock that showed the beardless Republican. On that basis, several Lincoln scholars discount the story that Grace Bedell persuaded the president-elect to cover his gaunt chin.

By the time Lincoln departed Springfield for Washington, he was displaying the beginning of his famous beard. Not a man to leave a political stone unturned, he nevertheless paid a public tribute to little Grace when he reached her hometown. That was the sort of thing good reporters would pick up and describe to their readers, and Lincoln knew he would get favorable coverage from the incident. And he truly did, for the *Inquirer* story was reprinted in numerous cities. Only Honest Abe knew, however, if Grace Bedell was really responsible for his decision to grow whiskers.

A LAST KISS

ABOLITIONIST JOHN BROWN was captured at Harpers Ferry, Virginia (now West Virginia) by a detachment of U.S. Marines

Thomas Hovenden's imaginative interpretation depicts a tenderhearted John Brown despite the fact that Brown was known as a cold-blooded killer in Kansas.

under the command of Lt. Col. R. E. Lee. Imprisoned at nearby Charles Town, Brown was tried and convicted of treason against the state of Virginia. His statements from jail, made after he knew he would be hanged, increased the zeal of abolitionists everywhere.

A wealthy New Yorker who admired Brown commissioned a painting of the condemned man stooping to kiss a small child as he was being led from the courthouse to the gallows. The myth of Brown's kissing a child had circulated throughout the North, offsetting reports that Brown and his followers had been fiendish, brutal murderers. The image of the tenderhearted Brown and the innocent child was a far cry from the cold-blooded murderer who ordered his followers in 1856 to hack five men to pieces with artillery broadswords.

This image of John Brown is more accurate, depicting him as an angry zealot.

JOHN STEUART CURRY MURAL

The artwork served its propaganda purpose well. Brown hated slavery with a passion, but he was anything but gentle or forgiving. He fled from Kansas because of his reputation as a cunning and cold-blooded killer. His image as a benevolent opponent of slavery was boosted by the painting of the kiss that did not happen.

WHY WAS LEE'S "RIGHT ARM" CUT OFF?

CONFEDERATE GEN. Thomas Jonathan Jackson was wounded by accidental fire from some of his own men, North Carolinians. The general was struck three times in the waning hours of May 2, 1863. He died of pneumonia on May 10, almost a week later.

For more than a century every devotee of the Civil War has learned these elementary facts about the dramatic wounding of the man Robert E. Lee called his "right arm." Numerous scholars have speculated about how the war might have been different had Jackson not been shot that evening.

Only recently has anyone asked if Jackson's wounding was not accidental. Part of the legacy of the Vietnam era, the term "friendly fire" has entered our language, meaning the accidental wounding or killing of soldiers by one's comrades. The Vietnam War also introduced the public to "fragging," which was the premeditated murdering of lower echelon officers by their subordinates who used grenades to make it appear as if the death was caused by the enemy. There are also a few firsthand accounts of incidents in which despised officers were killed outright by their own men. Could something similar to this have occurred on the Chancellorsville battlefield that fateful spring night in 1863?

There is no easy answer to that question, but a tentative answer can be pieced together from the following questions: (1) At what instant was Jackson hit? (2) What was the visibility at the time the shots were fired? (3) Was there anything distinctive about Jackson's silhouette on horseback? (4) How many men were in Jackson's party that night? (5) What company fired on the gen-

Stonewall Jackson (left) and Robert E. Lee (right) formed one of the most potent military partnerships the world has ever seen.

eral's party? (6) How did the former Virginia Military Institute professor get along with his subordinates? (7) What did Jackson do to endear himself to rank-and-file soldiers? (8) Did Jackson ever anger his men so that they would want to see him dead?

At what instant was Jackson hit? Capt. Benjamin W. Leigh, third man on the scene after the shots were fired, was a member of Gen. A. P. Hill's staff. He wrote a detailed description of the incident just ten days after the event. Leigh mentions that the men of Hill's command were in position late in the afternoon of May 2. Jackson issued the order to attack close to 6 P.M., and the fight went on for nearly three and a half hours. They "marched in line of battle through the woods filled with thick undergrowth and across ravines at a rapid pace" while men in blue "ran like sheep—throwing away their arms, knapsacks and everything of which they could divest themselves." Well behind what had been the Federal battle line, the attackers discovered abandoned entrenchments.

Rebel units ranged all over the rough terrain and became "mixed together." When the attack was halted so that they might regroup, Jackson and A. P. Hill rode forward in what Leigh interpreted as an effort to scout the Federal batteries as a prelude to a renewed attack.

According to Leigh, "suddenly a musketry fire opened to our right in the wood." Ten days later he still did not know whether that fire erupted "because our troops mistook us for a body of Federal cavalry, or for some other reason." Leigh hit the ground and lay there briefly before learning that Jackson had been hit. Then he moved to the side of the stricken general. It is interesting that Leigh alluded to the possibility of "some other reason" for the burst of fire, possibly suggesting that afterward no one was sure why a band of Tar Heels had fired on the riders.

Leigh's account suggests that the shots hit Jackson about 9:45 P.M. He may have been estimating time, because most of those who have analyzed Jackson's wounding lean toward the

Jackson demanded absolute obedience and unquestioning trust from his subordinates. At Front Royal, Virginia, he was unhappy with the performance of one of his colonels and ordered the man's arrest and court-martial. Such were not unique instances and did not endear him to his commanders.

THE SOLDIER IN OUR CIVIL WAR

opinion that Leigh was off by as much as an hour. They contend that the incident occurred shortly before 9 P.M.

What was the visibility at the time the shots were fired? Byron Farwell's 1992 biography of Jackson confronts this aspect of the dreadful affair head-on by noting "a curious disparity" in what the men who were there that night later said. A member of the Fourth Georgia recalled it as the darkest night he ever saw, but John C. West of the Fourth Texas was positive that it was "a beautiful moonlight night."

West may be more reliable than his comrade from Georgia. A full moon shone during part of the night of May 2, and if there was no cloud cover, the battlefield would have been brightly illuminated for several hours. In *Mighty Stonewall,* Frank E. Vandiver reports that Old Jack read a dispatch from Jeb Stuart in "silvered dimness." He also believes that every time Stonewall and his party passed through the clearings in the woods, they were briefly in full moonlight. Douglas Southall Freeman, in his *Lee's Lieutenants,* thought the night was very dark except where moonlight had the upper hand.

Turner Ashby (center), the head of Jackson's cavalry, was reprimanded by his commander. To his credit, Jackson's discipline was swift and he bore no grudges. The same could not be said of most of those who felt their general's wrath. Ashby was killed in action during the Shenandoah campaign of 1862.

ROBERTS ENGRAVING

Stonewall Jackson's distinctive cap helped to give him an instantly recognizable profile.

JOHN A. ELDER PAINTING, CORCORAN GALLERY OF ART

Since the path believed to have been taken by Jackson and his entourage ran through dense woods dotted with clearings, the visibility at the moment of the incident cannot be determined.

Was there anything distinctive about Jackson's silhouette on horseback? Astride Little Sorrel, Stonewall Jackson's silhouette was unmistakable. There are innumerable comments by the general's subordinates as to his eccentric horsemanship, which was rooted in his upbringing on his uncle's horse farm. Jackson leaned forward like a jockey, and that was a distinctive image atop the short horse the general rode. Wearing a visored VMI cap that was noticeably different from other Rebel headgear, the big man on the little horse was instantly recognizable in silhouette even in limited light. Men close enough to take aim on Jackson's party should have recognized the general and Little Sorrel the instant they were spotted.

How many men were in Jackson's party that night? A. P. Hill and some of his staff, including Leigh, were among those who accompanied Jackson. Three of Stonewall's aides were noticed by Henry Kyd Douglas: Lt. James K. Boswell, Lt. J. G. Slaughter, and Capt. R. E. Wilbourn. The party also included Capt. Keith Boswell, Maj. William H. Palmer, and courier David J. Kyle. Among the dozens of authorities who have described the fatal wounding of Jackson there is little disagreement that his party numbered close to twenty riders.

What company fired on the general's party? The fatal burst of gunfire was delivered by Gen. James H. Lane's brigade and probably came from the Eighteenth North Carolina. This has been the subject of little debate. The position of the troops plus the direction from which the volley ripped into Jackson's party pinpoint the Eighteenth North Carolina as the shooters.

How did the former Virginia Military Institute professor get along with his subordinates? Many of Stonewall's officers hated him as much as they admired him. Few if any of Jackson's biographers try to conceal or gloss over the fact that he was a tyrannical commander. He was severe in his judgments, and at one time tried to have Gens. Richard B. Garnett and William W. Loring cashiered.

Loring was the focus of a bitter quarrel that also involved Confederate Secretary of War Judah P. Benjamin. Despite his protestations that he despised anything resembling politicking, Stonewall brought Virginia Gov. John Letcher into the controversy that ended only when Loring was transferred out of Jackson's command in February 1862.

Garnett was arrested for having used his best judgment and withdrawing his brigade at Kernstown in the Shenandoah Valley. After about three months he went on trial, but the proceedings were halted when Jackson's corps was dispatched from the Virginia Peninsula in the first movements of the Second Manassas campaign in August 1862. Nearly a year later Garnett

died during Pickett's Charge at Gettysburg.

Col. William Gilham was a prewar friend and VMI colleague of Jackson. In 1862 his leadership at Sir John's Run, Virginia, so angered Stonewall that he brought formal charges against his peacetime friend and charged him with neglect

Artist Everett B. D. Julio's widely circulated painting of Lee and Jackson is probably the most well-known Southern icon of the war.

of duty. Since the charges rested solely upon Gilham's judgment in the face of a complex situation, they were dropped.

Col. Zephaniah T. Conner was brought up on charges after an engagement at Front Royal. Quizzed by his commander, he admitted he had suffered no casualties in the affair. Jackson saw to it that his commission was withdrawn. Col. Turner Ashby, Maj. John A. Harman, Gen. Charles S. Winder, Maj. Oliver R. Funston, and Gen. A. P. Hill were only a few of the officers with whom Jackson quarreled. Most or all of them admired him as a leader, but occasionally they loathed him as a person.

What did Jackson do to endear himself to rank-and-file soldiers? The men of Jackson's corps generally lauded their commander for his many victories. Stonewall rarely tasted defeat or even a drawn battle except at Kernstown and Falling Waters (or Hoke's Run), Virginia (now West Virginia). Jackson's men were inordinately proud that their commander often won against seemingly overwhelming odds. To them, he was the embodiment of the spirit of the South, able to outwit and outfight any force thrown up against him. Membership in the Stonewall Brigade was a great honor, but the entirety of the Army of Northern Virginia praised the general for his victories.

Did Jackson ever anger his men so that they would want to see him dead? Although thousands admired Jackson the victor in battle, many despised him when he seemed to show no mercy when it came to military discipline. Throughout Lee's army, the "foot cavalry" was a common designation for Jackson's infantry because they

The Chancellorsville battlefield was dotted with large trees and clumps of smaller ones.

HARPER'S PICTORIAL HISTORY OF THE GREAT REBELLION

KURZ AND ALLISON

Bright moonlight, cited by most observers at the time of Jackson's wounding, was featured in this lithograph of the tragic moment.

marched as rapidly and covered as much ground as mounted men. Drenching rain, ankle-deep mud, searing sun, choking dust, and howling winter winds were ignored when marching orders were issued. As if this were not enough to rankle a few men, they were ordered always to polish their weapons before turning in for a few hours of sleep.

Any deviation from orders was not tolerated. Men who displayed any unwillingness to do exactly as they were told were likely to be accused of mutiny. When one of Jackson's generals was faced with a group of troublemakers, Jackson ordered them shot. Stonewall directed his army without blinking an eye. Such discipline seems unduly harsh, but Jackson's stern and unwavering chastening of his army was not unlike that of the commander of the Army of Northern Virginia, R. E. Lee.

In his recent biography of Jackson, James I. Robertson suggests that one can best understand the general as a throwback to the dedicated general of the army of the Lord in the Old

Testament. One dared not show mercy to one's enemies when God declared a holy war. And that is the mind-set Jackson had of the war between the states: It was a crucible in which the Lord was purifying the nation. Woe be to anyone who might hinder or try to alter that, regardless of how justifiable a grievance might be.

Whenever a battle faced him, this commander in Lee's army seemed oblivious of the odds of success. Whatever the outcome, in Jackson's mind, it was the Lord's will, but that did not discount the devotion and determination of the participants. At Chancellorsville, Stonewall ordered Gen. Jubal Early's ten thousand men to form a five-mile line to confront at least forty thousand Union soldiers.

The acute scarcity of food meant nothing to Jackson; he drove hungry men as rapidly and as hard as if they were well fed. Many Northern abolitionists expressed a heartfelt concern for the Southern slaves who worked the plantations. Compared with Jackson's soldiers, these slaves were treated better. Although nearly all of his men admired and lauded Jackson the victor in battle, many of them suffered in agony to obey because they dared not complain or protest. At times they utterly despised Jackson the commander.

There is no way of knowing if Jackson's wounding was deliberate. But the question is intriguing and should invite similar questioning of other long-accepted and unquestioned explanations of other events during the Civil War.

DID LINCOLN FORESEE THE WAR IN 1858?

ON JUNE 16, 1858, Illinois Republicans held their state convention at Springfield and picked attorney Abraham Lincoln to challenge Stephen A. Douglas for his seat in the U.S. Senate. As soon as the tall and ungainly candidate addressed the crowd, he had the audience in the palm of his hand.

Most of that address has been forgotten, but some of his opening remarks were powerful and were remembered, pondered, and quoted. Lincoln began by saying that the country was like a group of children lost in a forest, not knowing which way to go to get out. Quickly he mentioned the importance of the slavery issue, which was growing instead of diminishing, and indicated that he did not think the matter would be resolved short of a major national crisis.

Lincoln then pronounced four of the most widely quoted sentences ever spoken by this master orator: "A house divided against itself cannot stand. I believe this government cannot endure, permanently half slave and half free. I do not expect the Union to be dissolved—I do not expect the house to fall—but I do expect it will cease to be divided. It will become all one thing, or all the other." Once war erupted, these sentences were reprinted many times and his words were taken to mean that division would be brought to an end on the battlefield.

Before Lincoln addressed those convention delegates in June 1858, he expressed his conviction that the Founding Fathers had not abolished slavery under the Constitution

An artist's interpretation of the "House Divided" showed a shackled slave between his owner (left) and an abolitionist.

because they believed it would die a natural death. Specifically, his appreciation of Thomas Jefferson was almost reverential, and he believed that Jefferson was among those who expected time to bring an end to slavery. To himself, Lincoln eagerly anticipated the day when the issue of slavery no longer divided the country, and he was certain that such a day was not far off.

Two years later he faced the bitter reality of a divided Union and took it upon himself to put the broken pieces back together by whatever means it might take. At Springfield in 1858 he had just been selected to joust with Douglas for a seat in the U.S. Senate. In 1861 he was the chief executive who confronted the dilemma of what to do about Fort Sumter and whatever might happen afterward. This was not what he had in mind when he spoke as a senatorial candidate; he expected natural processes to bring healing and unity to the "divided house." Instead time had driven the country apart and armies were forming. If anything, Lincoln's crystal ball was cloudy at best.

CHAPTER SIX ≈

FIRST HAPPENINGS
ᴀɴᴅ
DOINGS

LIGHTER-THAN-AIR CRAFT CONCEIVED

FOREIGN OBSERVERS, crackpots, and zealots swarmed into the war departments of both North and South as soon as war seemed inevitable. Many of them managed to meet with Abraham Lincoln, and a few got inside the door of the Confederate White House in Richmond. Those who never met either chief executive face to face found some officer with an interested or sympathetic ear.

Thaddeus Sobieski Constantine Lowe ranked high on the list of zealots. Strong winds often blew in his native New Hampshire, and as an adolescent he became interested in air currents. Despite his limited formal training, Lowe succeeded in building and testing experimental hot-air balloons.

Lowe made several efforts to reach Europe by air, but he never got far enough to be in serious danger when his craft

147

failed and dropped him to the ground or water. In mid-April 1861 one of his voyages ended at Unionville, South Carolina, a few days after Fort Sumter surrendered.

As soon as the Confederates released Lowe, who called himself "Professor," he headed for Washington. With an eagerness he could not conceal, he offered his unique services to Gen. Winfield Scott, but the aging head of the U.S. Army did not think much of crackpots regardless of their ideas.

Undaunted, Lowe managed to get a balloon up on June 18— taking a telegraph wire along for the ride. He reportedly sent from the air "the first telegram ever dispatched from an aerial station." It was addressed to the occupant of 1600 Pennsylvania Avenue, who did not respond immediately. On July 25, however, Abraham Lincoln sent a one-sentence message to the War Department: "Will Lieut. Genl. Scott please see Professor Lowe, once more about his balloon?"

Professor Lowe was made a colonel in August, given that rank by the president, and named chief of army aeronautics. In his new rank and position, Lowe soon discovered that most of the Union commanders considered him a lunatic when he

Detective-turned-master-spy Allan Pinkerton (left) confers with Union Gen. George B. McClellan during the Peninsula campaign. McClellan also chose to take advantage of the aerial reconnaissance that balloons could offer.

THE SPY OF THE REBELLION

HARPER'S WEEKLY

"Professor" Thaddeus S. C. Lowe, a noted balloonist, shown in this engraving at age twenty-seven, offered his services to the Union army.

claimed that his balloons could make a significant contribution to a Federal victory.

Of the numerous high-ranking officers he managed to see, Gen. George B. McClellan demonstrated the most interest. "The Young Napoleon" was ambitious and presumptuous, and in the spring of 1862 he was entirely too dependent upon the faulty intelligence provided by Allan Pinkerton and his operatives. McClellan did not want to engage his army until it had become an unstoppable force. In addition to the admiration and loyalty of his officers and men, the general also had an open mind about innovations.

Largely as a result of McClellan's interest, on September 24, 1861, Lowe became the first person to give firing directions to gunners from the air. He was the first person to take military photographs from a balloon, but the date on which he made this enduring record is not known. In the spring of 1862 McClellan lauded Lowe as "the intelligent and enterprising astronaut, who had the management of the balloons" and to whom he was "greatly indebted for valuable information obtained during his ascensions."

Until Gen. Joseph Hooker took command of the Army of the Potomac, the professor was in the air almost daily. Naturally he was quizzed by curiosity seekers in and out of uniform. One of his many foreign observers was a German, Ferdinand von Zeppelin. A professional soldier who had graduated from the Ludwigsburg Military Academy, Zeppelin had crossed the Atlantic to get a firsthand look at the kind of fighting that was going on between the North and the South. After being briefly attached to the Army of the Potomac, Zeppelin lost interest in battlefield strategy and tactics because Lowe's balloons had set his mind on fire. Leaving the war behind, he headed west, and at Saint Paul, Minnesota, he managed to get an upward trip in a balloon of the same type as those he had seen in action in Virginia.

Thaddeus Lowe conducted aerial reconnaissance throughout McClellan's Peninsula campaign and saw his funding increased until he was master of a "fleet" of seven balloons. For health reasons he was of little help during the Antietam campaign, but he returned to the air during Ambrose Burnside's campaign that crumbled at Fredericksburg. When command of the Union army passed to Joseph Hooker, Lowe was subordinated to the chief engineer of the army and his assets were reduced. On May 8, 1863, Lowe resigned and went west where he dabbled anew with new experiments in refrigeration and energy.

Zeppelin returned to Prussia and participated in the Austro-Prussian War of 1866 and the Franco-Prussian War of 1870. He retired from the German army in 1891 and devoted himself to

At Yorktown, Virginia, one of Lowe's balloons soared to one thousand feet to spy upon Confederate forts and camps.

At Harrison's Landing, Virginia, a balloon rose from the deck of a river boat in a reconnoitering expedition.

aeronautics. Zeppelin designed cigar-shaped lighter-than-air vehicles that were called by his name. These aircraft were utilized in World War I as bombers, and in May 1937 they came to a fiery end when the greatest zeppelin of the day, the *Hindenberg*, exploded in a ball of flame at Lakehurst Naval Air Station in New Jersey.

TRAILBLAZER IN PETTICOATS

WASHINGTON WAS in a heady state in 1854 following passage of the Kansas-Nebraska Act. A few observers feared that the legislation would lead to greater tension between the North and the South, but most Capitol Hill watchers were very optimistic that the struggle over the extension of slavery into the new territories would soon end and a new era of goodwill would be launched.

Clara Barton was the first person to systematically seek MIAs and notify the families of her findings.

Into that heady atmosphere a demure thirty-three-year-old woman arrived in search of a job. Clarissa Harlowe Barton had been born on Christmas Day in 1821 in North Oxford. Massachusetts, the youngest of five children. Had she been a little taller, she most likely would have been employed in one of the region's textile mills. There were few other options for a working woman in those days, however, and so Clara taught school. Her first day as a teacher was, in her words, "a disaster," but she muddled through.

Ten years later, Barton enrolled in the Liberal Institute, a school for teachers, in Clinton, New York. A year later she took a teaching position in Bordentown, New Jersey. This was a difficult time for the young woman from Massachusetts: her father was seriously ill, and her mother died in 1852. Rather than look inward, she looked at the community in which she lived and grasped the need for a school for the poor. She solicited funds for a nonprofit school that became the first public school in the state. Within two years it grew to more than six hundred students, but a newly formed school board preferred not to have a woman in charge and forced Barton to resign.

Prior to Clara Barton's arrival in Washington, no woman had been regularly employed by any government department. (Women did fill-in work for their fathers and husbands but received pay in the men's names, not their own.) Barton hoped and expected to do something new, and she was savvy enough to know she could not do it alone. She first visited with Alex DeWitt, the congressman from her home district in Massachusetts. At the time, Charles Mason, the Patent Office commissioner, believed that women would be efficient copyists of patents, records, and annual reports. Clara accepted the job at eight cents per hundred words, not to exceed nine hundred dollars a year. Mason was sufficiently impressed with her work to promote her to "regular 'temporary clerk'" and increase her annual salary to fourteen hundred dollars.

Barton's co-workers were not happy with her achievement and subjected her to a great deal of harassment. To Mason they complained that she was immoral and the mother of "negroid" children. When one formally complained to Mason that Clara's moral behavior was unacceptable, the commissioner demanded proof of the accusation. He told the man that if the charges were proved, Barton would be released; if not, the accuser would lose his job. The man lost his position, and the harassment stopped.

What prejudice failed to do, however, politics accomplished. In 1857 a Democratic and pro-Southern administration came to office. Barton was an outspoken Republican. She returned depressed and angry to Massachusetts and lived in her father's house, performing household chores and helping to care for her ailing father. At the same time she wrote letters applying for any position as a postmistress, since the Post Office was known to hire women in that capacity. Again she ran headlong into the Buchanan administration. She applied for every position of which she heard, including the register of deeds in Boston. The one thing she did not want to do was to teach school again. "I have outgrown that," she told her friends. In June 1860 she suffered an emotional and physical collapse and went to convalesce with a friend in upstate New York.

Lincoln's election revived her efforts. With the help of some friends, she was reinstated at the Patent Office in December 1860, but at a lower grade. When war came, she survived the round of layoffs at the Patent Office. Clara kept her job because she impressed D. P. Holloway, the new Republican commissioner, and because she realized that to survive in the bureaucracy she must have the support of the Massachusetts congressional delegation, which included Charles Sumner and Henry Wilson.

Wilson became Clara's best supporter. They first met in March 1861, and she charmed him. As it turned out, he was very well connected. When the Southern ranks of Congress abandoned the capital, the Republicans held the majority, and the amiable Wilson was named chairmen of the Committee on Military Affairs.

Clara wanted to enlist. Although other women did join the armies in the North and the South, Clara was not one of them—she was too shy to attempt to mask her gender and her sense of propriety forbade it. Nor was she anxious to answer the call of Dorothea Dix, who formed a nurses corps for the army. Dix's first criteria was to find "plain looking" women, which might weed Barton out. Dix was also an authoritarian whom her nurses described as "a stern woman of few words"; others christened her "Dragon Dix." This was not an arrangement under which Clara could contribute.

The atmosphere in Washington was tense during the week following the surrender of Fort Sumter. The president had called for seventy-five thousand volunteers, then news came that a Massachusetts regiment had been assaulted in Baltimore while en route to the capital. Clara rushed to the train depot with her sister, Sally Vassall, and then led a small group of woman to clean the wounds of the thirty men who were being unloaded at the platform. Not only were these Massachusetts men, Clara and Sally recognized some as former schoolmates and playmates. Some of the wounded were taken to a small infirmary; the rest were taken to Sally's home where Clara bandaged wounds and listened to stories of the small skirmish in Baltimore.

She scoured her home for anything to treat the wounded and brought it all to wherever the wounded men were laid. The next day she solicited food, hospital supplies, and assistance in the capital streets. She wrote to Massachusetts newspapers requesting aid, and it began to pour in. When her rooms could no longer hold it all, she rented warehouse space and started a distribution service. A friend in the Patent Office covered her desk for her so she could manage the supplies that were coming in. Her greatest obstacle, however, was the army, but she found officers who occasionally agreed to work with her to distribute the materials she gathered.

Her final hurdle was getting permission to visit the front lines. No officer was willing to accept the responsibility. Finally, in August 1862, Maj. D. H. Rucker, an assistant quartermaster general, relented and issued her a pass. Clara quickly oversaw the loading of a wagon and then, forsaking her ladylike predisposition, wore a man's jacket and drove the four-mule team to Cedar Mountain, Virginia. She arrived at the battlefield just as surgeon James Dunn was about to exhaust his supply of dressings. Her opportune arrival led the surgeon to dub her "the angel of the battlefield." Dunn later wrote, "I thought that night if heaven ever sent out a holy angel, she must be one."

After Cedar Mountain, Clara appeared or followed the army to Second Manassas, Fairfax Court House, Antietam, Fredericksburg, and throughout the Overland campaign. Barton traveled as far south as Charleston while the war raged and in 1864 became the first female superintendent of nurses for Benjamin F. Butler's Army of the James. To the men in uniform, she was "everybody's old maid aunt." To Barton the soldiers were "my boys."

Long before Appomattox, Clara realized that nothing had been done to bring solace to the families from which so many of "her boys" had gone off to war. With the highly focused energy that later led her to found the American Red Cross, she

Under battle and prison conditions it was often impossible to provide simple burials in wooden coffins.

NATIONAL ARCHIVES

established an "Office of Correspondence with the Friends of Missing Men of the United States Army." When she could not gain the necessary authorization from the army, she appealed to Lincoln. He granted her request in March 1865.

Barton was the first person to seek information systematically about soldiers who were missing in action and to relay her findings to their relatives. She was technically the first woman to direct the work of a federal agency, but she opened this office at her own expense and operated it from her rooms at 437 Seventh Street NW, roughly halfway between the White House and the Capitol. The government eventually paid her fifteen thousand dollars for her work there.

The office received letters from families inquiring about lost soldiers. The servicemen's names were compiled into a master list, with the names grouped by state. Barton's list was then published in newspapers nationwide and posted in other public places. Anyone with information was asked to contact Barton's

Thousands of wretched inmates of Andersonville Prison had no shelter except crude tents.

Harper's Pictorial History of the Great Rebellion

About fourteen thousand bodies were identified and reinterred in the burial ground at Andersonville, Georgia. Clara Barton raised the flag at the August 17, 1865, dedication ceremony.

office, which would then contact the soldiers' families. Most often the soldiers were confirmed to be dead, but a small number were found to be alive.

By June 1865 the list had grown to twenty thousand names. At the end of that month, a former inmate of Andersonville appeared at Clara's office. His name was Dorence Atwater. He had been captured in 1863 and had been held at Belle Isle and other Richmond prisons before being sent to the notorious camp in Georgia. While there he had been given the grim task of recording the names of the prisoners who died and were buried at the camp—and he surreptitiously made a copy of the listings. The graves were only numbered, but Atwater's ledgers listed the names of thirteen thousand casualties of Andersonville.

In July 1865 Barton, Atwater, and a work crew under the command of Capt. James Moore traveled to Andersonville. Using Atwater's lists, they identified and marked the graves of the camp's cemetery. Only 460 were left unidentified. The task was completed on August 17, 1865, and Barton raised the American flag over the newly established national cemetery.

In 1868 Clara Barton presented a final report of her work to Congress: 63,182 inquiries were received by her office, 41,855 replies were made, and 99,057 copies of her lists were published. Of the 62,000 missing Union soldiers, she was able to identify 22,000. Of the remaining 40,000 soldiers, she asked Congress to declare them dead so that their survivors could receive the death benefits they were due.

Of this work, Barton said: "The heart-broken friends appealed to me for help, and by the aid of surviving comrades, I gained intelligence of the fate of nearly one-half the number of soldiers: I greatly fear there are some whose name stands today on the rolls against the dark word—Deserter—who were never faithless to their trust, who fell in the stern path of duty on the lonely picket line, perhaps, or wounded, and left in some tangled ravine to perish alone."

After she delivered her report, Barton closed her office and shortly afterward moved to a house on Pennsylvania Avenue. In 1869 she traveled to Europe and worked with the International Red Cross during the Franco-Prussian War. When she returned she founded the American Red Cross and oversaw its operation until 1904. Clara Barton died in 1912.

In November 1997 a workman discovered papers and personal effects in a Seventh Street NW building—just across the street from the Patent Office—being prepared for demolition in Washington. What he uncovered were the remains of Barton's Office of Correspondence, including a tin sign that once hung on one of the room's doors. After the find was reported to the National Park Service, twenty boxes of newspapers, letters, books, and clothing were taken to Ford's Theatre National Historic Site. The plans to demolish the building were changed, and a new plan was formulated to sell the building with the stipulation that the third floor be preserved.

The recovered items include two boxes of men's clothing and two hundred letters addressed to Edward Shaw, the Patent Office worker who helped to cover Barton's desk so that she would be free to engage in her relief efforts during the war. The clothes may have belonged to him, since he lived in the room across the hall from Barton, or possibly to Dorence Atwater, who also lived on the third floor.

The discovery surprised Washington historians. Gary Scott, the National Park Service's chief historian in the area, described Barton's room as tattered but intact, creating an impression of both Barton and life in Washington in the years just after the war. A spokesman for the General Services Administration, which owns the building, said that it is not impossible that Barton's former office may be opened to the public after the restoration.

Once again Clara Barton may lead the nation into remembering the vast numbers of soldiers who never returned home. At the same time, her selfless work on and off the battlefield underscores her singular remarkable contribution to the Union war effort—the efforts of an individual with nothing to rely on but the power of her own will in the face of the needs around her.

REWARDS FOR FIRST GREAT VICTORY

THE FIRST great Federal victory on land was achieved by U. S. Grant at Forts Henry and Donelson, Tennessee. It was no great stretch to link the general's initials with his demand for unconditional surrender. From New Hampshire to Minnesota and from Wisconsin to Pennsylvania, backers of the Union war effort congratulated Grant with a veritable shower of cigars.

Grant received countless packages of these sought-after smokes. Some contained two or three dozen, others held only one or two. The outpouring is believed to have reached at least ten thousand.

Many of these gifts were shared with his aides and other officers, but Grant had such an abundant supply that he kept a cigar in his mouth from daybreak until after midnight for month after month. No one knows how many he consumed himself. These tokens of appreciation caused Grant to be far more firmly addicted to tobacco than during his hard-luck years when he could rarely afford a smoke.

Ulysses S. Grant, our eighteenth president, died in 1885 of throat cancer.

GENERALS BAPTIZED BY A GENERAL

IN MID-MAY 1864 Gen. Leonidas Polk brought his Army of Mississippi to reinforce the Army of Tennessee, led by Gen. Joseph E. Johnston, as Union Gen. William T. Sherman inexorably pushed his way into Georgia. Commanding one of Johnston's corps was John Bell Hood, who had lost the use of his left arm at Gettysburg and whose right leg had been amputated after the battle of Chickamauga. These three Confederate generals participated in a drama not usually associated with the battlefield.

While riding to Dalton, Georgia, with Polk, who had been an Episcopal bishop prior to the war, Hood asked to receive the rite of baptism. Polk had not relinquished his post in the Protestant Episcopal Church, and so he suggested that they have a simple ceremony that night. Hood assented at once but added that he wanted to inform his commanding general in advance, so they made their way to Johnston's headquarters.

Hood remained with Johnston until after midnight, then went to his room for the baptism. Polk was waiting for him, wearing a stained surplice over an old gray hunting shirt. The room was simply furnished, having in it only a mess table, four rickety chairs, and a single candle.

The baptismal font was a battered tin basin into which the bishop had poured a cup of water. Hobbling in very early on the morning of May 13, Hood apologized for the lateness of the hour. Polk told him to think nothing of it and

The bishop-general, Leonidas Polk, officiated at hastily arranged baptisms of Confederate generals.

WILLIAM SARTAIN ENGRAVING

NICOLAY & HAY, ABRAHAM LINCOLN

Joseph E. Johnston was baptized through the intercession of his wife.

invited his comrade to sit for the ceremony. Shaking his head, the one-legged general leaned on his crutches and bowed his head reverently. It took only two or three minutes for the bishop of Louisiana to administer the rite of holy baptism, America's first such ceremony administered by one general to another general.

News of the unusual religious ceremony traveled fast. Thus, on the following Monday, May 16, Johnston's wife penned a letter from Atlanta to Polk. She wrote: "You seem never too much occupied to pause to perform a good deed. General Johnston has never been baptized, and it is the dearest wish of my heart that he should be. I hope you perform the ceremony for him soon, for it would be great gratification to me."

As soon as he learned of his wife's request, the commander of the Army of Tennessee assented to her wish with what some of his aides considered to be joy. Hood sent word that he'd like to be present for the ceremony. His request was unusual, for it was well known that he was jealous of Johnston and considered him to be fighting the wrong kind of campaign. Johnston expressed his pleasure that a subordinate wished to be involved with him at a high and holy moment and made arrangements for Gen. William Hardee to be his official sponsor.

Polk, Hood, and Hardee came to Johnston's headquarters wearing full uniforms. Johnston, who was a permanent full general ranking from August 31, 1861, knelt and received baptism from his subordinate and comrade.

On June 14, Leonidas Polk was killed by an artillery shell while reconnoitering Union positions atop Pine Mountain.

A Battle at Gaines's Mill

DURING HIS first thirty-three years as a professional soldier, Robert E. Lee did not win a military engagement of any importance until June 27, 1862. Called by Virginia Gov. John Letcher to take command of the state's military establishment, Lee was promoted from colonel in the U.S. Army to general of militia. Some reference works say that he quickly busied himself with organizing his forces, but it glosses over a period that admirers of the general would rather forget about.

The former U.S. Army officer was soon sent over the mountains into the western half of the state, where his job was to defeat the Federals seeking to foster the secession of the western counties from the Old Dominion. Lee's most decisive defeat was at Cheat Mountain in early September 1861. Even Douglas Southall Freeman had to admit that this first campaign ended ingloriously—for Lee did not win a battle in what is now West Virginia. He later spent a period supervising coastal defenses in South Carolina and Georgia. When Jefferson Davis called him to Richmond in March 1862, he had never scored a victory.

While sparring with forces under the command of George B. McClellan, Confederate Gen. Joseph E. Johnston was taken out of action when he was wounded at the battle of Seven Pines on May 31, 1862. Davis had few options when he sat down with his advisers to choose a replacement for Johnston, who could not return to his command for several weeks. In this dilemma he selected Lee. Almost as soon as he took command, Lee completed the reorganization of the Confederate army begun by Johnston and changed the name of the Army of the Potomac to the Army of Northern Virginia. At the same time, this unproved general summoned the former Virginia Military Institute professor Thomas J. Jackson from the Shenandoah Valley.

A. P. Hill, one of Lee's new subordinates, struck the Union army hard at Mechanicsville, Virginia, on June 26. Despite the fact that D. H. Hill and many of his men came to his aid, the

Southerners did not break the Union line forming around the outskirts of Richmond. On the following day the Army of Northern Virginia began the violent campaign that is generally known as the Seven Days' battles. Lee won his first victory at Gaines's Mill. That had to have been an intoxicating day for the professional soldier who had decided to engage in the aggressive warfare for which he gained lasting fame.

His record at the end of the Seven Days was not anything to brag about, however. He and his men had relieved the Federal pressure upon Richmond, but they paid a dear price for this. When the casualty lists were tallied after the final battle of the series, Malvern Hill, on July 1, the Army of Northern Virginia had about twenty thousand fewer effectives than on June 26. Union Gen. George B. McClellan, who was constantly scolded and prodded by his commander in chief in Washington, had seen the ranks of the Army of Potomac thinned by about one-fourth as many men during the brief period in which Lee is credited with one win after another.

AN INDEPENDENT REPUBLIC WITHIN THE COUNTRY

DURING COLONIAL and Revolutionary days, a number of futile attempts were made to establish governmental entities in addition to the thirteen original British colonies. One of the best known was an effort to create the state of Franklin in eastern Tennessee. It never really gained its independence, however.

That was not the case with a republic established late in 1860. South Carolina led the secession parade by withdrawing from the Union on December 20 as a result of an enthusiastic unanimous vote by members of a convention held in Charleston. Since the Palmetto State was alone in her stance until a ripple effect took out several sister states that went into the provisional Confederacy, its leaders formally transformed the first maverick into the Republic of South Carolina.

Though the new political loner soon yielded its sovereignty to the Confederacy, its governor had stationery printed for use by officials of the republic. In addition, steps were taken to select commissioners and send them to Britain and Europe to represent the Republic of South Carolina.

MOST UNUSUAL TRIBUTE TO AN AMERICAN INDIAN

ATTORNEY CHARLES SHERMAN, a native of Connecticut, struck out for the West soon after he married and settled at New Lancaster, Ohio. When he arrived at his new home in 1810, the great Shawnee warrior Tecumseh was the talk of the territory. Tecumseh failed in his attempt to unite all western tribes in all-out war with the white man, but he was no ordinary chieftain.

Widely known as Shooting Star, Tecumseh could read as well as write. He had a personal secretary, a Potawatami leader named Billy Caldwell, who looked after his correspondence and decrees. About the time Charles Sherman was beginning to think of himself as an Ohioan, news spread through the region that Shooting Star had decreed that his warriors must spare the lives of women and children.

During the War of 1812, Tecumseh became a British brigadier general and won the respect of some Americans by denouncing the inhumanity of the Redcoats. Numerous settlers came to admire the warrior, after a fashion. Charles Sherman went a lot further than most of his new acquaintances. When his sixth child came along in 1820, the boy was baptized as Tecumseh Sherman. Years later, looking back upon the career of the Civil War general who could have been nominated for president had he not been disdainful of politics and politicians, it was apparent that he had taken Tecumseh's name to new heights by his military feats.

As a child, his brothers and sisters found that Indian name too long for everyday use. So the boy grew up as "Cump," with the abbreviated form of his baptismal name being used by members of the family and most of the approximately one thousand residents of New Lancaster. If any of them wondered why a prospering attorney would name one of his sons for a tribal chieftain, they probably kept quiet about it when Cump's father was around. Usage of the time led many a man to identify himself by his first name, middle initial, and surname.

Just as Tecumseh left an unforgettable memory for most of the pioneers of Ohio, the young Cump went on to blaze his name in the history of the Civil War. From the battle of First Manassas to the surrender of Confederate forces in North Carolina, William Tecumseh Sherman's name lived in infamy in portions of the South for decades after the war.

A CONGRESSMAN AND PIRATE

BEAUFORT, SOUTH CAROLINA, native Robert Smalls was the first former slave from his state to have a notable political career. Partly because the war had started in Charleston, partly because the leaders of the Palmetto State were notoriously cantankerous, the so-called Reconstruction did not follow the chronological path of secession. South Carolina was not readmitted to the Union until the state adopted a radically revised constitution three years after Appomattox.

Smalls was a delegate to the all-important constitutional convention of 1868, and during the same year he won a two-year term in the South Carolina House of Representatives. With two years of legislative experience under his belt, he was almost guaranteed to be elected to a six-year stint in the state senate. Years later he characterized these eight years as an apprenticeship that prepared him to go to Washington for the first of seven terms in the U.S. House of Representatives.

Robert Smalls was also the first black congressman to be accused of accepting a bribe. Almost unbelievably, in the light of much that took place in the Palmetto State, Smalls was cleared of the charges through the diligent work of William Dunlap Simpson, who in 1879 served briefly as governor of South Carolina.

Smalls capped his eventful career by still another first accomplishment. Immediately after the war, he enrolled in the South Carolina State Militia. He was active in that military body for a dozen years, during which he became the first African American to hold the rank of major general.

His exploits prior to his first term in the South Carolina legislature are not well known, so he is rarely listed as being central to more than one significant first event. The majority of Charlestonians know a little about him now, however, for he has become a local hero of sorts and his career is summarized in *The Civil War at Charleston,* a perennially popular publication of the *Charleston Post-Courier,* which is first in age among newspapers of the nation. His boyhood home in Beaufort became a National Historic Landmark on May 30, 1973.

Only a handful of Charleston's white residents knew that Small existed until May 13, 1862, despite the fact that his owner took him to the city well before the outbreak of war. As an adult he was a member of the crew of a transport steamer.

Every working day the *Planter* could be seen chugging around Charleston Harbor, often pulling out to take a cargo to Georgetown or Edisto. Hardly anyone paid any attention to the movements of the vessel because they were familiar and commonplace.

Very early on the morning of a fateful spring day, Smalls smuggled his wife and three children aboard the *Planter.* Once they were safely below deck, he took command of his twelve fellow slaves who constituted the remainder of the crew. Directed by Smalls, the vessel moved from her slip much earlier than usual and headed toward open water.

Confederate guards were stationed at several points near which incoming and outgoing ships had to pass. They were on duty around the clock and were responsible for checking each passing vessel to be sure it did not carry Yankees before allowing it to proceed. Each guard station had a small battery of guns, loaded and ready for use.

Smalls, who never bragged about his exploit, somehow managed to imitate the voice of the ship's master well enough to be waved past each of the guard stations the *Planter* had to pass on its way to a brand-new destination. This time, the ship had no guano or hemp aboard—for it was headed directly toward the Union vessels of the South Atlantic Blockading Squadron. Its chance of reaching a Federal warship would have been judged to be minute had the scheme been divulged to one who knew those waters well.

By seizing the *Planter,* Smalls became a mutineer despite the fact that he did not wear a uniform. Once he passed out of the harbor and headed into the open sea, he became a pirate as well. The first successful African-American mutineer-pirate was soon alongside a Yankee warship. When he, his crew, and his family climbed aboard, the seventeen slaves became contrabands of war. Two months later Congress passed its Second Confiscation Act and made this band of African Americans free under the law.

To those who have never taken a tour of Charleston Harbor, the Smalls feat might be thought to have been easily accomplished. Anyone who remembers that in 1862 this immense sheltered body of water could have held at anchor every warship of every fleet in the world will recognize how far the *Planter* had to go to get past the Confederate guard stations. Because it was an epochal happening and the first and only one of its kind during 1861–62, Abraham Lincoln personally instructed the War Department to put Smalls on the Federal payroll as a pilot. In addition, he was given a cash award when the value of the *Planter* was assessed in a prize court—for the vessel he took out of Charleston became a prize of war as soon as it reached the Federal fleet.

During the long and bitterly contested siege of Charleston by Union warships, the *Planter* was swirled into Rebel-held waters again. In December 1863 Smalls managed to guide the vessel to safety once more. For this feat he was commissioned a captain, making him not only the first black to hold this rank but also the only African American to receive such a commission until Reconstruction was well under way. Yet Smalls has been overlooked as the central character in great Civil War literature.

LARGEST SEABORNE MOVEMENT BEFORE WORLD WAR I

LATE IN March 1862, Gen. George B. McClellan took decisive steps to implement action against the Confederate armies in Virginia after a zany plan of his own concoction failed. Instead of marching from Washington to Richmond, he proposed to move his army by water to the Federal fort at the tip of the Virginia peninsula and march up to Richmond to capture the capital of the Confederacy.

The assembly of transport vessels began around February 27, when their destination was to be the tiny tobacco port of Urbanna, Virginia. Though forced to give up his "Urbanna plan," McClellan continued to commandeer ships of several kinds. On March 15, according to one account, his fleet of schooners, barges, and steamers numbered 389 vessels. Some of them were used to transport supplies, and horses went aboard others. Officers and men of the Army of the Potomac crowded aboard a majority of the vessels, however.

Though McClellan was seen by his contemporaries as one of the worst commanders who wore blue, there is no denying that he scored a logistical triumph without equal. During a period of only twenty days, he moved approximately 105,000 men plus their equipment and animals from Washington to Fort Monroe. At the only major installation in Virginia that remained in Federal hands throughout the war, McClellan launched the disastrous northwestern move by land that became famous as the Peninsula campaign. Not until World War I was a larger body of troops transported anywhere in the world by water.

KNIGHTHOOD FOR A DRIFTER

AN ILLEGITIMATE boy who grew up in Denbigh, Wales, never knew a permanent home. From age three he was shifted back and

Henry M. Stanley was a three-way veteran of the Civil War. He served in the Confederate army and the Union army and navy.

forth between ne'er-do-well relatives and a tax-supported workhouse for the indigent. Constant change during his formative years may have contributed largely to his practice of drifting from place to place and niche to niche as an adult. Typical cabin boys of this period were about nine to twelve years of age, but at age twenty John Rowlands took on this role as a member of the company of a vessel bound for America.

At New Orleans the cabin boy jumped ship. Ravenously hungry and dressed in rags, the illegal immigrant was found by well-to-do merchant Henry M. Stanley, who took him into his home. By the time the native of Wales was on the way to Arkansas to take charge of one of his benefactor's establishments, he had taken on the merchant's name without bothering with the legal formalities.

When war broke out, Stanley became a Confederate soldier at a recruitment center close to his business post. As a member of the Dixie Grays, or the Sixth Arkansas, he fought at Shiloh and was captured. By the time he reached Camp Douglas as a prisoner of war, he discovered that it would be to his advantage to change sides. Soon after having reached Chicago, he volunteered to enlist in Federal forces and was assigned to an artillery unit.

This service lasted until he became seriously ill and received a medical discharge. No longer under duress of any sort, he managed to get passage to Wales for a brief visit then returned and enlisted in the U.S. Navy, where he became acting ensign on the USS *Ticonderoga,* which took part in the 1865 assault upon Fort Fisher at Wilmington, North Carolina. Stanley was

British Missionary David Livingstone was found in Africa by a journalist with the New York Herald.

one of the few men known to have served on both sides and to have spent time in three different branches of service.

Given an honorary discharge, the twenty-four-year-old drifted to New York. His unusually varied experience probably contributed to his finding a job with James Gordon Bennett's *New York Herald.* Though Joseph Pulitzer had not yet become a major force in journalism, sensationalism was already the key to circulation. Even if you are not well acquainted with a life story that can only be called bizarre, by now you have probably connected with the world-famous exploit of the Civil War veteran.

That's right—it was the ex-Rebel, ex-Union infantryman-artillerist-sailor who on November 10, 1871, reached Ujiji on Lake Tanganyika. There he extended his hand to a white man who had been lost in the wilds of Africa for two years and said, "Dr. Livingstone, I presume." As a result, Henry M. Stanley became the first Civil War veteran to be knighted by Queen Victoria.

KILLER WON MEDAL OF HONOR

CONTROVERSY STILL swirls around the action of Union Gen. Daniel E. Sickles at Gettysburg. As the Federal line solidified on the second day, he doubted the wisdom of holding his corps in position in the middle of Cemetery Ridge when there was, in his estimation, a better position in front of him. Without clearing his movement with the field commander of the Army of the

HARPER'S PICTORIAL HISTORY OF THE GREAT REBELLION

Union Gen. Daniel Edgar Sickles was described as "a good-looking cuss" even by his critics.

Potomac, George Gordon Meade, Sickles ordered his men from the long, low spot he occupied toward the slightly higher peach orchard to his front. By doing so he clearly exposed his numerous regiments to enemy fire. At the same time, however, his unauthorized movement may have dulled the impact of James Longstreet's simultaneous attack upon the center of the Federal position on the ridge.

Sickles took a direct hit in his right leg from a Confederate cannon. His wound was so bad that the surgeons did not consider trying to save it; they amputated the limb less than an hour after he was struck. Military and public sympathy ran high for the man who now reveled in posing for photographers so that his one-leggedness showed. At the same time, his detached leg attracted tremendous publicity when he ostentatiously donated it to a medical museum. Every time he paid a visit to the severed limb, he made headlines. Some people suggested that his injury and his way of often underscoring it may have prevented jealous rivals from forcing him to face a court-martial for his conduct in the battle in which he lost the leg.

By 1867 one-legged Dan Sickles had become a folk hero of a sort. As a tribute to his valor, he was made a brevet major general in the U.S. Army that year. Lawmakers later saw to it that he received the Medal of Honor for the way he handled his command at Gettysburg. After a few years passed, virtually all criticism of his generalship was stilled.

Most of his admirers and some of his harshest critics knew that as a member of the U.S. House of Representatives he had made legal history just prior to the outbreak of war. Before moving to Washington from New York, Sickles married Teresa Bagioli, the sixteen-year-old daughter of his landlord. He was more than twice her age and had a reputation as a notorious womanizer, and she was pregnant. Sickles was a highly ambitious politician as well, and so when the two arrived in Washington he easily neglected Teresa as he pursued his career.

At the time, Washington society centered as much on parties as it did on politics. Unescorted women at these parties, however, were scandalous, and so it was not unusual to see a woman in attendance with a man other than her husband. Teresa had no difficulty attracting escorts, all with her husband's knowledge and within the bounds of acceptable behavior. One of these was Philip Barton Key, the son of Francis Scott Key and the district attorney for Washington. It was not long, however, before the neglected Teresa and the distinguished Key were lovers. The affair went on for more than a year with most of Washington society aware of the scandal. Sickles, for some reason, seemed unaware. Finally, a "friend" sent the congressman a letter informing him of the infidelity.

Sickles confronted Teresa, and she confessed. Not satisfied with her ending the affair, the young congressman from New York demanded a written confession and stood over her as she wrote it.

The next day Philip Barton Key appeared and signaled for Teresa as he usually did prior to their trysts. Unfortunately for him, Sickles happened to see him. Enraged, he flew out of the house and accosted Key in the street. Key merely turned to avoid the confrontation, but Sickles drew a pistol and the two men briefly scuffled. The encounter drew a great deal of attention since it occurred in Lafayette Square, directly across Pennsylvania Avenue from the White House.

Sickles fired at Key, but the bullet only grazed him. The two men grappled with one another, and Sickles dropped his pistol. He pulled another from his coat and coolly pulled the trigger, this time striking Key in the upper leg, and Key fell to the ground. Key begged for his life, but Sickles stood over him, aimed his pistol, and pulled the trigger. The weapon misfired. Despite the fallen man's pleadings—he was a widower with four children—Sickles pressed his weapon against Key's chest and fired again.

Key was taken to a nearby men's club where he died. Sickles walked calmly to the house of the U.S. attorney and surrendered. The murder shocked the city. Numerous eyewitnesses viewed the fatal encounter. There was no question of Sickles's guilt; all that remained was the formality of a legal decision.

Sickles hired Edwin McMaster Stanton, a rising star in the legal community, to defend him. The twenty-two-day trial concluded with a pair of first happenings.

The jealous husband who claimed he had acted on impulse to protect the sanctity of his home became the first American killer to win acquittal on the grounds of temporary insanity. Some time in December 1861, Abraham Lincoln decided to replace his secretary of war, Simon Cameron, and on January 15, 1862, the first attorney to frame a successful temporary insanity defense for a client accused of murder became the U.S. secretary of war.

Dan Sickles shot and killed Philip Barton Key in broad daylight not far from the White House, with an eyewitness only a few feet away.

LIBRARY OF CONGRESS

No man to forgive and forget, Stanton nursed a lasting grudge against his opponent in the Sickles trial, Robert Ould, the U.S. district attorney for the District of Columbia. Soon after the outbreak of war, Ould declared his allegiance to the South and subsequently became involved in the efforts to exchange prisoners of war between the two sides. In this official capacity, he dealt constantly with Federal agents and was the only Confederate official whose office was recognized formally by the North.

At the war's end, Stanton ordered Ould arrested, jailed, and charged with treason. Ould was investigated by a military commission and, after only two months of imprisonment, became the first top-level Confederate official to be released. In the years afterward, during which Ould held office as a judge, he admitted that he never found it possible to forgive fully the man who had been his legal foe during the Sickles trial.

The sequence of events that led to the death of Key and the acquittal of his murderer made Sickles the first known murderer to be decorated with the Medal of Honor.

COMMANDER IN CHIEF UNDER FIRE

ABRAHAM LINCOLN was the first American chief executive to come under enemy fire. James Madison would have had that unenviable honor had he been at home when the British raided Washington during the War of 1812. (His wife, Dolley, however, was in the residence and saved many of the mansion's irreplaceable treasures, such as the famous Gilbert Stuart portrait of Washington.)

On July 11, 1864, our sixteenth president came under Rebel fire when Confederate Gen. Jubal Early raided the Washington area in an attempt to divert Union troops from the siege of Petersburg. The Federal capital was ringed with sixty enclosed forts and ninety-three batteries when Early brought his army in front of Fort Stevens and began to probe the Washington defenses. Lincoln was no stranger to the capital forts, and he visited Fort Stevens twice during the engagement with Early. Several reports indicate that he stood on the parapet, watching the troops engaged on the field as bullets plinked near him and struck down a man near the president. Oliver Wendell Holmes Jr., an officer with the Twentieth Massachusetts, allegedly shouted to the tall target, "Get down, you fool!"

Though there's little doubt that a Confederate bullet might have brought Lincoln's life to an end that summer day in 1864, it was not the first instance in which this chief executive tempted fate in front of the foe. That first happened on May 8, 1862.

The president's son Willie had died in February 1862, and Lincoln had not ventured far from Washington for a while afterward. The Union army, however, had finally renewed the offensive in Virginia, and George B. McClellan engineered the movement of his men from the capital camps to the Virginia Peninsula, but the offensive had stalled in front of Yorktown and McClellan had hunkered down for a siege.

In May, Lincoln decided to have a face-to-face talk with his general. The commander in chief was less than satisfied with McClellan's leadership; the cautious general did not move nearly as quickly as the president hoped he would. To demonstrate to his general that "the slows" could be remedied, Lincoln impetuously sailed from Washington for the Federal foothold on the Virginia Peninsula, Fort Monroe.

NATIONAL ARCHIVES

Joining the president aboard the revenue cutter *Miami* were cabinet members Salmon P. Chase and Edwin M. Stanton. At about 10 P.M. on May 6 the steamer tied up at the fort's

Abraham Lincoln was not content to remain in Washington while his army was marching up the Virginia Peninsula. He ventured to Fort Monroe to see for himself how the fighting was progressing.

wharf. Etiquette required that the president visit the quarters of John Wool, the fort's commander. McClellan could not join them; the Confederates had withdrawn from Yorktown to the old Virginia capital city of Williamsburg, and the Union army had succeeded in overwhelming that position that day.

During his conversations with Wool and the other general officers at Monroe, Lincoln learned that no effort had yet been mounted to seize the Confederate base across the bay at Norfolk. Taken aback by this bit of incompetence, the president and his advisers met with several naval officers whose vessels were moored close to the fort. Lincoln's suspicions of Norfolk's vulnerability were confirmed by reports that the Southerners had already begun to evacuate the port city.

Although we know a great deal about what Lincoln did and said, he was a highly secretive man who managed to mask his feelings and motives. It is possible that he had the capture of Norfolk in mind before embarking on his expedition, but there is nothing to confirm this suspicion. On May 8, however, Lincoln announced that the fall of Norfolk would be hastened by a thrust at the Rebel batteries at Sewell's Point, close to the vital Southern naval base—and home port to the Confederate ironclad *Virginia*.

Chase executed an evening reconnaissance to find a suitable landing site for the attack force; Lincoln remained at the fort and studied maps. When Chase returned with a suggestion for the landing, another reconnaissance across Hampton Roads was planned for the next night, this time with Lin-

LIBRARY OF CONGRESS

Secretary of War Edwin M. Stanton accompanied the president and walked ashore with Lincoln on a Virginia beach to scout a landing site for the assault force that would claim Norfolk.

coln and Stanton undertaking a closer inspection of the ground while Chase directed the *Miami* as it protected the president's party. That moonlit evening, Lincoln waded ashore and strolled the Virginia beach. Whatever resistance the two vessels and landing party encountered were minimal.

The landing was planned for the next day. Support vessels included the USS *Monitor,* the paddle sloop *Susquehanna,* and the screw-driven *San Jacinto, Oneida,* and *Dacotah.* Chase joined the forces in the field, while Lincoln and Stanton remained at Fort Monroe. Chase boarded the tug *Tigress* to watch the action firsthand and landed with the troops.

Lincoln remained at Fort Monroe and took an active part in directing reinforcements as they boarded transports. One of the soldiers commented, "Abe was rushing about, hollering to someone on the wharf—dressed in a black suit with a very seedy crepe on his hat, and hanging over the railing, he looked like some hoosier just starting for home from California, with store clothes and a biled shirt on."

As the last Confederates boarded the last train out of town, Chase and Wool accepted the surrender of the city from the mayor, who thought to give them the key to the city as symbolic of the capitulation. The hurried evacuation, however, did not give

the *Virginia's* crew the time it needed to lighten the vessel so it could navigate the shallows and the sandbars of the James River to a safe port. The vessel had to be destroyed, and the explosion could be heard by the Union troops and their president at Fort Monroe.

Secretary of the Treasury Salmon P. Chase demonstrated tremendous verve when he scouted a landing site one night and then directed the gun crews that watched over Lincoln and Stanton when they landed in Virginia.

Lincoln's timing of the initiative to secure Norfolk upset the timetable of the evacuating Confederates. One Southern casualty was the ironclad Virginia.

Chase wrote in a letter to his daughter, "So has ended a brilliant week's campaign of the President, for I think it quite certain that if he had not come down, [Norfolk] would still have been in possession of the enemy and the [*Virginia*] as grim and defiant and as much a terror as ever." Military experts contend that Lincoln's life was not in danger during "the week's campaign," but the moonlit foray across Hampton Roads on May 8, 1862, rather than the president's visit to Fort Stevens marks the first instance in which a sitting chief executive of the United States came under hostile fire.

CHAPTER SEVEN

JOHNNY REB
& BILLY YANK

TWO KINDS OF FORAGING

LONG BEFORE William T. Sherman's bummers began foraging in
central Georgia for horses, mules, pigs, preserves, quilts, salt,
and just about everything else a rural household was likely to
have, troops on both sides habitually scoured the countryside
looking for horses. Officers and cavalry rode them; wagon dri-
vers whipped them; and common soldiers looked after them.

Decades before self-propelled vehicles began to chug along
the roads of the North and the South, there were just four kinds
of transportation for civilians and soldiers. If a railroad happened
to be running in the right direction, a train might help one to
reach his destination within four or five days. Steamers navigated
the country's waterways. A person could walk maybe ten miles a
day in good weather (or march a whole lot faster on orders from

Ulysses S. Grant or Thomas J. Jackson). The remaining mode of travel was by horse power and was perhaps the most widespread mode of transportation.

Without horses, the Civil War would have been a wholly different conflict. Central corrals in Federal military departments often held thousands of them. Once an animal had been allocated for duty, it became the job of Johnny Reb or Billy Yank to see that the animal was cared for. Horses preferred to eat grass or hay, but when neither was available, they would chomp on fodder or leaves from mature cornstalks. A hungry horse would graze on almost anything.

Early Federal incursions into Virginia saw many units exhaust their supply of forage in the field. Confederate units encountered the same predicament, so it was natural for commanders on both sides to send out foraging parties. To foragers on either side, it made little difference whether these supplies were found on the property of a dyed-in-the-wool Rebel or a true-blue Unionist trapped within a seceded state.

Bummers who followed in the wake of Sherman's forces looted and stole anything and everything of value.

HARPER'S WEEKLY

HARPER'S WEEKLY

This corral in Washington was typical of hundreds that were scattered throughout the theaters of war.

The word *forage* rates 3,372 mentions in the *Official Records*. *Foragers* are discussed 154 times, and *foraging* is a topic in 960 reports and dispatches. Several times, news of good forage prompted a skirmish when elements of both sides appeared at the same time to claim it.

Gradually foraging expanded in meaning beyond food for animals. Foragers began hunting chickens, geese, turkeys, hats, shirts, pants, clocks, watches, rings, necklaces, shotguns, pistols, hunting rifles, anything that looked valuable, and worthless souvenirs (except for the memories linked with them).

When Johnny Reb or Billy Yank sneaked off in the night to go home or was furloughed as a reward for reenlisting, he was likely to have a tale or two to tell about foraging. The folks at home probably did not understand how horses could use sheets and featherbeds and butter and eggs. It's likely they just nodded their heads at the tales of adventure and never asked how those things came into camp after a foraging expedition.

U.S. ARMY MILITARY HISTORY INSTITUTE

Medical corpsmen, such as these men of the Federal Ninth Corps, struggled against sickness and disease as much as against battle wounds.

BETTER THEN THAN NOW

INITIALLY, SOLDIERS on both sides seemed to have been willing and eager to take shots at one another. Some of that enthusiasm wore off early, so both the South and the North had to resort to conscription when the armies lost manpower to combat. There were so many loopholes in the draft, however, that very soon the conflict came to be called a "rich man's war, poor man's fight."

Very few soldiers died as a result of bayonet wounds, despite the frequency with which officers bragged of having ordered their units to fix bayonets and charge. Millions of pounds of metal were hurled by field artillery, naval batteries, and assorted big guns. By far the greatest number of deaths and mortal wounds came from the lead projectiles propelled from muskets, rifles, carbines, and pistols. More men, however, lost their lives to the diseases of diarrhea, malaria, dysentery, pneumonia, yellow fever, typhoid fever, typhus, smallpox, measles, and other maladies than they did to combat.

Battle, disease, and malnutrition cost the warring sections the lives of about 620,000 men. Before South Carolina seceded in December 1860, the census of 1860 estimated the national population at 31.5 million. Without factoring in estimates of the number of immigrants that arrived during the war years, wartime deaths wiped out almost 2 percent of the total population.

The census of 1990 reported that the country's population was 248,709,873. If the Civil War had been launched in 1991 and the mortality rate had matched that of 1861–65, the fifty states would have experienced almost five million dead—and that does not take into account the more lethal manner in which war is waged today.

MOST DISTINGUISHED PRIVATE

QUITE A few prominent civilians enlisted as common soldiers, making no effort to gain commissions. Hannibal Hamlin ranks as the most distinguished officeholder in this select group. The former congressman and senator from Maine, who became vice president of the United States in 1861, could easily have finagled an appointment as a colonel or a brigadier. Instead he became a

Vice President Hannibal Hamblin served briefly as an enlisted man in the Maine Coast Guard.

NICOLAY & HAY, ABRAHAM LINCOLN

buck private in Company A of the Maine Coast Guard and remained undistinguished during the two months he spent in camp.

ONE OF A KIND

WHEN JOHN SUMMERFIELD STAPLES of Pennsylvania enlisted in the Union army in the fall of 1864, few of his comrades realized that he was like no other among the approximately three million men in blue. His name appears in the *Official Records* just once, in one of the most unusual documents included in this unique collection. A Northern "List of persons who put in representative recruits, and names of recruits," runs to nineteen pages of miniature print. Ordinary folk rarely used a highfalutin term like *representative recruit*. Instead, they called men who were paid to fight for someone else "substitutes."

A widely circulated list of Civil War substitutes holds that five prominent men each bought his way out of military service. They have been identified many times as Chester A. Arthur, Andrew Carnegie, Grover Cleveland, J. Pierpont Morgan, and John D. Rockefeller. Carnegie was born in Scotland and may not have been subject to the draft. Arthur, Morgan, and Rockefeller each could have paid $300, more or less, to stay out of uniform, but there's no certainty that they did.

Grover Cleveland's record is a different matter. In a New York State lottery, his name was drawn from a pool of potential fighting men, and he would have been expected to join the ranks had he not had enough money to meet another criteria of the draft. He found a Polish immigrant, variously identified as George Benninsky or George Brinske, who needed money. Evidence suggests that Cleveland got a bargain, for he probably did not pay George more than $150 to fight in his stead.

Only eight residents of the District of Columbia are listed as having bought their way out of military service. Seven of the principals—men whose money bought "substitutes"—are obscure, but the eighth is widely familiar after nearly 150 years. His substitute was John Summerfield Staples, whose enlistment is credited to the quota of the capital's third subdistrict, courtesy of the fellow who hung his tall black hat at 1600 Pennsylvania Avenue.

Why Staples got at least $500 and perhaps as much as $750 to become the military substitute of Abraham Lincoln is anybody's guess. We know a lot about the public Lincoln but hardly anything about why he made the decisions and acted as he did. Indisputably exempt from the draft, he nevertheless paid for the services of one of the approximately 118,000 men who laid their lives on the line for what to them seemed to be big money.

The twenty-year-old Staples is listed among the hundreds of "representative recruits" whose names have been preserved. As a substitute for the commander in chief of all military and naval forces of the Union, the Pennsylvanian was no ordinary Billy Yank, but he did little to distinguish himself during the war. Shortly after his enlistment—which was his second—his regiment

Future President Grover Cleveland (left) hired a substitute to fill his place in the ranks of the Union army. By the time Lincoln (right) hired a substitute, his face hinted that he might have preferred that the substitute stay in the White House while he joined the fight on the battlefield.

was stationed across the Potomac in Alexandria. He served under the provost marshal both as a clerk and occasionally as a prison guard. In the spring of 1865 he fell ill and was furloughed home to recover. He was there when Lee surrendered to Grant on April 9 at Appomattox Court House. Staples was still home when news came of the president's assassination. In September 1865 he was mustered out of the service with little fanfare.

The life of John Summerfield Staples remained unspectacular until his death in 1888. He returned to the family business in Stroudsburg, Pennsylvania. He married twice, but both wives died, leaving him with a son and a daughter. Staples left the children with his parents and began drifting from job to job across Pennsylvania and New York. His health failed in 1884, and citing his service in the war, he applied for a disability pension from the federal government. It was not approved; the illness had not been related to his military duties. At the age of forty-three, John Summerfield Staples, the soldier substitute for Abraham Lincoln, died of a heart attack. His hometown of Stroudsburg erected a memorial in his honor.

TRAMP, TRAMP, TRAMP . . .

ALTHOUGH THE famous marching song referred to in the title of this section is generally associated with World War I, it was a song of the Civil War. Whatever else a common soldier of the Civil War may have done, marching was his reality. Horses, railroads, and steamers did not log a fraction of the almost two billion miles the soldiers marched across the country. The vast majority of Northerners were able to do so in the relative comfort of shoes, but the soldiers of the South were largely barefoot.

The word *march* appears in the *Official Records* 11,222 times, followed by 4,394 references to marching and 7,971 instances in which men are reported as having marched.

If we arbitrarily assume that the average march was 5 miles— a conservative estimate—and that each march involved ten thou-

Harpers Ferry, recently captured by Stonewall Jackson's corps, was the starting point for the epic march to the Antietam battlefield by A. P. Hill's men.

U.S. ARMY MILITARY HISTORY INSTITUTE

sand men, how many miles would the troops have totaled? Using the 23,587 instances listed in the *Official Records*, this would equal 1.179 billion miles.

Most commanders preferred that their men march four abreast at a rate of about 2.5 miles per hour. Although the troops were seldom required to keep in step during a short march, many found that the journey was a trifle easier if they walked in cadence with each other.

That did not necessarily hold true for long marches, however. On these treks, the attrition could be terrible. Stragglers fell out of the ranks at the rate of one every minute, and another soldier would have to change position to fill the gap. This made marching in step impossible.

Reporting from Pulaski, Tennessee, on May 8, 1864, Union Gen. W. Q. Gresham casually noted that the Seventeenth Wisconsin and the Fourteenth Illinois had marched 27 miles that day. In October 1862 the Fifteenth Illinois, Twelfth Michigan, and Sixty-

Union Gen. Nathaniel P. Banks claimed that his men once marched at the rate of two and a half miles per hour for fourteen hours without a stop.

eighth Ohio covered 28 miles. In March 1862 Maj. Joseph Conrad reported that his command became too fatigued to continue after having marched 30 miles from sunup to sundown. Gen. Isaac J. Wistar noted in October 1863 that the entire "Fourth United States infantry (colored) made thirty miles in one day, with no stragglers." Chaplain H. S. White of a Rhode Island heavy artillery unit did not seem surprised to learn that his group had covered 40 miles in one day, since they moved at the double-quick for several miles.

If the focus is on speed rather than distance, then the achievements of the Southerners comes to the fore. At Harpers Ferry, Confederate Gen. Ambrose Powell Hill received the urgent call to join the September 17, 1862, battle at Sharpsburg, Maryland. He hurried his entire command to the scene and possibly set a record of sorts. Although hundreds of men fell out along the way, about three thousand men covered 17 miles in roughly eight hours. The sight of the long gray column behind the Virginia and Confederate flags brought more than a sense of relief to those Southerners who managed to get a look at men who joined the right side of Lee's line just as it seemed to be on the verge of collapsing.

It's probably impossible to arrive at a definite "speed record" made by marching men, but some of the contenders would include the soldiers under Union Gen. Robert C. Schenck, who traversed 34 miles in twenty-three hours in May 1862. In contention would also be Nathaniel P. Banks's men who hurried from Winchester, Virginia, to Williamsport, Maryland, marching 35 miles in fourteen hours. (Banks's claim sounds like an exaggeration until one realizes that he was trying to get away from Stonewall Jackson.)

A march led by Union Gen. Francis J. Herron was described in greater detail than that by Banks. Departing from Springfield, Missouri, Herron's command reached Prairie Grove, Arkansas, within three long days during which his troops covered 112 miles. A similar feat was accomplished in March 1862 without setting foot outside the state of Missouri. Men of the Third, Twelfth, Fifteenth, and Seventeenth Missouri marched 125 miles in four days. One private of the Twelfth fell out, and thirteen men of the Fifteenth could not keep the pace; the rest arrived at Keetsville with blistered feet and high spirits. Some of the veterans of these long marches were later captured and reportedly forced to move 85 miles in fifty hours "with hardly any food at all." Confederate Gen. Jubal Early and his men were so eager to attack the Federal capital at the height of summer heat in 1864 that they raised a choking dust cloud for a total of 42 miles in a little more than a day.

The average speed of an army on the march was cut drastically when vast distances were involved. Had the men under Stonewall Jackson and A. P. Hill been forced to cover twice as many miles as

they did during the Shenandoah campaign of 1862 and the march from Harpers Ferry to the battlefield around Sharpsburg, even they would have moderated their pace before reaching their destinations.

Stonewall Jackson's men reputedly adored him, despite

Prior to the first major battle of the war, Union Gen. Irvin McDowell set a record of sorts when he moved his command toward Centreville, Virginia, at the rate of only a third of a mile per hour.

Men under Union Gen. John Sedgwick marched about 41 miles without a halt when he led them to the battle at Gettysburg, Pennsylvania.

PICTORIAL FIELD BOOK OF THE CIVIL WAR

the manner in which he drove them so relentlessly. In March 1862 his famous "foot cavalry" covered 25 miles one day and 16 more the next day in order to reach Kernstown, Virginia, and immediately fall into line to fight a battle. Their ranks were thin, however, since an estimated fifteen hundred stragglers fell out during the march.

There is no reason to challenge the claim of Yale-educated Union Gen. William Birney that one brigade of his Twenty-fifth Corps completed a 96-mile march in eighty-four hours "without losing a single straggler." In Virginia in 1863 an unidentified USCT (U.S. Colored Troops) regiment reputedly marched 60 miles in forty hours during a raid.

Union Gen. John Sedgwick was very late in hearing that a battle was forming around the Pennsylvania town of Gettysburg. He did not want to disappoint the new commander of the Army of the Potomac, George G. Meade, so he raced the entire Sixth Corps toward the scene from its camp at Manchester, Maryland. His men did not begin the move until about 10 P.M. on July 1, 1861, and had neither a reliable map nor a dependable guide. Counting the approximately 8 miles lost by going astray, this body of men tramped 41 miles to get to the battlefield. Some say this march ended after nineteen hours, but others insist that it took only seventeen.

During the long retreat three days later, numerous units of Lee's Army of Northern Virginia distanced themselves from Gettysburg by 30 to 40 miles during a forty-eight-hour constant rain.

German-born Union Gen. Franz Sigel permitted his men to saunter toward their objectives.

HARPER'S PICTORIAL HISTORY OF THE GREAT REBELLION

Lots of marches were anything but fast. Approaching Centreville, Virginia, prior to the battle of First Bull Run, Irvin McDowell's men in blue marched only 22 miles in sixty hours. Moving cautiously up the Shenandoah Valley, Union Gen. Franz Sigel's men took seventy-two hours to cover the 22-mile stretch between Martinsburg and Winchester. At that rate, the Federals were lightning fast compared with Confederate Gen. Braxton Bragg and his forces during part of September 1863. In the aftermath of Chickamauga, Bragg's men took sixty hours to march 12 miles from that battlefield to Chattanooga.

Even Bragg's command did not come close to challenging a record of sorts that was set by Union Gen. Ambrose E. Burnside and the Army of the Potomac in January 1863. On the heels of the defeat at Fredericksburg, the man with the muttonchops whiskers decided to move his army north to a crossing of the Rappahannock River to strike the Rebel rear. Having been born and reared in Indiana, Burnside should have known that January weather can play havoc with the shrewdest of maneuvers. Rain pelted his army relentlessly on January 19 and did not let up. As a result the sudden strike turned into the infamous Mud March in which thousands of men became bogged down and found it impossible to go forward and nearly as hard to retreat. Burnside scrapped the attack plans early on January 23, and it took his men two days to muck their way back to their old camp opposite Fredericksburg. Shortly after the inglorious end of the Mud March, Burnside was relieved and Gen. Joseph Hooker took command of the filthy, hungry, and exhausted army that had

During the highly publicized Mud March of the Army of the Potomac under Union Gen. Ambrose Burnside, the feet and ankles of soldiers and horses often disappeared in the mud.

HARPER'S PICTORIAL HISTORY OF THE GREAT REBELLION

marched nowhere during a 120-hour period.

There is no way to ascertain which commander led his men the fastest from one point to another, but there were some remarkable achievements of what the professors of West Point called *celerity,* which Nathan Bedford Forrest summarized as "getting the mostest there the fastest." During a period of just over six weeks in the Shenandoah Valley, Stonewall Jackson reported that his men averaged 13.5 miles every day for a total of 646 miles.

Men of the Twelfth Wisconsin claimed to have made 22 miles in six hours so as to reach Hannibal, Missouri, in January 1862. This remarkable unit may have been the only one to keep meticulous marching records from start to finish. Organized at Madison, the Twelfth Wisconsin did not leave the state until January 31, 1862, and its men had their first taste of combat at the April 1862 battle of Shiloh. A little more than three years later, the regiment marched in

NATIONAL ARCHIVES

When rain and mud delayed his army's advance, Ambrose Burnside was forced to abandon his second campaign to march on Richmond. He also lost his job as commander of the Army of the Potomac.

the grand review up Pennsylvania Avenue on May 24, 1865, before riding the rails home. Once back in Madison, the regimental record keepers toted up their figures and reported that the Twelfth had marched a total of 3,380 miles.

STATUS SYMBOL

MANY AN officer was inordinately proud of his gold braid and his bars or stars. The average soldier, however, rarely had occasion to display a symbol of rank of this sort. According to Lonnie R. Speer, under special circumstances a few soldiers did strut their stuff because they displayed maybe the most unusual of military status symbols.

In his book *Portals to Hell,* Speer reports that among the thousands of Yanks who spent time in Richmond's infamous Libby Prison, only a handful had toothbrushes. Inmate George

At Richmond's Libby Prison thousands of prisoners of war came and went— mostly to other prisons around the Confederate capital, but in the last eighteen months of the conflict to prisons farther south, like Andersonville and Cahaba.

NATIONAL ARCHIVES

Putnam wrote that there were only about a dozen in the entire prison population. These privileged few wore their toothbrushes in buttonholes of their shirts "to emphasize a sense of aristocratic opulence."

COMRADES READY TO KILL

EVIDENTLY EVERY man in uniform quickly came to know what file closers were ordered to do, but there seems to have been a conspiracy of silence concerning this functionary. In the approximately 133,000 pages of the *Official Records,* file closers are mentioned only eighteen times. Most of these are casual to the point of meaninglessness, asserting that the file closers did their duty without hinting at what that duty was.

The functional title of these men seems perfectly clear. Obviously, it was their duty to see that the men making up a file did not spread out and mess up a line that was supposed to be straight

The majority of Civil War field commanders—including Robert E. Lee (center)—seemed to have had hearts of stone when they issued orders concerning the duties of file closers.

and tight. In the second edition of *Webster's New International Dictionary of the English Language* (1934) a terse description of this role describes a file closer as "A commissioned or noncommissioned officer in the rear of a line, or on the flank of a column, to rectify mistakes and insure steadiness in the ranks."

During the Civil War file closers were noncommissioned officers. Officers might occasionally serve in this capacity, but only when they had no one else to do the job. File closers were handpicked men who were not allowed to question the task to which they were assigned.

At least as early as the spring of 1862, the file closers' job description was expanded. They were given the added task of following behind the lines in battle and ensuring that the men fought and did not run. Anyone who attempted to flee the front line was forced back at sword- or gunpoint. File closers were also empowered to execute any man who failed to do his duty.

During the siege of Petersburg, on February 22, 1865, R. E. Lee included a circular to his General Orders No. 4. It was distributed throughout the Army of Northern Virginia and underscored the need for keen military discipline in the face of internecine fighting along the siege lines. With regard to file closers, he wrote:

> I call your attention particularly to the following order with reference to the duties of file closers, which you will immediately carry into execution. . . . The whole number of file closers in each company shall be one for every ten men. . . . They will be required to prevent straggling and be held responsible for their respective squads of ten. In action they will keep two paces behind the rear rank of their several squads, . . . with loaded guns and fixed bayonets. They will be diligently instructed to aid in preserving order in the ranks and enforcing obedience to commands, and to permit no man to leave his place unless wounded, excused in writing by the medical officer of the regiment, or by order of the regimental commander. For this purpose they will use such degree of force as may be necessary. If any refuse to advance, disobey orders, or leave the ranks to plunder or to retreat, the file

closer will promptly cut down or fire upon the delinquents.
They will treat in the same manner any man who uses words
or actions calculated to produce alarm among the troops. . . .
[I]t will be enjoined upon file closers that they shall make the
evasion of duty more dangerous than its performance.

In light of Lee's instructions, the role of file closer was not a
popular one. Although the *Official Records* gives no hint that
soldiers sometimes turned on file closers in combat, it is not
unlikely such actions occurred frequently enough to prevent
most men from hankering for the job.

CHAPTER EIGHT

RECORD MAKERS AND BREAKERS

TOP SOCIAL EVENT

CHARLES S. STRATTON was born at Bridgeport, Connecticut, in 1838. When he was six months old, he appeared to be a normal child who then weighed more than nine pounds. His growth slowed dramatically, however, before he was one year old and eventually halted altogether. At age four, he weighed only fifteen pounds and was just twenty-eight inches tall.

Because of changes in his travel schedule occasioned by severe weather, showman Phineas T. Barnum passed through Bridgeport late in 1842 and spent the night there. He learned about the little Stratton and immediately entered into a contract with the boy's parents. Advertised as a dwarf of "perfect physical proportions and high intelligence," the youth from Connecticut was billed by Barnum as Tom Thumb.

Charles S. Stratton became known as Tom Thumb.

When Tom turned eighteen, Barnum took him to England and arranged for him to be presented to Queen Victoria and the royal family. He was a great success as a performer in London, and later in Paris he was lauded by the rich and famous. Back in the United States, he met Lavinia Warren (also a dwarf) and created great excitement with the announcement of their marriage.

The 1863 wedding of Tom Thumb and Lavinia Warren was by every standard the outstanding social event of the war years. President and Mrs. Lincoln, who regretted their inability to attend the ceremony, sent a gift of Chinese fire screens to the bride and groom.

On February 10 New York's Grace Church was filled with two thousand well-wishers who had either received invitations or been lucky enough to purchase a pair for $120. The assembly was made up of the very wealthy plus generals, governors, congressmen, and their wives. Everybody who was anybody tried to be on hand for the ceremony that had caught the interest of the whole North.

Showman Phineas T. Barnum made Tom Thumb a world celebrity.

GLEASON'S PICTORIAL

GLEASON'S PICTORIAL

The wedding of Lavinia Warren and Charles Stratton was one of the top social events of the war years. The couple toured the world for the rest of the century, and young children conducted "Tom Thumb weddings" into the next.

Soon after the ceremony, the wee couple was received by the Lincolns at the White House. Later that year they sailed for London, the first stop on a fifty-six-thousand-mile world tour during which King Victor Emmanuel of Italy, Napoleon III of France, and Pope Pius IX received them. Noted engineer-builder Peter Cooper built for a wealthy client a miniature train complete with a steam locomotive that was widely publicized as the Tom Thumb. The impact of the wartime ceremony was such that in many parts of the country, carefully coached boys and girls were performing "Tom Thumb weddings" as late as the 1930s.

APPOMATTOX RANKS SECOND

THE SYMBOLIC importance of R. E. Lee's surrender at Appomattox Court House is unequaled, yet it did not involve as many

Union Gen. Philip Sheridan (shown long after the war) won a spectacular battle at Five Forks, Virginia, and R. E. Lee realized there was little else he could do militarily.

LIBRARY OF CONGRESS

fighting men as the surrender of other Southern armies. By March 31, 1865, the once nearly invincible Army of Northern Virginia had been reduced to an estimated fifty thousand men. They faced adversaries who outnumbered them by more than two and a half to one, so the Appomattox campaign was doomed from the beginning.

In some respects, the word *campaign* is a misnomer to describe the actions that took place after the assaults of April 2 outside Petersburg. As the Confederate government was evacuating Richmond, Lee's army began a withdrawal intended to bring them together with the Army of Tennessee in North Carolina.

Union Gen. Philip H. Sheridan's April 1 victory at Five Forks, however, made it impossible for Lee's army to withdraw into the Deep South. Retreating northward across the James River, the Army of Northern Virginia waged a rear-guard struggle that was no more than a futile attempt to slow or obstruct the Federal pursuit. During a two-day period, engagements took place at Beaver Pond Creek, Namozine Church, and Amelia Court House. In retrospect, Lee saw the delay that took place at Amelia Court House as having been fatal and "beyond retrieval."

Several separate but significant actions in the region of Sayler's Creek on April 6 significantly reduced the ranks of the retreating Southerners. U. S. Grant initiated a correspondence with Lee on the following day. Lee's response to Grant's overture amounted to a thinly veiled request for terms of surrender.

The exact number of officers and men still following Lee when the two commanders and their aides came together at the McLean house on Palm Sunday, April 9, cannot be determined. At least twelve thousand Confederates had been captured at Petersburg and during the course of the retreat. Half as many had become casualties, and deserters may have numbered as many as four thousand. That left Lee with no more than twenty-eight thousand men under his command at the time of the Appomattox surrender, and the number was probably closer to twenty-six thousand.

In North Carolina, Confederate Gen. Joseph E. Johnston was in frequent contact with the fleeing Confederate president, Jefferson Davis. Still trying to seem hopeful and belligerent, Davis was reluctant to approve the surrender of the Army of Tennessee even after "a basis of agreement"—in effect, an armistice—was signed on April 18. Johnston's formal surrender was delayed eight more days, but during this interval no significant military action took place in this region.

Final negotiations between Johnston and Gen. William T. Sherman were conducted in a farmhouse that belonged to James

The surrender of the Army of Northern Virginia, signed by Robert E. Lee at Appomattox Court House, involved fewer than thirty thousand men.

CENTURY WAR BOOK

and Nancy Bennett, near Durham Station, North Carolina. The chief executive of the Confederacy, who demanded that Johnston continue to fight, chose to empower Johnston with command of all Southern forces in North Carolina, South Carolina, Georgia, and Florida.

Johnston reasoned that additional battles would accomplish nothing except a senseless loss of many lives. He therefore disobeyed Davis and on April 26 signed articles of capitulation. An estimated thirty thousand officers and men who constituted what was left of the Army of Tennessee were directly affected by the surrender. Although it did not affect forces farther west under E. Kirby Smith and Richard Taylor, all Confederate soldiers in four states were included in the Sherman-Johnston pact.

Estimates of the total number of soldiers who were surrendered on Wednesday, April 26, run as high as ninety thousand, but that figure is probably exaggerated. If the total were cut in half, Johnston surrendered at least forty-five

Although he is generally depicted as pugnacious, Union Gen. William T. Sherman was conciliatory and generous when he met with Confederate Gen. Joseph E. Johnston in Durham Station, North Carolina.

CURRIER & IVES LITHOGRAPH

thousand men at Durham Station—almost twice as many as were yielded by Lee at Appomattox Court House.

CIVIL OFFICIALS RAN RINGS AROUND MILITARY OFFICERS

DURING THE war, at least four Confederate generals surrendered entire armies. Dozens of commanders on both sides capitulated and surrendered their men in the wake of battles and sieges. For example, Vicksburg, Mississippi, was the largest city surrendered by a general—John C. Pemberton, who happened to be a native of Pennsylvania.

Only two significant surrenders occurred in the North. The first was a town where the Confederates met no resistance.

CHAMBERSBURG, PENNSYLVANIA—OCTOBER 10, 1862

On or about October 8, R. E. Lee authorized Gen. Jeb Stuart to lead his cavalry into Maryland and, if circumstances warranted, to

Defended to the end, Vicksburg was eventually surrendered by a northern-born Confederate general.

HARPER'S WEEKLY

go a short distance into Pennsylvania. An estimated eighteen hundred horsemen crossed the Potomac River just above Harpers Ferry and rode hell-for-leather toward the north. Stuart's troopers cut across the Maryland panhandle and reached Chambersburg, Pennsylvania, well before dark.

The defense of the town had been entrusted to A. K. McClure, editor of the local newspaper, but he had only a handful of home guards whom he described as being "scattered and bewildered." A rider bearing an improvised flag of truce approached the town and demanded to meet with someone in authority. Led to McClure, the rider refused to identify his unit or name his commander, but he offered to serve as go-between.

McClure huddled with a few prominent men. Since they had no choice, they agreed to give up their town and learned later that Gen. Wade Hampton would take command. According to McClure, stories implying that Chambersburg suffered severe damage during the occupation are incorrect. He said that only the property of the United States was a legitimate target, but no wanton destruction was permitted. In addition, Hampton offered to have his men give receipts for any property that was seized, so that claims could be made against the Federal government.

McClure later wrote that several Confederates who tried to seize private property were arrested and remanded to Stuart's provost marshal. Several boxes of clothing, a quantity of ammunition, and about two hundred pairs of shoes were taken from a warehouse. An estimated eight hundred horses were impressed; U.S. government and railroad property valued at about $250,000 was destroyed. Describing his experiences during this "invasion" of Pennsylvania, McClure said of Rebels, "Our people generally feel that, bad as they are, they are not so bad as they might be."

YORK, PENNSYLVANIA—JUNE 27, 1863

Thinking the Keystone State was almost certain to be invaded, Pennsylvanians established a Committee of Safety. The leaders of this body, however, had virtually no military resources. When the Confederates reached the town of York and demanded its surrender, the mayor and other elected officials deferred to the Committee of Safety and formally gave up the place to the men under Confederate Gen. Jubal Early.

ALEXANDRIA, VIRGINIA—MAY 24, 1861

The first Federal invasion of Southern territory was at Alexandria, Virginia, on May 24, 1861. The arrival of the enemy had been expected for several weeks, for warnings of the impending move had come from Roger A. Pryor at Petersburg on May 2. Any defense of the city would be difficult, for it lay across the Potomac River from Washington in what river pilots called "the convex side of the re-entering curve" of the river. Having pondered his alternatives, Gen. Robert E. Lee of the Provisional Army of Virginia reluctantly concluded that the chief result of "an abortive attempt at defense" would be "to hazard the destruction of the city."

At 5:30 A.M. Col. O. B. Willcox of the First Michigan reported to Gen. Joseph Mansfield, commander of the Department of Washington, "Alexandria is ours." The occupation had been almost bloodless, but one of the men killed was Col. Elmer Ellsworth, who had been shot "by a person in a house."

VIRGINIA ARCHIVES AND HISTORY

Ellsworth was something of a protégé of Abraham Lincoln. He had gained renown as a military drill organizer in Chicago and had toured the world with his U.S. Zouaves. Just before the war he had worked in Lincoln's law office in Springfield, and Ellsworth had accompanied the president-elect to Washington. In that

Prior to his service with the Confederate army, Roger Pryor often alerted Southern military leaders about the expected moves of Federal forces.

time he had endeared himself to the Lincoln family. When the war broke out, he organized a Zouave unit in New York City and led his men to Washington in answer to the president's call for troops.

The dashing Ellsworth crossed with his men to Alexandria. Noticing a Confederate flag at the top of a hotel, he led a small detachment and a newspaper writer to the roof of the building and hauled the banner down. Inside he encountered the owner of the establishment, James T. Jackson, who fired a shotgun into the Union officer's chest. Jackson was bayoneted by one of the men in Ellsworth's entourage.

Ellsworth was by far the most notable casualty of the assault upon the river town that had been defended by only a handful of cavalrymen. Earlier Alexandria had housed an estimated seven hundred infantry, but they had been evacuated by the Orange and Alexandria Railway and burned the bridges behind them as they fled. A small band of citizens—none of them officeholders—met with Federal officers before noon and turned the city over to them.

MEMPHIS, TENNESSEE—JUNE 6, 1862

After a series of reverses in Tennessee during May 1862, Confederate troops were withdrawn from Memphis. The defense of the city was relegated to a river flotilla led by Capt. James E. Montgomery of the Confederate navy and Gen. M. Jeff Thompson. Thompson's tiny band of fighting men was encamped near one of the most important river ports in the Confederacy; Montgomery was in charge of several gunboats. It was clear that the fight for the city would take place on the river rather than on land.

The naval guns commenced firing shortly after 5 A.M. on June 6 and continued until only the CSS *Van Dorn* was able to escape to the Yazoo River. Col. Charles Ellet, who had made his reputation as an engineer and shipbuilder, led the Federal fleet in the attack. He took a hit above his knee, and the wound proved fatal. No other Yankees died during the fight upon the water, but Rebel casualties were estimated at two hundred.

Once the Mississippi River had been cleared of enemy vessels, Lt. Charles Ellet—son of the mortally wounded Colonel Ellet—and two enlisted men marched ashore. They took down the Confederate flag flying above the heart of the city and then demanded the town's surrender from Mayor John Park. The mayor offered no resistance or delay, but Ellet's action was regarded by his fellow officers as unofficial. Hence Capt. Charles H. Davis, who had succeeded Andrew H. Foote in command of the Union river fleet, went into the city shortly after 10 A.M. This time the surrender by the mayor was treated as official, and the Federal occupation of Memphis began immediately.

FREDERICKSBURG, VIRGINIA—NOVEMBER 21, 1861

Union Gen. E. V. Sumner made plans to take Fredericksburg for the second time, since it had been recaptured by Southerners. He ordered two batteries into position, ready to fire upon the river port at daylight on November 21.

Mayor M. Slaughter, who was warned of the Federal plan at 4:40 P.M. on Wednesday, November 20, protested that he did

The once-peaceful river town of Fredericksburg, Virginia, was largely in ruins a little more than a year after it was first surrendered to Federal forces.

PICTORIAL FIELD BOOK OF THE CIVIL WAR

not have sufficient time to convene the city council and reply to Sumner's surrender demand by the 5 P.M. deadline. Slaughter promised that the city would be surrendered peaceably, and the citizenry was warned not to fire upon the Union troops. He was given sixteen hours to move "the women and children, the sick, wounded, and aged" from the town. That was not sufficient, he protested, so Sumner extended his deadline before taking physical possession of the place noted for the battle that would occur here in December 1862.

BILOXI, MISSISSIPPI—DECEMBER 31, 1861

Three Union gunboats with a large contingent of marines left Ship Island for Biloxi at 7 A.M. on the last day of the first year of the war. Their attack upon the town probably stemmed from the fact that a vessel out of Biloxi bound for Honduras had been captured in late November. She carried a cargo of 301 barrels of

Atlanta saw heavy fighting on all sides before the railroad center was surrendered to William Tecumseh Sherman's army.

GEORGIA ARCHIVES AND HISTORY

turpentine and 100 barrels of tar, both commodities in great demand among seamen.

The majority of marines and sailors remained aboard the *Water Witch* and the *New London*. Lt. Thomas McKean Buchanan of the USS *Henry Lewis* led a landing party of sixty men and encountered no resistance. They called upon the mayor to surrender forthwith, but he insisted upon having an hour to consult "some prominent citizens." When the conclave was over, he gave Buchanan "free navigation of surrounding waters" and formally surrendered the town.

NEW ORLEANS, LOUISIANA—APRIL 26, 1862

About 1:30 P.M. on April 25, Mayor John T. Monroe was waited upon by Capt. Theodorus Bailey of the U.S. Navy who delivered a message from Flag Officer David G. Farragut that demanded the unconditional surrender of the city and the raising of the U.S. flag over the customshouse, post office, and mint. Monroe did not act, so he received a written note from Farragut on the following day.

The mayor responded that he did not know how to surrender an undefended place, since the Confederate garrison had already left. "To surrender such a place were an idle and unmeaning ceremony," he said. Farragut did not agree; he insisted upon a formal capitulation. The official surrender occurred in the mayor's office before nightfall.

A few of many other cities and towns surrendered by civilians were: Norfolk, May 10, 1862; Natchez, Mississippi, September 3, 1862; Fredericksburg, May 21, 1864; Atlanta, September 2, 1864; Charleston, February 18, 1865; Georgetown, South Carolina, February 25, 1865; Richmond, April 3, 1865; Cahawba, Alabama, April 5, 1865; Mobile, April 12, 1865; and Raleigh, North Carolina, April 13, 1865.

Many local officials and town leaders took part in surrender ceremonies because there were no military brass present, and they were the sole representatives of authority. Collectively, these civilians turned over to the enemy at least four hundred thousand persons—more than the total number surrendered by all the Confederate military commanders.

MOST OUTSPOKEN UNIONIST

ATTORNEY JAMES LOUIS PETIGRU was close to the top of the list of "most plain-spoken men in Charleston, South Carolina" and is today remembered as the most stout-hearted Unionist who stayed in a Confederate city. His rise to the top in this respect began at least as early as 1832, when he openly and vigorously denounced John C. Calhoun's nullification doctrine by which states could at will choose not to enforce federal laws.

When secession dominated all political discourse in the Palmetto State in 1860, many members of Charleston's elite boasted about their eagerness for the state to sever ties with Washington and become an independent nation. Petigru, who never tried to keep quiet about controversial issues, scoffed, "South Carolina is too small to be a republic and too large to be an insane asylum."

Numerous advertisements and articles in the city's two newspapers pointed out that it would soon be very difficult for Unionists to live there. A paid advertisement in the *Mercury* promised, "If Lincoln is Elected South Carolina Will Lead Boldly for a Southern Confederacy." Petigru too conceded that civil war would be inevitable if a Republican should become the nation's chief executive.

Soon after Lincoln's election, the new president sent his long-time friend Ward Hill Lamon to assess the situation in the port city. Lamon approached Petigru for guidance, which in itself led to renewed publicity in Charleston and throughout the state.

A notice sent from Washington on April 6, 1861, did not go to the mayor or to the commander of military forces in the city. Instead it was sent to Petigru, who was expected to share the message with the three other prominent Unionists in Charleston.

When the rest were driven out, Petigru not only remained but continued to publicly condemn secession and the Confederacy.

Strangely, the man who swam against the current of public opinion kept the respect, if not the liking, of his fellow citizens. In 1862 the renowned diarist Mary Boykin Chesnut wrote: "He is as much respected as ever. Maybe his astounding pluck has raised him in the estimation of the people he flouts and contradicts in their tenderest points."

LARGEST NORTHERN CITY THREATENED

COMPETING WITH Boston for the rank of second largest colonial city, Philadelphia still ranked among the largest cities in the nation in 1860. Rumors that R. E. Lee's Army of Northern Virginia might be headed into Pennsylvania in 1862 struck the state like a bolt of lightning. In Philadelphia, civil leaders hurriedly arranged to purchase cannon, and every unit of the state guard was alerted.

These fears, however, were groundless. The Confederates never came close to the city and never targeted it. Yet because of these groundless fears, Philadelphia was by far the largest Northern city that many believed would be threatened by invaders from the South.

OLDEST PRISON GUARD

A PROMINENT citizen of Muscatine, Iowa, conceived the idea of organizing a unique regiment requiring its members to be forty-five years old or older. Mustered in on December 15, 1862, the volunteers were known as the Graybeard Regiment. Surgeon John F. Marsh, who checked the physical condition of some of the graybeards, called them "decrepit old men" who were the most unpromising subjects for soldiers he'd ever seen.

Undaunted, the colonel of the regiment cheerfully accepted an invitation to put his men to work as guards at Gratiot Street Prison in Saint Louis. They performed this task so admirably that they were shifted from one prison to another: Alton, Illinois; Rock Island, Illinois; Camp Chase, Ohio; Camp Morton, Indiana; and several other prisoner of war camps.

Three members of the regiment had celebrated their eightieth birthdays before enlisting. Since all were within a few weeks of one another in age, their comrades proudly said that their regiment included "the nation's oldest prison guard"—who could have been any one of the trio.

SOUTHERNMOST MILITARY ENCOUNTER

NEITHER FLORIDA nor Texas come close to being the southernmost site for a Civil War encounter. Bahia, Brazil, holds that undisputed title. Naturally the matter had to do with commerce raiding.

Built under contract at Liverpool, England, by William C. Miller and Sons, the twin-blade screw steamer *Oreto* was taken out of port by a British crew late in March 1862. At Nassau, John N. Maffitt took command and revealed that the vessel had been designed to be a Confederate raider. With batteries installed on her gun decks, the vessel put to sea in mid-August—this time as the CSS *Florida*.

Few Southern raiders had so large a dose of luck, both good and bad, as did the *Florida*. Most of her officers and crew came down with yellow fever, and a skeleton crew barely managed to get her into Mobile to be refitted. On February 12, 1863, she captured her first prize, the *Jacob Bell*, which was carrying cargo worth well over one million dollars—making the seizure the most valuable prize captured by any of the Rebel raiders.

Sailing to Brest, France, for repairs, the *Florida* lost her commander. His successor lasted less than a month, after which Lt. Charles M. Morris took over the ship. After making thirty-seven captures, the *Florida* had become unseaworthy. Navigation was so chaotic that officers of a Federal warship who watched her progress from a distance mistakenly thought the crew had mutinied.

On October 4, 1864, the now-famous raider put into Bahia, Brazil. Knowing that they were in international waters, Morris brazenly instructed members of his crew to slip into a berth adjacent to the USS *Wachusett*. Maritime laws prohibited the 1,032-ton Federal warship from disturbing the *Florida* while she lay in Brazilian waters.

Shortly after midnight during the Confederate vessel's third day in port, a rowdy bunch of U.S. sailors decided to take matters into their own hands, despite international law. With many of their comrades on shore leave, this band of self-styled patriots rammed the Southern raider and towed her into international waters.

Brazilian authorities registered strong protests and demanded that the ship captured at Bahia, along with all members of her crew, should be returned to that port. Communication was slow, but a dispatch from Washington finally reached Brazil with a promise that the ship would be dispatched from her anchorage in Chesapeake Bay for the Southern Hemisphere.

On November 19, 1864, the *Florida* received what the master of the U.S. Army transport *Alliance* reported as "a heavy accidental blow that did considerable damage." The Confederate raider began taking on water immediately and was towed to Newport News, but no repairs were done. Consequently she sank on November 28. Brazil eventually received a lamely phrased apology, but the up-and-down career of the raider that was central to the southernmost military encounter of the war had already come to an end by then.

MOST BRAZEN EFFRONTERY

CONFEDERATE ARCHIVES seized at war's end took months to sort and classify. Many were eventually published in the *Official Records*. A lengthy document, dated October 29, 1861, was addressed to Judah P. Benjamin, then the Confederate secretary of war, and included detailed information sent to Richmond by John F. Callan, a clerk of the U.S. Senate Military Committee.

Callan had come into the position during Jefferson Davis's tenure as secretary of war. Callan's ability as a clerk was said to be "without rival." He had had no communication with Davis since the senator had left Washington following Mississippi's withdrawal from the union.

On February 21, 1861, Davis was swamped with the duties of putting together a government. Among his first messages was the initial communication in a series of telegrams to Callan, seeking to convince his former clerk to come to Montgomery as the chief clerk of the Confederate War Department.

Callan was keenly interested but had some reservations. As a result, telegrams kept coming to him for two months, during which the Confederate capital was moved to Richmond and Davis was inaugurated as president of the Confederate States of America. The clerk eventually opted to remain in the Federal capital. At any time during at least sixty days in which he was receiving frequent messages from Davis, a censored telegram would have revealed what the former secretary of war was trying to do. Davis's messages flowed without interruption, no one apparently heeding what was taking place. After he decided not to go to Richmond, Callan became an important spy for the South.

ULTIMATE IN COLOR RISK

AT CHARLESTON, Maj. Robert Anderson surrendered Fort Sumter on Sunday, April 14. On the same day in faraway Minnesota, the services of a regiment of ninety-day volunteers that had been organized at Fort Snelling were tendered to Washington. Virtually all authorities recognize the First Minnesota as leading the entire four-year procession of troops raised at the state level and then turned over to the federal government.

Approximately nine hundred officers and men of this regiment took part in the first Federal invasion of Confederate terri-

THE WAY IT WAS

Fort Snelling, Minnesota, was the point of departure for the first volunteers headed to Washington after the surrender of Fort Sumter.

tory at Alexandria, Virginia. Col. Willis A. Gorman and his command went to the important Potomac River port by boat accompanied by a seventeen-member cornet band, all of whom wore uniforms "of plain gray cashmere, trimmed with black, and a black felt hat."

They were not alone in the wearing of the gray. Members of the First Wisconsin reported to Washington with uniforms of cadet gray, and the First Iowa drilled in gray uniforms.

The use of what was already known as "the Rebel color" was not limited to the initial units to arrive in Washington in answer to the president's call for men. When the Twenty-first New York reached the Federal capital in mid-June 1861, its officers and men wore uniforms "of gray cloth." A week or so later, when the Fifth Maine passed through New York on the way to the front, a newspaper account of the 1,046-man regiment reported, "Their uniform is gray throughout, with drab felt hats, regulation pattern."

According to Maj. George L. Paddock, the Twelfth Illinois trained at Caseyville after having been organized throughout the surrounding county. Paddock wrote that the men eagerly looked

Mary Ann "Mother" Bickerdyke was one of the most tireless organizers of the war. She formed sewing circles to generate uniforms and then founded a group of volunteer nurses.

WOMEN OF THE WAR

forward to receiving the uniforms provided by the state. When they arrived, however, many were glum because all "were of a color not at all welcome—gray."

The famous Union nurse organizer Mary Ann "Mother" Bickerdyke said that one of the first organized war efforts by women led to the establishment of sewing circles around Cairo, Illinois. These groups spent much of their time making uniforms for Federal fighting men. "If good cloth was not available in army blue," said Bickerdyke, "they chose brown, gray, Scotch plaid, or any other serviceable color."

Small wonder that the uniform colors contributed to the major confusion at the battle of First Manassas. Several instances in which men fired into the ranks of their comrades stemmed from this confusion over uniforms. Yet the first major battle of the war did not bring about the standardization of uniform colors on either side. During the month after the battle of First Bull Run, Col. Charles Devens led the Fifteenth Massachusetts to Washington, dressed, according to the *New York Herald* in "the regular army uniform—gray pantaloons, blue coats, and hat." A few days later, the Fourteenth Massachusetts stepped off the train in Washington wearing "light brown pants, deep blue jacket."

Confederate fighting men faced textile color problems of equal magnitude. At Shiloh, the Second Texas went into battle wearing undyed white uniforms. Described as "greatly resembling shrouds," the color of these garments practically invited other units on both sides to take them for the enemy. Also at

Shiloh, a volunteer battalion that became known as the Orleans Guards was outfitted with what one officer described as "stylish blue uniforms." After having been mistaken for Yankees more than once, they reputedly turned their coats inside out and continued to fight "with the white linings showing."

Southern men in blue uniforms, however, were not limited to the units from New Orleans. The official regulations of the Richmond government called for uniform trousers to be "sky blue." A few officers are known to have worn these, but there is no record that they were ever issued in quantity to the troops. At least one unit that played a prominent part at Fort Sumter could have been mistaken for Yankees, however. The soldiers of the Flying Artillery volunteers wore blue uniforms even when they posed for photographs.

The yellow sashes that many Northern generals wore as a symbol of rank made some of them prime targets for Southern sharpshooters. Yellow lace was used to trim seams and edges of jackets worn by the First New Jersey Hussars. Their uniforms also displayed yellow stripes across the chest; small wonder that derisive comrades of other units mocked the men as "butterflies."

They were far less easily identified by color, though, than were Hiram Berdan's Sharpshooters, who wore "green frock coats, gray pantaloons, and green caps." After having taken part in combat a few times, the sharpshooters discarded their gray pants in favor of green pants.

Elaborate dress was not the norm for many men who had

Disorganized fighting at the July 1861 battle of First Manassas failed immediately to dissuade some Federal units from using gray uniforms.

WINSLOW HOMER IN HARPER'S WEEKLY

been trained in the regular army before the war. Ulysses S. Grant frequently appeared with only a semblance of a uniform and no insignia of rank. His close friend William T. Sherman was sometimes taken for a civilian because he dressed so casually. On the other hand, some men took great pride in their appearance. Confederate Gen. Jeb Stuart wore a hat with a huge plume that made it easy for enemy marksmen to identify him at a distance. His comrade A. P. Hill allegedly went into battle wearing a shirt of flaming red that identified him from far away.

By far the most colorful units on the battlefield were those that modeled their garb after the French Zouaves of North Africa. Some regiments in both the Confederate and the Union armies opted for this stylish and multicolored fashion. These were never standardized on either side, and the wearers were susceptible to fire from both friends and foes. Over time Southern Zouave units disappeared. The majority of these came from the Creole ranks of Louisiana, and shortages brought about by

The chaos of the April 1862 battle of Shiloh was compounded by the variety of uniforms and colors used by the units that fought there.

Gov. Zebulon Vance of North Carolina ran into a problem when the supply of gray dye for uniforms was exhausted.

the war included the colorful cloth from which Zouave uniforms could be made.

Gov. Zebulon Vance of North Carolina was responsible for the last set of large-scale uniform problems. Textile factories in the state exhausted their supplies of gray dye in the fall of 1864. Vance ordered the entire batch of Confederate uniforms to be dyed blue—to facilitate getting the badly needed clothing to the troops before winter set in.

THE MOST BELLICOSE GOVERNOR

WITHOUT TRYING, Georgia Gov. Joseph E. Brown set a lasting record as the governor whose attitude toward his central government was the most bellicose. From the day the war started until it ended, the Yale Law School graduate never tired of proclaiming that he had as little use for the Confederate capital and its officials as he had for their Union counterparts.

His attitude stemmed from a rock-hard conviction that states' rights superseded those of the central government. He fought the taxes imposed by the Confederate States of America and attempted to thwart the conscription acts adopted by the Southern Congress.

More violently than any other prominent politician in the South, Brown lashed out at all moves to suspend habeas corpus. He is credited with the fact that violations of long-established civil rights by Jefferson Davis were much less numerous and extensive than were those of Abraham Lincoln. In some respects, Brown's supreme act of defiance was to withhold large numbers of men from the armies of the Confederacy. He armed a special force under his control with pikes rather than muskets or rifles and adamantly refused to let them fight anywhere except in Georgia.

He was captured at the end of the war and briefly imprisoned in the Federal capital. He returned home after his release as the first southerner of his political stature to turn Republican. He later established another record that cannot be broken. On behalf of the state-owned Western and Atlantic Railroad, he wrote and published one of the first travel-oriented Civil War books.

His publication was entitled *War Scenes on the W&A: Mountain Campaigns in Georgia* and was designed to induce tourists from the North to visit the mountains of the state by rail. The groundbreaking volume was illustrated by a trio of talented Yankee artists: William A. Waud, Thure de Thulstrup, and Joseph Fleming. As a final gesture of contempt toward the now-defunct Confederacy, the privately produced first edition was printed and bound by the Matthews-Northrup Company of Buffalo, New York.

NORTHERNER WITH THE GREATEST IMPACT

WELL BEFORE most of the generation that fought the Civil War first saw the light of day, a genuine Yankee delivered a double whammy to the Cotton Belt. Headed toward a job in Charleston, twenty-seven-year-old Eli Whitney paused at what was then considered a nice spread in Georgia. It had been given to Revolutionary Gen. Nathanael Greene as a token of gratitude and in 1792 was being run by Greene's lovely young widow. Whitney never reached Charleston. Reputedly enamored with Caty Greene, after having stayed with her for three months, he gave up his plan to report for work as a tutor.

Whitney's education in New Haven, Connecticut, had done little if anything to enhance his mechanical skill. In this field, he had a natural aptitude that bordered on genius. He began to repair broken implements and tools he found on the Widow Greene's property. Even if such a chore had been given up by others as too complicated, this Yankee fixed the damaged household object or plantation gear quickly.

When she noted Whitney's mechanical proficiency, Caty Greene asked if he could perfect a machine to pull lint from the seeds of her upland or "green" cotton. Unlike long-staple Sea Island cotton produced in limited quantity, this upland variety yielded short fibers that had to be picked from seeds by hand. So much labor was involved in this tedious process that upland cotton was diminishing rapidly as a cash crop, which also threatened to undermine southern slavery as unprofitable.

Whitney did not turn out the special gift for his hostess overnight; it took him a week of intensive effort to solve the problem to his satisfaction. Supposedly the idea came to him while he walked with the Widow Greene one afternoon and the two noticed a cat trying to catch a chicken by reaching through the slats of a cage to grab the bird. The feline missed the poultry by less than an inch, but it did grab a paw full of feathers.

The young man raced to his workshop. Three days later he emerged with a model of a machine that would revolutionize the cotton industry and breathe new life into the dying institution of slavery.

Whitney's almost absurdly simple device consisted of two rollers set in a small wooden box. One roller had wire spikes

Eli Whitney stopped at a Georgia plantation en route to a job as a tutor, and the economic history of the South was changed.

GEORGIA ARCHIVES AND HISTORY

that were similar to the paws of the cat. The surface of the other roller was covered with bristles. When rotated as cotton was being fed into it, the first roller pulled the lint from the seeds. Simultaneously, the second roller brushed the lint from the first roller and dropped it into a container. This simple cotton-cleaning machine, whose name was soon clipped to gin, was offered to neighboring cotton farmers for their use at a toll of half the lint it collected.

The simplicity of the device was such that any good mechanic or blacksmith could duplicate it easily. As a result, a host of imitations of the original gin were in use before Whitney was issued a patent. South Carolina lawmakers took an unprecedented step and voted to reward the inventor fifty thousand dollars, but the inventor spent all of that and more in a futile attempt to defend his patent against infringement.

Slaves planted upland cotton, harvested it, then separated lint from seeds with cotton gins.

The radical innovation of interchangeable parts is believed to have been developed in Whitney's machine shop in Connecticut.

Meanwhile, slave labor took an abrupt upward turn because cotton could now be cleaned in a matter of minutes instead of weeks. Slavery might have been abandoned in the Cotton Belt had it not been for the lovesick genius of a fellow from the North.

Whitney's second contribution to have a radical impact on the South came when he was awarded a government contract to produce firearms. He devised an ultra-radical concept. In his factory he began producing interchangeable parts, all of which functioned flawlessly in any weapon he produced, instead of following the centuries-old practice of hand-producing weapons one by one. The rapid spread of interchangeable parts helped to convert the once-agrarian North into an industrial region of immense size and diversity. Meanwhile, cotton farmers used slaves and Whitney's gin so profitably that they did not show a lot of interest in putting up manufacturing plants of any kind.

Slavery, flourishing as never before as a direct result of the invention made at Mulberry Plantation, was the one insoluble

Parts of guns manufactured and sold by the inventor of the cotton gin were interchangeable from one weapon to another.

issue over which the North and the South quarreled. When the sectional split came and war raged, its manufacturing plants made the North virtually independent—while the South remained dependent upon a constant flow of goods imported from England and Europe. Combined, these two factors had an impact that was more profound and sweeping than any battle won by a Northern general.

CHAPTER NINE

FRESH AND SALT WATER

FOOTE NAMED HIS CASUALTIES

THE HUNDREDS of reports in the archives of the Union army usually include a note regarding the number of casualties suffered in an engagement or battle. Frequently, these reports list the names of the officers who were killed or wounded in the action. Rarely, however, do they include the names of the enlisted men who were casualties. These men are merely numbers. Any effort to enumerate them is limited to the categories of killed, wounded, and missing.

The Federal navy, however, listed all of its casualties by name. Andrew H. Foote, commander of U.S. naval forces on the western waters, enclosed a complete casualty list with his February 15, 1862, report to Gideon Welles in Washington. Dispatched from the flagship *Saint Louis,* it summarized the

Gideon Welles, the U.S. secretary of the navy, received a complete casualty list from Andrew H. Foote regarding the action of February 14, 1862.

naval attack of the previous day made by his vessel and the *Carondelet, Louisville, Pittsburgh, Tyler,* and *Conestoga.*

Foote meticulously noted the names and fates of the fifty-six men who were killed or wounded at the battle of Fort Donelson on the Cumberland River. His list of casualties aboard his own vessel includes: "Killed: Charles W. Baker, ship cook; F. A. Riley, pilot. Wounded: Flag-officer A. H. Foote; R. G. Baldwin, pilot; Charles Smith, boatswain's mate; Antonio Calderio, Thomas Kirkham, seamen; R. H. Medill, carpenter; U. S. Coon, John Thompson, seamen."

The USS Carondelet *was heavily involved in the action at Fort Donelson.*

EVERY STEAMER HAD AN ACHILLES HEEL

ABRAHAM LINCOLN issued his first proclamation concerning a blockade of the ports of the seceded states on April 13, 1861. He knew that he was bluffing, for the U.S. Navy had only three vessels in port that day. Even had they been on hand and ready for duty, most warships then in North American waters would have been dependent upon the wind. One of the few steam-powered ships belonging to the U.S. government at that time was the revenue cutter *Harriet Lane,* named for the niece of President James Buchanan.

The transition from sail to steam was extremely rapid. At first, shipbuilders were reluctant to trust in steam alone. Therefore numerous ships that distinguished themselves early in the war were equipped with both sails and an auxiliary steam system.

Once sails were abandoned, the most vulnerable compo-nent—or Achilles heel—of a vessel was its steam plant. A typical

Southerners had a warship under construction in New Orleans within weeks after the battle of First Bull Run.

warship was equipped with several boilers. In the South, an as yet unnamed steamer was under construction at New Orleans in September 1861 that was expected to be fitted with "eleven boilers, 32 feet long, 42 inches in diameter, 2 return flues, with mat drum 24 inches in diameter, steam driver 30 inches in diameter, about 41 feet long."

The naval architects of this warship, which became the CSS *Mississippi,* informed Richmond in October that they were unable to get enough steam to operate the ship from "one set of boilers ranged side by side." Without formal authorization, they installed two sets of eight thirty-inch boilers that were expected to generate about fifteen hundred horsepower. This change made it necessary to lengthen the middle section of the vessel by twenty feet.

Early the following year, New Orleans shipbuilders E. M. Ivens and John Clarke were given precise instructions concerning the boilers for two "steam gunboats." They were told that each small vessel must have four boilers with these specifications: "42 inches diameter, 26 feet long, with two return flues, 15.5 inches diameter, with steam and mud drums, two safety valves, with all necessary check valves, steam exhaust, blow-off, feed, and other necessary pipes, three gauge cocks to each boiler, and one steam gauge for each boat. Steam pipes to be of copper or wrought iron, and covered with felt or some other non-conducting material."

Leaders in Richmond, who knew that enormous quantities of specially made boilerplate would be needed, made ambitious plans to build rolling mills capable of daily turning out four to six tons of this plate. When they set out to create fifty "light-draft steam propellers [steam-powered ships]" in March 1862, they estimated that "3,000 tons of first-class boiler-plate iron" would be needed.

The industrial capacity of the Confederacy was far too low to meet requirements of this sort, so a great deal of special metal was imported. In October 1863 the steam-powered blockade-runner *Bonita* reached Nassau from Liverpool with three sailing vessels following her. Collectively, these small oceangoing ships carried one thousand tons of precious boiler iron.

Nassau was a haven for blockade-runners and an occasional Confederate warship.

Boilers became worn with use, damaged by sand and mud, and crippled by the intricate systems that conveyed water and steam. Small wonder, therefore, that the naval volumes of the *Official Records* include nearly seven hundred references to boilers. During several engagements on rivers and open seas, a single shot from an enemy disabled a warship by putting its steam plant out of commission. Too much coal, not enough water, clogged pipes, and defective valves could and did cause numerous explosions. When the boilers of the CSS *Chattahoochee* exploded in May 1863, eighteen members of her crew died instantly. Their names and occupations were duly listed in the casualty report, but "others of the crew" who were injured were too numerous to identify.

REBEL DERRING-DO ON THE HIGH SEAS

SOON AFTER South Carolina seceded, Confederate authorities in Charleston seized a merchant steamer with the idea of converting

Capt. John Wilkes of the USS San Jacinto *seized two passengers from a British royal mail steamer and risked war with England.*

CENTURY WAR BOOK

her into a commerce raider. A side-wheel brig of 1,221 tons, the wooden vessel was fitted with two or more 26-pounder rifles and became the Confederate vessel *Nashville*.

Possibly without having received formal authorization from Richmond, Lt. James W. Pegram of the fledgling Confederate navy offered to take commissioners James Mason and John Slidell to England aboard the *Nashville*. They declined his offer in order to take passage on a British vessel, the mail steamer *Trent,* but on November 8 this vessel was stopped on the high sea and Mason and Slidell were taken prisoner aboard the USS *San Jacinto* by Capt. John Wilkes. Shackled, the two diplomats were transported to Boston and imprisoned.

Meanwhile, Pegram managed to slip through the Federal blockade. After taking on coal in Bermuda, he headed east across the Atlantic but avoided well-traveled sea lanes.

Eleven days after Mason and Slidell had been seized, the lookout of the *Nashville* spotted a merchantman headed toward their vessel. Although the master of the improvised raider did not know that the high-ranking Confederate officials had been seized in international waters, he was intent on showing the world that the Confederate navy was no laughing matter.

When the vessels came within hailing distance, Pegram demanded and quickly received the surrender of the *Harvey Birch,* which he claimed as a prize. Owned in New York and bound for her home port in ballast from Le Havre, the fifteen-hundred-ton merchantman was valued at $125,000. All thirty-one officers and crew of the Federal vessel were transferred to the *Nashville*.

Confederate commissioners James M. Mason (left) and John Slidell (right) were removed from the British vessel Trent *in international waters.*

Not having sufficient manpower to handle both vessels, Pegram set his prize afire and watched as she burned to the water line. He then continued on his course and on November 21 anchored off Southampton, England. Officers and crew of the *Harvey Birch* were released and preliminary arrangements were made for the *Nashville* to go into dry dock for repairs.

This brash exploit on the part of a man who carried a commission on which the ink was barely dry created a tremendous uproar on both sides of the Atlantic. Many newspapers devoted much space to the accounts of how a Confederate naval vessel had effected a capture so far from home. Numerous artists depicted the destruction of the *Harvey Birch,* and some claimed that the Rebel exploit had taken place almost within sight of London. A laudatory *Morning Post* editorial was believed to have been written by the prime minister, Lord Palmerston, while an account in the *London Times* bore the hallmarks of the British Foreign Office.

Telegrams from New York demanded that Lincoln protect Northern commercial interests on the sea by dispatching "armed steamers of sufficient power [and] forthwith ordered to cruise in the British and Irish channels and off the Straits of Gibraltar to protect the commerce of the United States." In Washington, Secretary of the Navy Gideon Welles denounced the "wanton destruction of the property of our merchants upon the high seas." He ordered Cmdr. T. A. M. Craven of the USS *Tuscarora* to "proceed without delay to the English coast" and capture the *Nashville*.

Early in December 1861, Welles indicated that he intended "to keep an armed vessel on the other side of the Atlantic to protect American commerce and guard American interests." Having decided that the "necessities of the case" demanded unconventional action, Welles informed Craven that he had been given "great discretionary power."

When the *Tuscarora* dropped anchor at Southampton, there was great indignation in England. Public feeling was aroused by an "attempt by one belligerent vessel to blockade another in a neutral port," Pegram reported to Richmond. This led the British authorities to take drastic action. The masters of both

Seized aboard a British vessel, two Confederate commissioners were taken aboard the U.S. warship San Jacinto *under arrest.*

FRANK LESLIE'S ILLUSTRATED WEEKLY

The Confederate commerce raider Nashville *(left) captured and burned the merchantman* Harvey Birch.

vessels were notified that they would have to leave, with the *Nashville* being given a twenty-four-hour head start. Uncertain that Craven would respect this stipulation, British naval officials sent the frigate *Shannon* to lie alongside the Union vessel "with steam up and guns shotted."

Although not nearly so well known today as some other Confederate warships, the *Nashville* had demonstrated that Southerners were willing to take great risks for their cause. She left Southampton on February 3, successfully eluded the *Tuscarora*, and after a seventeen-day voyage reached Saint George, Bermuda. Four days later, now heavily laden with coal, the clumsy little warship headed for Beaufort, North Carolina.

En route to safety in a Confederate port, Pegram saw off the port bow of his vessel a merchantman of unknown identity. He had the American flag hoisted and watched as similar action was taken aboard the *Robert Gilfillan*. Once he knew he again had a Federal ship within gunshot, the Confederate demanded its surrender and again received it almost instantly. When the seven members of the captured ship's company had been taken aboard along with their personal effects, the *Robert Gilfillan* was torched just as the *Harvey Birch* had been.

That should have ended the saga of a virtually forgotten Confederate warship, but it did not. From London, Confederate commissioner James D. Bulloch ruefully notified Stephen Mallory, the Confederate secretary of the navy, "The *Harvey Birch* turns out to have been owned by a warm sympathizer with our cause."

Having been battered by strong winds and high seas, the *Nashville* did not seem worth refitting for additional service in the Confederate navy. Sold to private parties, she became the blockade-runner *Thomas L. Wragg* and was later converted into the privateer *Rattlesnake*. Early in 1863 a Federal ironclad trapped her in Florida's Ogeechee River and mercilessly destroyed her.

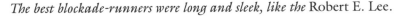

The best blockade-runners were long and sleek, like the Robert E. Lee.

USS MONITOR WAS TOWED TO HISTORIC FIGHT

WHEN ABRAHAM LINCOLN announced the blockade of Southern ports, Northern shipbuilders were fast at work. This rapid buildup in firepower of Union naval vessels was a major but not always fully appreciated factor in the ultimate Federal victory.

In Richmond, Confederate Secretary of the Navy Stephen Mallory had no warships. This desperate situation contributed largely to his willingness to experiment with many ideas that had never been tried before. In a fashion never equaled by his counterpart in Washington, Gideon Welles, the Southern naval leader accepted and encouraged experiments and innovations.

When Virginia state forces seized the Norfolk Navy Yard on the heels of the state's secession, the Federal commander of the largest facility of its sort in North America tried to destroy everything the Confederacy might be able to use. Some facilities were totally destroyed, but others escaped with minor damage.

The USS *Merrimack* was fired with apparent thoroughness, but it burned only to the water line. Some naval policy makers would have dismissed the hulk as too badly damaged to be worth salvaging. Not so Mallory. He quickly authorized the rebuilding of the Federal vessel and found approximately six thousand dollars with which to fund the job. He also ordered that the craft should be given something brand-new. A few insignificant experiments had been made in England and Europe, but no warship that plied North American waters had ever before been covered with iron. When completed, the salvaged warship would be the first of its kind on the continent.

Word that the ironclad vessel would be renamed for the state in which it was captured reached Washington before work on the CSS *Virginia* had reached the halfway point. Secretary of the Navy Gideon Welles recognized the gravity of the situation and authorized the naval review board to solicit designs for a Federal ironclad. Three contracts were awarded for three different designs. The most unusual and far-fetched was that of

Partly burned, the fifty-gun USS Merrimack *was converted into the ironclad* Virginia *by Confederate naval architects.*

eccentric inventor John Ericsson, which the builder agreed to have ready for use no later than February 1862.

His "cheese box on a raft" was armed with only two 11-inch Dahlgren smoothbores, but Ericsson insisted that its revolving turret would double or triple the firepower of his craft. The resulting duel between the *Virginia* and Ericsson's *Monitor* revolutionized naval warfare on March 9, 1862.

Remarkably few commentators on the epic fight between the pioneer ironclads or upon the prebattle saga of the *Monitor* call attention to a record scored by the Federal craft. It was the first North American vessel of its sort to stage an epic contest at a place where it had not been ordered to be. When the *Monitor* left New York on March 4, she was to join the North Atlantic Blockading Squadron based in North Carolina. Diverted to Hampton Roads because of the destructive work of the *Virginia* on March 8, the *Monitor* never reached North Carolina. Then, after having been used on the James River for a period, she sank off Cape Hatteras on December 29.

The *Monitor*'s inglorious end was not the only seldommentioned first scored by the craft. She was the world's first

FRANK LESLIE'S ILLUSTRATED WEEKLY

The Seth Low, *a tugboat much like the one illustrated above (left), was used to tow the USS* Monitor *into Virginia waters.*

vessel of her category that did not sail or steam against the enemy under her own power. A little tugboat, the *Seth Low,* pulled the great warship from New York Harbor all the way to Hampton Roads because high-level authorities doubted the ironclad's ability to make a long journey under her own steam.

SUDDEN DEATH NEAR MEMPHIS

MILITARY NEWS dominated newspapers across the country from their front pages to the bottoms of their last pages, from Bull Run to Appomattox. Consequently, the public was likely to know what was taking place at Malvern Hill or Hatcher's Run while remaining ignorant of matters that would ordinarily have been reported with banner headlines.

That's why a river disaster that still ranks first in the number of casualties among all U.S. accidents of its sort got hardly any attention at the time. A northbound steamboat on the Mississippi River went down on a balmy spring night when a boiler exploded. Though its passenger list was neither complete nor accurate, it's all but certain that more people died from this accident than in the *Titanic* disaster in 1912, the most famous shipwreck of modern times that made headlines for weeks. There was another difference in the casualties from the sinking of the North Atlantic liner and the riverboat *Sultana*. The earlier disaster cost the lives of more than fifteen hundred ordinary and all but nameless men; the *Titanic* claimed the lives of many of the wealthiest and best-known persons of the Western world.

On Friday, April 21, 1865, the anchor of the 719-ton *Sultana* was hoisted, and she started on her long voyage up the Mississippi River to its confluence with the Ohio at Cairo, Illinois. Though the vessel was small by comparison with many warships, she was old and clumsy and hence required a crew of about 200 men. Her cabins were scant in number and small in size, so they held no more than 75 or so first-class passengers.

In addition to these 275 or more persons, an estimated 1,900 passengers for whom the U.S. government was paying the passage were jammed and packed below decks. Eager to make as profitable a voyage as possible, the master of the river boat ignored restrictions and stopped gesturing for the Union veterans to go below only when his narrow stairway was full to the top. Rated to transport no more than 376 persons, substantially more than 150 tons of passengers and horses were aboard when the *Sultana* made an unusually slow and ponderous exit from her berth at Vicksburg, Mississippi. Numerous members of the crew noticed shudders that warned the vessel was loaded far beyond capacity.

Firemen poured on the coal. Boiler repairs at Vicksburg had taken nearly two days, so they were almost as eager to be on the move as were the jam-packed passengers. The firemen did not need to be told that if they didn't work extra hard to keep the steam pressure at its maximum, their vessel would swing around and start back to Vicksburg when caught by a heavy current in a sharp bend of the river.

Crowded as they were, the passengers in the least comfortable quarters were exultant with the thought of going home. A majority of them had spent time in more than one Confederate prison, and now they were en route to their homes and families! This realization overshadowed every other aspect of the voyage. Soldiers who for months had been cold and hungry and crowded almost beyond belief were not bothered by conditions below the deck of the *Sultana.*

At a point south of Memphis, an overtaxed and overworked component of the ship's propulsion system could not take the strain any longer. No one ever discovered whether the terrific blast was caused by superheated steam, by defects in hastily repaired boilers, or by the shoveling of more coal into furnaces than they could handle. Whatever the case, the *Sultana* was ripped apart in a predawn explosion.

As was the case much later with the legendary *Titanic,* only one ship deliberately came to the rescue. Having heard that there was trouble on the river, the master of the USS *Essex* raced for the scene of the disaster at top speed. Members of the crew of the *Essex* manned a yawl and two boats, found sixty men and one woman in the dark water, and pulled them aboard. A bit later the merchant steamer *Bostonia,* out of Cincinnati and headed downriver to New Orleans, happened upon some swimmers and effected as many rescues as possible.

Since no accurate records were made at the debarkation point, the number of men who went to the bottom of the river because they could not swim or were crushed by the timbers of the *Sultana* or were ripped apart by red-hot fragments of the propulsion system is not known. Eventually the U.S. Customs Service had staffers review the available records and announced an official death toll of 1,547 persons. Unofficial estimates by maritime experts and prisoner-of-war workers suggest that the *Sultana* disaster cost around 1,750 lives. U.S. Secretary of War Edwin M. Stanton, who had general oversight of transportation of veterans, piously attributed the disaster to Providence and insisted that no one under his authority played any role in the tragedy.

Six days before the ship went down, John Wilkes Booth had shot and fatally wounded the wartime president, so newspapers were filled with stories about the assassination, death, and last train journey of Abraham Lincoln. Editors could devote only meager space to reports about the deaths on the Mississippi. As a result, the story of the fatal last voyage of the *Sultana* became the first major disaster of modern times to receive so little coverage by the media.

A Ship and a Shot

NEARLY ALL histories of the Civil War note that either the *Pocahontas* or the *Harriet Lane* was the first ship to be fired upon at Charleston in April 1861. There is some disagreement among these authorities concerning who pulled the lanyard and launched the first shot toward Fort Sumter. Nevertheless, that first shot arced across Charleston Harbor at around 4:30 A.M. on April 12, and Lincoln's resulting call for seventy-five thousand ninety-day volunteers marked the beginning of the war. Yet both the name of the ship and the date of the shot are incorrect if cannon fire directed at an enemy is the focal point of discussion.

President James Buchanan of Pennsylvania did not want civil war under any circumstances, and he dreaded the possibility that he might make a move that would ignite a blaze that could not be extinguished. He turned down suggestions that he use Whiskey Rebellion legislation to authorize a call for volunteers to augment the small U.S. Army. He knew that Maj. Robert Anderson and the garrison at Fort Sumter would be starved into surrender unless they received rations and that the small force needed to be strengthened if the installation was to be held for the Union. Still he procrastinated about dealing with "the Fort Sumter issue" so long that his secretary of war, Joseph Holt, resigned in fury.

The political pressure eventually became so great that Buchanan felt he had no choice; he must try to send provisions. The resulting expedition failed, but it—rather than the later one sent by Lincoln—was the first to provoke the roar of South Carolina batteries.

On January 5 the USS *Star of the West* set out from New York with papers saying she was making a routine trip to New Orleans. Since the *Star* regularly made this voyage with cargo, many dockworkers regarded her departure as routine. Some observant fellows noticed, however, that a great many soldiers had been herded below decks shortly before the ship left the dock. That little item became an interesting story before the *Star* had sailed very far.

A staffer of the *New York Herald* investigated the story and found that the side-wheeler had been chartered by the U.S. government at $1,250 a day. His account of the vessel and its covert voyage reached Charleston as the first significant newspaper leak of the war years about thirty hours before the *Star* was within sight of her goal.

Partly influenced by the *Herald*'s account of the supposedly secret voyage, but earlier having kept a weather eye open for a nor'easter, an official at the Citadel Military Academy in Charleston was prepared for the *Star* when she hove into sight with her load of provisions and hidden soldiers. Sometime soon after midnight on Wednesday, January 8, the Yankee vessel anchored close to the entrance to Charleston Harbor.

The Citadel, Charleston's military college, sent cadets to a hastily erected battery of guns guarding the harbor. One of them fired the first shot of the war.

CHARLESTON PUBLIC LIBRARY

Edmund Ruffin, a fiery Secessionist from Virginia, is often credited with firing the first shot on Fort Sumter in April 1861.

Civilian John McGowan, master of the vessel, instructed his crew to cautiously begin working their way toward the harbor fort before first light. Having no idea that his name and destination had already appeared in a nationally circulating newspaper, McGowan hoped that the *Star* would attract no notice.

He found out how wrong he was when a cannonball hurtled from Morris Island across the bow of his vessel around 7:15 A.M. There's no question about who fired that first shot, for Citadel records were meticulous and complete. Cadet G. W. Haynesworth pulled the all-important lanyard that morning. He did so upon receiving the nod from Maj. P. F. Stevens, commander of a hastily improvised battery. Along with thirty-eight other cadets, Haynesworth had been sent to the island south of the harbor to watch for and halt the approach of the expected Yankee vessel.

For McGowan aboard the first Northern vessel to come under fire from Southern cannon, one shot was enough to make him fearful of risking his vessel and passengers. He had sense enough to know that he was an easy target for the gunners on Morris Island, so he correctly interpreted the splashing shell as a warning shot.

The commander of the troops aboard the vessel, Lt. Charles R. Wood, also realized that his men would go to the bottom before they would have a chance to get to the fort. He ordered the soldiers to stay below, but not before two or three additional shots had been fired from Fort Moultrie, on the opposite end of the harbor from Morris Island.

Although a dispatch had been sent from Washington to Anderson alerting him of the mission of the *Star* so he would be able to offer some assistance should trouble erupt, it did not arrive prior to the vessel's appearance. Maybe this was by accident or maybe it was cunning on the part of James Buchanan; the dispatch had gone out by ordinary mail. Unaware that he was under orders to help the ship if necessary, Anderson ordered that the fort's flag be lowered and raised several times quickly.

Even an ordinary seaman who knew nothing of military affairs ought to interpret the flag movement as a signal, Anderson reasoned. He was probably right, but the scheme failed, the first failed signal attempt of the war. Twisted halyards prevented the men from lowering the flag, so the *Star* turned around and distanced herself from the fort without realizing that the guns at Sumter were willing to respond to the warning shots from South Carolina's gunners. By 8 A.M. the first U.S. ship to come under hostile fire in the struggle was on her way back to New York. Lieutenant Wood's men were disappointed, but they were free to lounge on deck until they docked.

ONE WARSHIP AND FIVE LAKES

THE USS *Michigan* was launched at Erie, Pennsylvania, in 1844, a fourth-rate barkentine of 582 tons with only one gun. This decrepit wooden vessel was the only Union warship on the Great Lakes during the Civil War, the result of restrictive stipulations in an old treaty between the United States and Canada. Perched at a single spot in the largest connected body of freshwater in the world, the *Michigan* guarded Johnson's Island near Sandusky, Ohio, where three thousand Confederate officers were imprisoned in 1864.

Had half a dozen vessels been anchored near the prison, it is unlikely that a Southerner would have picked this spot for a raid. With a single aging vessel charged with guarding almost ninety-five thousand square miles, a daring Rebel adventurer pondered the possibilities.

When her officers went ashore, a small party could swarm aboard the little *Michigan* in a matter of minutes. Once her gun was turned upon the three-hundred-acre prison, John Y. Beall was sure its fences could be blasted away. Then the prisoners could escape aboard the captured vessel. Quickly these officers could be landed in Canada and make their way back to their old commands. No doubt this feasible exploit could profoundly affect the course of the war.

Beall plotted the possibilities as he recuperated from a wound suffered when he served as a private in the Second Virginia. It was fairly easy for him to get a post as master's mate in the Confederate navy, but Secretary of the Navy Stephen Mallory and his advisers in Richmond were leery of the Johnson's Island scheme. They assigned the Virginia native to duty as a raider in Chesapeake Bay, where he quickly became so successful that his name became well known to his Federal opponents.

Subsequently, when Beall was captured during a raid, he and his crew were tried and convicted of piracy—a crime carrying an automatic death sentence. Beall, however, had come to be highly valued by his superiors. Reminiscent of the tactics enlisted to rescue the first captured Southern privateers, Beall's commanders notified the Federal authorities that seventeen prisoners—Lt. Cmdr. Edward P. Williams, Ens. Benjamin H. Porter, and fifteen Yankee seamen—would serve as hostages for the safe return of the Chesapeake Bay "pirates."

According to the *Richmond Examiner,* it took only a day or two for the two sides to arrange the exchange of prisoners. Once free, Beall badgered his superiors for permission to launch his scheme regarding the USS *Michigan* and the Confederate prisoners on Johnson Island. With their permission, he went to Canada and began to enlist a crew. Unfortunately he had to compromise on the idea of finding a force of determined men and accepted almost any man willing to take the risk for a few gold coins.

The raiders boarded the lake steamer *Philo Parsons* at various points in small groups. When they were assembled, they had no difficulty in taking over the ship. Johnson's Island was barely

The editors of The Confederate Veteran *published this rare image of John Y. Beall.*

visible beyond the *Michigan* when Beall issued last-minute instructions to the boarding party. To the consternation of his hastily recruited men, a pre-arranged signal from shore did not appear. Unnerved now, most of the raiders refused to follow through with the plan. The plot to seize the Federal vessel ended before it began.

Reluctantly giving up on one of the most ingenious and elaborate schemes of the war, Beall went to New York State and devised another plan to rescue Confederate prisoners who were being transported by railroad. Before it could be executed, he was captured near the Canadian border on December 16, 1864, probably as a result of having recruited a Federal spy into his operation. After a perfunctory trial, the mastermind of the great Johnson's Island raid was condemned as a spy and hanged on February 24, 1865.

REBEL IRONCLAD THROWS WASHINGTON INTO PANIC

THE CONVERSION of the scuttled *Merrimack* into the CSS *Virginia* launched the era of ironclad warships leading to the epic battle with the USS *Monitor*. Until U.S. Secretary of the Navy Gideon Welles told the story long afterward, few Confederate military or naval leaders knew the extent to which their ironclad had thrown the Federal capital into chaos. Welles's detailed account offers a rare inside look at the Lincoln administration and constitutes the first chapter of the 1879 volume entitled *Annals of the War*.

HARPER'S WEEKLY

News of the first mission of the Confederate ironclad Virginia *in Hampton Roads
threw Washington's power brokers into a panic.*

Early on Sunday morning, March 9, 1862, a telegram from
Gen. John E. Wool relayed word that on the previous day the CSS
Virginia had destroyed a ship of the line in the Federal blockading
fleet at Hampton Roads and left another in flames, sending shivers
throughout the Federal navy. Both Union frigates *Cumberland*
and *Congress* were not simply defeated, they were sent to the
bottom. Wool's telegram conveyed his fear that the seemingly
invulnerable Rebel craft might target his command at Fort
Monroe and end the Federal presence on the Virginia Peninsula.

When news of the attack reached Secretary of War Edwin M.
Stanton, he raced to the White House. Other cabinet members
were urged to attend a special meeting.

By the time Welles reached the mansion, Secretary of State
William H. Seward and Secretary of the Treasury Salmon P.
Chase were engaged in an excited conversation with Stanton
and Lincoln. All four men turned expectantly to Welles, eager to
know what he planned to do to prevent the *Virginia* from
steaming up the Potomac River and shelling the capital.

Welles commented that his best man was Como. Louis
Goldsborough, who was in North Carolina, where the USS
Monitor was originally scheduled to go. Although the *Monitor*
had been diverted to Hampton Roads, Welles had not been
forewarned about her expected arrival. He recalled:

> Mr. Stanton, impulsive and always a sensationalist, was terribly
> excited, walked the room in great agitation, and gave brusque
> utterances, and deprecatory answers to all that was said, and

censured everything that had been done or was omitted to be done. Mr. Seward, usually buoyant and self-reliant, overwhelmed with the intelligence, listened in responsive sympathy to Stanton, and was greatly depressed, as indeed, were all the [cabinet] members, who, in the meantime had arrived, with the exception of Mr. Blair [postmaster general], as well as one or two others—naval and military officers—among them Commander [John A.] Dahlgren and Colonel [Montgomery] Meigs [who had just been made quartermaster general].

Stanton gloomily predicted that the Southern ironclad "will change the whole character of the war." He was convinced that it would "destroy, seriatim, every naval vessel" and then would "lay all the cities on the seaboard under contribution [ransom]." He announced that he would immediately recall Gen. Ambrose Burnside from North Carolina and would order the evacuation of Port Royal, South Carolina. He planned to "notify the Governors and municipal authorities in the North to take instant measures to protect their harbors."

Welles described his colleague's speech as "broken and denunciatory" and his manner as betraying the absolute fear that gripped him. Stanton looked out of a window and said he was sure that "the monster was at this moment on her way to Washington." To the chief executive and his top advisers, the secretary of war warned that they were likely to have "a shell or cannonball from one of her guns in the White House before we leave this room."

Welles tried to calm Stanton by pointing out that the extremely heavy Confederate craft could not possibly pass Kettle Bottom Shoals. This major obstruction in the Potomac River at a point about fifty miles below the capital greatly limited its navigation. The size and weight of the Confederate ironclad meant she also could not get into the sounds of North Carolina.

Instead of dispatching telegrams that would cause panic to spread throughout the North, Welles counseled consideration and concealment of alarm from the public. Chase agreed then modified that view by saying he thought it would be well to warn the governor of New York and the mayor of New York

City. Stanton took this as an opportunity to declare that "authorities in all the chief cities" should be warned.

As calmly as he could in this situation, Welles announced that he had to put his trust in the *Monitor*. Stanton instantly demanded, "How many guns does she carry?" Told that the vessel's battery consisted of two large-caliber pieces, he "turned away with a look of mingled amazement, contempt, and distress, that was painfully ludicrous." This emergency meeting broke up when Lincoln ordered his carriage so he could go to the Washington Navy Yard for a firsthand look at its defenses.

Later during that eventful Sunday, cabinet members returned to the president's office. Stanton announced triumphantly that he had summoned shipping magnate Cornelius Vanderbilt. He also enumerated his personal plans for further obstructing the Potomac River. Welles did not get the full import of this revelation until he learned that night that every available boat in Washington, Georgetown, and Alexandria had been purchased. Stanton directed Meigs to load them with ballast so they could be sunk at Kettle Bottom Shoals.

Welles returned to the White House and registered his protest against Stanton's plans. Lincoln listened attentively, pondered the alternatives, and agreed that "Stanton's squadron"

A single shot at full power from one of the Monitor's *guns would have broken through the side of the* Virginia—*but the crew had strict orders to underload the ordnance for fear of blowing up the guns.*

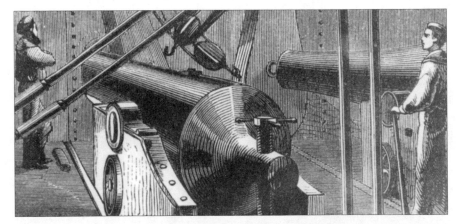

could be made ready, but no boats would be sunk in the Potomac until the *Virginia* entered the river.

When Vanderbilt arrived, he was met by Stanton, who told him that the War Department had little confidence in the *Monitor* and was prepared to take independent action to stop the seemingly invulnerable Rebel craft. Assured that naval officials would not interfere, Vanderbilt offered to ram the *Virginia* with his 3,360-ton side-wheel steamer.

Informed of this scheme, Lincoln—who had just learned of the inconclusive duel between the ironclads—suggested that such an attack could send the *Vanderbilt* to the bottom. The financier responded that he would cheerfully give the vessel to the United States, asking only that her crew be retained. Immensely pleased, Stanton quickly ordered both the *Vanderbilt*, the USS *Baltic*, and a small fleet of large merchant steamers to Hampton Roads. These vessels anchored at Fort Monroe and for two months waited for the Confederate ironclad to make an appearance.

During Lincoln's voyage to Fort Monroe in May 1862, the president's party noticed "a string of boats nearly a mile in length on the Maryland shore, some fifty miles below Washington." They learned that these were the vessels of "Stanton's navy." These watercraft never encountered the fearful *Virginia*. When the Confederates abandoned Norfolk, the Rebel ironclad had no port to call home. Her crew destroyed her rather than see her fall into Federal hands.

The panic that filled the halls of power in Washington in the wake of the *Virginia* subsided. Anxious as the capital remained throughout the war, which reached its highest point when Confederate Gen. Jubal Early raided Maryland and threatened Washington, the political and military leaders never again experienced the anxiety that led the secretary of war to form his own navy.

ABSOLUTELY NO ESCAPE

WRITING FROM the Ogeechee River on March 3, 1863, Union Comdr. John L. Worden again voiced to Rear Adm. Samuel F.

Du Pont a plea that had not as yet been heeded. On February 28 Worden's vessel, the USS *Montauk,* had been hit by a torpedo. Since the explosion took place under her keel, the warship was heavily damaged. Worden, however, was far more concerned about his crew than about the vessel. Consequently he wrote: "This report also mentions a fact of vital importance to those concerned, as well as to the efficient working of the ship, viz, the total absence of any means of escape from death by scalding of those in the engine room in the event of an accident causing an escape of steam. This is, in my opinion, true, and so serious a fact that I beg leave to urge a remedy may be applied if possible."

Du Pont was not unaware of this problem, for the boilers of one of the Federal vessels that helped to reduce Fort Donelson had been damaged by enemy fire. Although numerous sailors had been scalded to death that day, nothing had been done about the matter.

Worden pointed out that the impossibility of "instant exit" from the engine room of a warship was due to the standard design of such vessels. They were fitted with heavy, clumsy hatches that took several minutes to open. While attempting to escape an engine room mishap, the men were engulfed in lethal steam.

One of Worden's subordinates, engineer Thomas A. Stephens, suggested a remedy for this defect. The hatches could be refitted with "a simple lever, fulcrum, connecting rod, counterpoise, and trigger." When it was linked to a heavy hatch, pulling the trigger was "all that is necessary to give instant means of escape to those in the engine room at any moment."

Similar suggestions had gone to the Navy Department in Washington earlier and had not been acted upon. Worden and Stephens fared no better. Until well after the end of the war, nearly every warship was a death trap for the men stationed in the engine room.

CHAPTER TEN

LAWS AND POLITICS

BANISHMENT

ALTHOUGH SEVERAL kinds of punishment are enumerated in the Constitution of the United States, it makes no mention of banishment, a practice long common in the monarchies of Europe and Asia. During the Civil War several women and men were banished from the North by Federal authorities.

The first person to be banished from the North was Mrs. Rose O'Neal Greenhow of Washington. The famous detective Allan Pinkerton arrested her in August 1861 on suspicion that she had supplied valuable military information to Confederate Gen. P. G. T. Beauregard prior to the battle of First Manassas.

Along with her eight-year-old daughter, the Washington hostess was hustled off to Sixteenth Street and a prison improvised from the building that earlier had been the U.S. Capitol and a boarding

Washington socialite Rose O'Neal Greenhow, whose daughter went to prison with her, was banished because any other punishment might have embarrassed high-placed political leaders.

LIBRARY OF CONGRESS

house run by Greenhow's aunt. As was often the case with political prisoners, no formal charges were preferred—yet Greenhow and her daughter were treated as though she had been convicted of treason and was awaiting execution.

Since the attractive widow had numerous high-placed friends in the Federal government, it was dangerous even to consider sending Greenhow to the gallows. Union Gen. John A. Dix and judges Edwards Pierrepont and Joseph Holt interrogated her at length.

Although there was abundant evidence to prove her guilt, the government chose not to use it. A courtroom battle with Greenhow on the witness stand was the last thing the Lincoln administration wanted. Possibly the president was involved in deciding how to punish the woman. Because of the highly unusual nature of her offenses, her fate could not have been decided without his knowledge and consent.

In June 1862—about nine months after her arrest—Greenhow received a small group of official visitors in her cell. Seven soldiers and the prison warden formed a cordon around her and her daughter and escorted them out of the Old Capitol Prison and to a dock on the Potomac River. They were taken to Fort Monroe, where she was told that she would be given her freedom in exchange for her solemn vow never again to set foot on Union soil during "the present unpleasantness."

Greenhow gladly took the prescribed oath, of course, and made her way to Richmond. She quickly gained the ear of Jef-

Having once served as the U.S. Capitol, during the war this building came to be known as "The American Bastille."

ferson Davis, who selected her for a delicate mission to England whose nature was never disclosed. She remained in Europe for two years and published her autobiography, *My Imprisonment and the First Year of Abolition Rule in Washington.*

In October 1864 she took passage on the blockade-runner *Condor* and headed for Wilmington, North Carolina. Within sight of her destination, warships threatened to overtake the *Condor*, but the helmsman managed to outmaneuver them. Unfortunately the vessel grounded on a sandbar just two hundred yards from Fort Fisher. Greenhow was anxious that she might again be imprisoned by the Union authorities and asked to be taken ashore in the ship's longboat. Against the captain's wishes, she insisted until the boat was lowered into the rough waters. It wasn't long before the craft was swamped and overturned. The sailors who had manned the boat were able to cling to it until they were rescued. Greenhow might have been rescued too, but she had sewn dispatches and a quantity of gold into her dress. The weight carried her to the bottom and she drowned. Her body was recovered the next day, and she was buried with military honors.

A number of other political prisoners, among whom Clement L. Vallandigham was best known, were later banished by Federal authorities. There is no record that the U.S. Supreme Court was ever asked to rule on the legality of this ancient form of punishment. Had a case gone to the High Court after pro-Lincoln members gained a majority, it's likely that a precedent would have been set and that banishment would have become an authorized form of American punishment.

ALIEN ENEMIES

JEFFERSON DAVIS had so many spies in Washington that he probably knew that Rose Greenhow would be banished long before she was expelled from the Union. Under his leadership Southern lawmakers took formal steps to rid the eleven states of the Confederacy of its civilian enemies but did not label such action as banishment.

On August 8, 1861, the Confederate Congress approved Davis-sponsored legislation entitled "An Act Respecting Alien Enemies." Under its terms, men fourteen years of age or older who resided within the Confederacy and did not acknowledge its authority within forty days would be considered alien enemies. Davis was careful to note that this did not apply to a citizen of the United States who was residing in the Confederacy and who intended to formalize his allegiance.

Marshals were authorized to remove aliens and persons who remained loyal to the Union from the Confederacy. Should a person who had been banished return to Confederate territory and be captured, he was to "be at once delivered over to the nearest military authority to be dealt with as a spy or as a prisoner of war, as the case may require." Strangely, in the light of the high-profile case of Rose O'Neal Greenhow, women were not targeted.

DEPORTATION

FOR CENTURIES military leaders have had the authority to expell civilians from an occupied region—ostensibly for security purposes but often as a punitive measure. Expulsion, usually for a stipulated period of time but sometimes permanent, fell short of banishment since the persons involved were not required to go beyond national borders. Dozens of Federal commanders and a handful of Confederate officers resorted to this measure despite the fact that they were on questionable legal ground.

The most controversial expulsion of civilians occurred in Missouri. There a foster brother of Union Gen. William T. Sherman forced all the residents of a region in the southwestern corner of the state to pack up and leave their homes.

Thomas Ewing Jr. was a prominent prewar attorney and political leader who moved to Leavenworth, Kansas, in 1856. Earlier, he had been a U.S. senator and a member of the cabinets of two presidents.

A fiercely combative abolitionist, Ewing became the first chief justice of the new state soon after it was admitted to the

Union. In 1862 he resigned his office in order to recruit the Eleventh Kansas Cavalry and become its colonel. Less than a year later he was a brigadier in command of the military District of the Border.

All of Kansas was put under his control, and at his request a tier of Missouri counties running from south to north along

Guerrilla leader William C. Quantrill had followers throughout Kansas and western Missouri.

Unarmed civilians beg to be permitted to remain in their Kansas homes.

the border were added to the district. He wanted them under his command because he was convinced that residents in the southern tip of the Missouri segment were aiding the Confederate guerrilla leader William C. Quantrill.

Late in July 1863 some of Ewing's troops brought a number of "females of the bushwhacking persuasion" to Kansas City and placed them under guard in the Union Hotel. Soon the rooms in which these women were imprisoned were crowded with other captives. Frustrated because he could not gain full control in the section of Missouri for which he was responsible, Ewing journeyed to Saint Louis for permission to take drastic action.

Earlier he had gained the respect of Abraham Lincoln. Advocating a position unlike those held by numerous other prominent attorneys, Ewing had advised the president to order the release of the Confederate commissioners who had been seized aboard the British vessel *Trent*. In a telegram about possible treatments for the pair of Rebel envoys, Ewing warned, "There can be no contraband of war between neutral ports."

Lincoln, who initially leaned toward a public trial of James Mason and John Slidell, changed his mind when he sensed that public opinion might force Great Britain into the war as an ally of the Confederacy. Though Ewing did not know it at the time, when his telegram reached Washington, approximately fourteen thousand British troops were readying for transport to Canada.

Because of his ties with Lincoln, Ewing is believed to have had the unwritten approval of the chief executive before he drafted one of the most infamous documents of the war. Issued on August 25, 1863, his General Order No. 11 required every man, woman, and child in the Missouri counties of Cass, Jackson, and Bates "to remove from their present places of residence within 15 days." The same stipulation applied to all residents of a designated portion of Vernon County. Part of the text of the Ewing document was printed in the *Western Journal of Commerce*.

Since Confederate Arkansas was the closest place of refuge for these displaced persons, thousands of civilians had to pack their belongings and move across the state line. Ewing's agents hunted down pro-Southern civilians wherever they had taken refuge. A single order from his pen required sixty-four persons, "many of them heads of families," to leave Kansas City.

Union soldiers began sweeping through the four depopulated counties while their residents were still on the move. They destroyed crops and burned everything they could—homes, barns, outhouses, grist mills, bridges, and public buildings. By the time this program of systematic destruction ended, southwestern Missouri had come to be known as "the burnt district."

Virginia-born artist George Caleb Bingham was nationally renowned by the time he settled in Missouri as one of the state's most famous citizens. Outraged at what had been done by a military leader who was also a respected jurist, Bingham executed a painting in which he depicted unarmed civilians making futile pleas to be permitted to remain in their homes.

Soon after the war ended, Ewing was offered two cabinet posts in succession by President Andrew Johnson, but he declined both. During the next decade he was one of the most prominent Democrats of Ohio, and after moving to New York City in 1881 was a leading contender for a seat on the U.S. Supreme Court. Typical biographical profiles laud the jurist-soldier for his accomplishments—but they say little if anything about General Order No. 11.

CHIEF JUSTICE COULD NOT ENFORCE THE LAW

JOHN MERRYMAN of Maryland was placed under military arrest by order of Col. Samuel Yohe soon after a civilian mob fell on the Sixth Massachusetts Militia on April 19, 1861, while that unit was en route to Washington. Charged with having taken part in the riot and having helped to destroy bridges to prevent the passage of Federal troops, Merryman was confined in Fort McHenry at Baltimore.

Through influential friends he managed to get word of his plight to Chief Justice Roger B. Taney of the U.S. Supreme Court, who came to Baltimore for a session of the federal circuit court. Taney drew up a writ of habeas corpus and sent a message to Gen. George Cadwalader, commandant of Fort McHenry:

> You are hereby commanded to be and appear before the Hon. Roger B. Taney at the U.S. court room in the Masonic Hall on Monday, the 27th day of May, 1861, at 11 o'clock in the morning, and that you bring with you the body of John Merryman, now in your custody, and that you certify and make known the day and cause of the capture and detention of the said John Merryman, and that you then and there do submit to and receive whatsoever the said court shall determine upon concerning you on their behalf according to law.

Cadwalader sent one of his officers to deliver a written summary of charges against Merryman, after which his aide was interrogated by the chief justice:

> CHIEF JUSTICE: Have you brought with you the body of John Merryman?

COLONEL LEE: I have no instructions except to deliver this response to the court.

CHIEF JUSTICE: The commanding officer declines to obey the writ?

COLONEL LEE: After making that communication my duty is ended and my power is ended. (Rising and retiring.)

CHIEF JUSTICE: The Court orders an attachment to issues against George Cadwalader for disobedience to the high writ of the Court.

Taney then immediately wrote and delivered to the clerk of court: "*Ordered:* That an attachment forthwith issue against General George Cadwalader for a contempt in refusing to produce the body of John Merryman according to the command of the writ of *habeas corpus* returnable and returned before me today, and that said attachment be returned before me at twelve o'clock to-morrow, at the room of the Circuit Court."

Cadwalader informed the chief justice that he was "duly authorized by the President of the United States to suspend the writ of habeas corpus for the public safety." A copy of the correspondence was sent to Washington, where Asst. Adj. Gen. E. D. Townsend instructed Cadwalader: "In returns to writs of habeas corpus by whomsoever issued you will most respectfully decline for the time to produce the prisoners, but will say that when the present unhappy difficulties are at an end you will duly respond to the writs in question."

Since this regulation allowed no exceptions, the chief justice of the U.S. Supreme Court had no power to enforce the law when he clashed with Union military authorities.

ON THE EDGE OF A DICTATORSHIP

NO ONE involved in the celebrated Merryman case anticipated that the "unhappy difficulties" linked with it would drag on for almost four more years. Neither did anyone predict that Lincoln's "temporary suspension of the writ along a line between

Washington and Baltimore" would be extended and amplified numerous times. Wherever martial law was in force, as well as in numerous Union states far from any battle zones, habeas corpus was suspended from Washington.

By March 1863 lawmakers of the North were convinced that it was necessary to curtail personal liberty in order to win the war. On the same day that the first Union conscription act was passed, Congress attempted to sanction the president's prior violation of constitutional rights. Although the issue never went to the Supreme Court for a definitive ruling, suspension of habeas corpus took place so frequently and involved so many hundreds of thousands of persons that it became virtually commonplace.

Some authorities estimate that approximately eighteen thousand Northern civilians were arrested on suspicion and held without trial for various lengths of time. In 1865 editors of *The American Cyclopedia and Register of Important Events* for that year held that "from June, 1861, to January 1, 1866, the cases of some thirty-eight thousand" arrests in which citizens were refused the right of habeas corpus were reported to the office of the Provost Marshal in the capital." In *The Fate of Liberty,* Mark E. Neely argues that it is impossible to accurately determine how many persons in the North were deprived of their constitutional rights.

The Confederate Congress sanctioned suspension of habeas corpus by Jefferson Davis, and on three occasions the lawmakers took matters into their own hands. Their measures were limited in both geographical scope and duration; as a result of public outcry, their impact was minimal. Many Southerners considered suspension of the writ to be a giant step toward despotism, and hosts of them were almost as strongly anti-Richmond as they were anti-Washington. Comparatively few residents of the Confederacy were held without trial for lengthy periods after having been arrested on suspicion.

That was not the case with the enemy. It's doubtful that the president recognized the degree to which he placed the Union in peril. His *Collected Works,* an eight-volume set of books from which hundreds of speeches and documents are missing, deals with the suspension of habeas corpus twenty-one times. Campaigns, battles, and raids dominated newspaper headlines for four years during which the future of democracy was in grave peril. Whatever the true number of suspensions and "political prisoners" may have been, for months the Union teetered perilously close to military dictatorship. Democracy survived, not because long-standing laws and the U.S. Constitution were honored, but because no Federal general seized the opportunity to overthrow the Lincoln administration and launch a military regime.

PIRATES BY THE HUNDRED

PIRATES HAVE long been known to be men "without sanction from a political authority" who took part in violence or robbery "on the high seas beyond the jurisdiction of any nation." The traditional penalty of anyone convicted of piracy was death.

Skilled and knowledgeable as attorney Abraham Lincoln was, he seems to have ignored the field of maritime law. At his insistence, captured Confederate privateers who had been licensed by Richmond were treated, not as prisoners of war, but as pirates. Thomas Baker and twelve members of the crew of the privateer *Savannah* surrendered to the USS *Perry* early in June 1861. These captives were put in irons and taken to New York's infamous Tombs prison to await trial.

It took nearly four months for U.S. government attorneys to prepare their case against the captives, whose numbers had swelled in the meantime with the additional seizures of Rebel vessels. Jurors who heard the case in the U.S. Circuit Court of the Southern District of New York had no doubt that the accused had been engaged in seizures and attempted seizures of Union vessels. Some of them argued, however, that the men on trial were duly licensed by the Confederacy.

At least one member of the jury later confessed that he did not understand why a Confederate taken prisoner on land should become a prisoner of war, while a comrade captured on water was charged with piracy. These factors led to a hung jury, so at least two bands of men who had been captured on the high seas stayed in jail as accused pirates.

When Richmond responded by selecting a Federal hostage for each Southern sailor who faced the death penalty, Lincoln relented in his judgment that captured crews of licensed privateers had to be treated as pirates. Yet John Y. Beall and crewmen of the Confederate navy were put on trial for piracy after being taken prisoner in Chesapeake Bay in 1863. Their lives were saved when Southern authorities again resorted to the use of hostages who were exchanged for the accused men.

Despite these emotionally charged events, the president and his top aides continued to write and speak about Confederate piracy throughout the war. This usage is responsible for the multiple instances in which *pirate* or a variant of this term appears in the *Official Records* and the *Naval Official Records*.

FATE, PROVIDENCE, AND CUNNING IN CHICAGO

DELEGATES TO the 1860 Republican National Convention who converged upon Chicago and the building erected for their use considered the gathering to be all but perfunctory. It was assumed that William H. Seward of New York would be the presidential nominee.

They failed, however, to take into account the astute work of Judge David Davis of Illinois, chairman of the convention and campaign manager for the dark-horse candidate Abraham Lincoln. Davis had promised that if the party would hold the nominating convention in his state, Illinois would not field a favorite-son candidate. He may have had no part in the shenanigans by which attorney Lincoln suddenly became a popularist in the guise of a railsplitter, but by the time Republicans gathered on May 16 Davis knew that whoever they nominated would go to the White House. Three weeks earlier, meeting in Charleston, the Democrats had found themselves hopelessly divided for the

Judge David Davis may have made promises without Lincoln's knowledge or consent.

first time in many years. They were certain to field two candidates rather than one, and the fledgling Constitutional Union Party had nominated a man who was sure to be supported by another portion of the dissident Democrats.

Thurlow Weed, veteran political boss of New York, was confident that Seward would sweep to victory very early. Possibly at the suggestion of Weed, residents of Auburn, New York, brought a cannon to Seward's home so that it could be fired as soon as word of his nomination was received.

Reporting on some of the events during the first day of the convention, an observer noted that Seward's followers were so certain that he would win "that they urged an immediate ballot." They probably would have had it, had Davis not seen to it that the printer could not deliver the tally sheets that evening.

On the following morning a brass band displaying Seward banners paraded through the streets of Chicago to the cheers of the leading candidate's backers. By the time they returned to the convention site, they found it so crowded that many of them could not get inside. Davis had arranged for nearly every town close to the meeting place to send as many spectators as possible, and they had packed the hall.

From Springfield, Davis received a telegram instructing him to make no bargains. Whether that was what Lincoln wanted or was simply what he put on record, no one knows. Nevertheless, Davis made promises to almost everyone. Far too astute to seek upfront support for his candidate, he requested pledges for the second and third ballots. In return, he promised that Simon Cameron of

Thurlow Weed was a powerful political leader who wholeheartedly supported Seward's candidacy.

Pennsylvania and Salmon P. Chase of Ohio would be members of the Lincoln cabinet. Similar pledges were made to Edward Bates of Missouri and Montgomery Blair of Maryland. When Seward's support began to slip, he seems to have asked for and received assurance that upon Lincoln's election he would become secretary of state. Significantly, all five of these candidates for the nomination wound up as cabinet members.

From May 1860 until his untimely death, Lincoln reiterated that he was an instrument of Providence. He did not so much direct events as he was directed by them, he asserted time after time. Be that as it may, he saw to it that Judge Davis of the eighth judicial circuit of Illinois became an associate justice of the U.S. Supreme Court in 1862.

SHERMAN IGNORED

WHEN HIS armies began pushing south from Chattanooga, Gen. William T. Sherman hoped to quickly crush the Army of Tennessee then head for the nearest port to transport his army to join Grant in Virginia. After his March to the Sea, however, he opted to march his men northward rather than ship them. He would eventually reach Grant, and in the meantime he would tramp through the Carolinas, the "seed bed of secession."

By the time his troops were deep inside North Carolina, they had met and mastered several Rebel forces. By mid-April 1865 Confederate Gen. Joseph E. Johnston knew that additional combat would be futile and indicated his willingness to talk terms. Since Jefferson Davis was also in North Carolina, Johnston was frequently forced to consult with his president, who wanted impossible terms.

Sherman and Johnston met at the Bennett farm near Durham Station on April 17, eight days after R. E. Lee had surrendered at Appomattox Court House and three days after the assassination of Lincoln. Present-day southerners who still rankle at the mere mention of Sherman's name fail to remember that the Federal commander granted remarkably generous peace terms to his counterpart. Johnston's men were allowed to retain their weapons and deliver them to state arsenals and officers were allowed to keep their horses. Civilian officials were to retain their offices, and virtually universal amnesty was promised. Even Jefferson Davis, members of his cabinet, and Confederate commanders were included in this sweeping amnesty. Measured by any standard, the formula Sherman agreed to was generous to the point of being benevolent.

Joseph E. Johnston surrendered the Army of Tennessee and the rest of his commands to William Tecumseh Sherman at the Bennett farm in Durham Station, North Carolina. Many of the generous terms Sherman agreed to, however, were repudiated by Secretary of War Edwin M. Stanton.

Sherman knew he had gone beyond his authority, so he added at the end of the document a brief statement that both parties should quickly get the assent of their respective governments. Davis and his aides were privy to what was being offered and offered no objection to any clause.

It was no secret that Sherman despised politics and politicians and that he was not universally admired in Washington. The general would not have been surprised to learn that his decisions were being questioned, but he did not imagine that Congress would sabotage the agreement. He was summoned to Washington and interrogated by high-level officials, among whom Secretary of War Edwin M. Stanton was the most openly antagonistic.

At the two-day grand review in Washington, Sherman rode at the head of his staff and then was seated at the reviewing stand. He chose to ignore Stanton.

It quickly became apparent that many Northern leaders intended to beat the defeated South into the ground instead of extending a hand to lift the region to its feet. The generous terms given to Johnston by Sherman were ridiculed, scorned, and ultimately repudiated. Had the Bennett farm document been honored, the era known as Reconstruction would not have been as revenge-laden as it was for the next fourteen years.

Whether Sherman is despised or admired, there is no escaping the fact that he had both imagination and the courage of his convictions, for after seeing his surrender document revised with much less generous terms, he enjoyed a fine hour of his own. When the two-day grand review of Union forces was held in Washington, he was notified that he had a seat in the reviewing stand. As he stepped into the gallery of high-level dignitaries, with thousands of eyes upon him, Stanton moved forward and extended his hand. Sherman ignored him, turning his back on the secretary of war and focusing his attention upon the ranks of war-weary veterans.

FIRST SINCE WASHINGTON

GEORGE WASHINGTON began his long military career in 1754 as a lieutenant colonel in command of about 150 men. During the following year he took command of Virginia forces with the rank of colonel. Twenty years after he first donned an officer's uniform, he was commanding all Continental forces. Yet he did not reach his highest rank until after having served eight years as president and having retired from political life. In 1798 the infant United States faced a threat of war with France, then one of the three most powerful nations on earth. Out of loyalty to the nation he had helped to form, Washington accepted command of his nation's armed forces with the new rank of lieutenant general.

Winfield Scott, hero of the Mexican War, presidential contender, and long the top officer of the U.S. Army, was widely

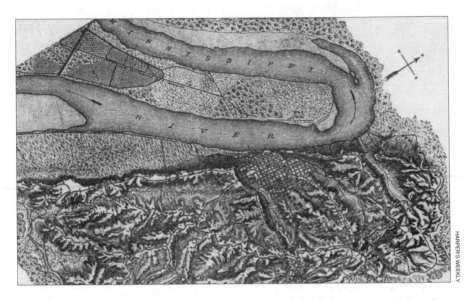

HARPER'S WEEKLY

Its location at a bend in the Mississippi River made Vicksburg especially hard for Federal forces to subdue.

addressed as a lieutenant general. His rank was honorary (by brevet), however. For nearly seven decades after the death of Washington, no other American was a full lieutenant general. That changed after the spectacular Federal victory at Vicksburg, which coincided with the victory at Gettysburg and effectively cut the Confederacy in half. Nine months after the surrender of the Mississippi River bastion, Ulysses S. Grant followed in the footsteps of Washington by donning the insignia of a lieutenant general.

Conventional wisdom explains the elevation of a man who had dropped out of the prewar U.S. Army and had been reduced to poverty by citing Abraham Lincoln's exultant tribute to him as a man who was willing and eager to fight. Beginning with George B. McClellan, characterized by the president as having a severe case of "the slows," the commander in chief of the Union forces had tried one general after another and had found all of them wanting. Almost as though he was in a state of despair, he made Henry W. Halleck his general in chief but continued personally to make major military decisions.

Democrat Horatio Seymour became governor of New York as a result of the midterm elections of 1862.

Important as were Vicksburg's surrender ceremonies on July 4, 1863, in Washington the military victory was overshadowed by growing fear that the Republican Party might soon be defeated at the polls. The midterm elections of 1862 were held in different states at different times that were spread out from spring until fall. When all the votes were tallied, the Democratic Party showed signs of having made significant gains.

Vital states that had gone for Lincoln in 1860 shifted away from the Republican Party two years later. Democrats gained three congressional seats in Indiana. Twenty-three out of New York's thirty-three members of the House were Republican in 1860, but two years later seven new Democratic congressmen went to Washington from the Empire State. Ohio had been heavily Republican in 1860, but just two years later the balance of power shifted to the Democrats. In 1860 Republicans held 80 percent of Pennsylvania's seats in the House; midterm elections left the state's congressional delegation split fifty-fifty. Four of New Jersey's five seats in the House of Representatives went to Democrats in 1862. In addition, Lincoln's political rivals won scores of state and local offices. In New York, Democrat Horatio Seymour gained the governorship by a slim margin. Increasing numbers of voters throughout the North were becoming weary of war and wondering if it might be wiser to let the South go.

The astute political observer who was temporarily residing in the White House knew he faced a tough fight in November 1864. Lincoln knew that he could not win a second term unless he devoted time and energy to his political campaign. To do that, he was forced to give less and less time to his day-to-day direction of the war effort. To a degree rarely recognized, the political dilemma faced by the chief executive heavily influenced his decision to hand the military reins to Grant and elevate him to George Washington's postpresidential rank.

LAND FOR LABOR

MILITARY EVENTS dominated the headlines during the war and have been endlessly examined ever since, but the political action on the domestic front has not received its due. On May 20, 1862, the U.S. Congress passed a nonmilitary measure that proved to be of great importance to the expanding postwar nation.

Under the terms of the Homestead Act, which went into effect January 1, 1863, hundreds of thousands of Americans were offered land in exchange for labor. Terms of the legislation promised anyone 160 acres of public land in what was then considered the far west. A citizen not yet twenty-one years of age had the same opportunity if he or she served as head of a household. A youngster of seventeen or eighteen who had a record of two full weeks in military service was treated as an adult under the act.

To receive clear title to the government-owned land, the person who settled on it was required to live there for five years and "to make improvements" whose nature and extent were not specified. A cash fee of ten dollars, less than seven cents per acre, had to be paid to a land agent of the government. Since no land could be claimed before January 1, 1863, and hundreds of thousands of men were in full-time military service, it would seem that government land would have sat idle until war's end. That was far from the case, however. During the eighteen months after the Homestead Act went into effect, at least 1.25 million acres were claimed. Even Gettysburg, Vicksburg, and Antietam did not have so sweeping an effect upon subsequent American life as did the political decision to open the West to settlement.

IRON FROM COAST TO COAST

EARLY IN the nineteenth century a few visionaries began dreaming of a railroad that would extend from east to west across the middle of North America. If the Atlantic Ocean could be bound to the Pacific with iron, the long and dangerous voyage from Boston to San Francisco by way of the southern tip of South America could be eliminated. Skeptics scoffed that such an undertaking was impossible, but a handful of leaders refused to give up the idea.

A dedicated band of lawmakers framed legislation designed to make possible the building of what was called the Pacific Railroad. After several modifications, the measure passed the U.S. Senate on June 20, 1862, and sailed through the House of Representatives four days later. Lincoln affixed his signature to the bill barely a week later.

Terms of the Pacific Railroad Act enabled investors to form the Union Pacific Company and to raise a staggering $100 million to fund the venture. Since the Central Pacific had been

Several lines of tracks ran through railroad centers such as Grafton, Virginia, but in 1861 all railroad lines were short.

B&O RAILROAD ARCHIVES

chartered a year earlier, this railroad line was given the green light to thrust eastward from Sacramento, California. The Union Pacific was to lay track westward from Omaha, Nebraska. Construction firms willing to recruit workers and buy essential equipment were promised government aid in the form of loans whose cumulative value could not exceed $50 million.

Railroad entrepreneurs became eligible for grants of as much as 12,800 acres of government land per mile of track completed. Although this land was considered to be all but worthless, it was hoped that some of it might become useful when hamlets and villages began to spring up along the railroad line. Work started at Sacramento early in 1863, and before the end of the year a few sections of track were under construction near Omaha.

Four years after Appomattox, the gigantic construction enterprise that was authorized when the war was only eighteen months old came to a climax in the Golden Spike ceremony at Promontory Point, Utah. Wartime legislation had led to that creation of a steel bond that linked two oceans.

A ONE-SHOT POLITICAL PARTY

WITH THE election of 1864 in the offing and Democrat George B. McClellan running on a peace platform, David Davis and other key leaders of the youthful Republican Party persuaded their colleagues to pursue a drastic course of action. For their national conclave scheduled to meet in Baltimore on June 7, the delegates were told that they would be attending the convention of the Union Party. Adopted in a bid for votes, the new name was virtually ignored by the general public. Posters distributed by Democrats warned voters against backing "Lincoln and the Black Republican Party."

Brief as was the life of the Union Party, it offered voters a vibrant platform. Significant segments said:

> We approve the determination of the Government of the United States not to compromise with the rebels, not to offer

them any terms of peace except such as may be based upon an unconditional surrender of their hostility and a return to their full allegiance to the Constitution and the laws of the United States. . . .

As slavery was the cause and now constitutes the strength of the rebellion, and as it must be always and everywhere hostile to the principles of republican government, justice and the national safety demand its utter and complete extirpation from the soil of the Republic.

Significant civil service legislation lay in the future. A major reason for seeking the presidency was the spoils system under which the dominant party had control of thousands of jobs. Every person holding a high or a low governmental post knew that someone else would get his or her job if the national balance of power were to shift. Because of this, relatively few employees of the Federal government protested when asked to make a standardized "payroll contribution" to the party whose goal was the reelection of Lincoln.

Bolstered by Northern military triumphs, Lincoln fared far better in the electoral college than among ordinary citizens. McClellan received 1.8 million votes, only 10 percent fewer than Lincoln. When the electors met, however, the Democrat got just 21 of 233 votes. Although it may have had the shortest life of a nationally recognized body of its sort, the Republican-rooted Union Party was a potent influence in the making of modern America because it returned Lincoln to the presidency.

JOHN SHERMAN WAS SMEARED BY A TARHEEL

THREE YEARS younger than his brother who led the March to the Sea, John Sherman of Ohio was poles apart from William Tecumseh Sherman when it came to politics. John was a born-and-bred professional politician who spent much of his career in Washington and who yearned for one of the key posts of the capital, Speaker of the House of Representatives.

John presided over Ohio's first Republican Convention at which Salmon P. Chase was nominated for governor in 1855. During the same year, the foster brother of Union Gen. Thomas Ewing Jr. went to Congress for the beginning of a term much longer than Abraham Lincoln's. As a member of the Committee of Inquiry, he went to "Bleeding Kansas" and wrote the congressional report about the state of affairs there.

On December 5, 1858, Sherman's political star began a rapid ascent. Nominated by Republican members of the House for the all-important post of Speaker, he appeared to be a shoo-in. His party held 114 seats against 92 occupied by Democrats, so every party-line vote by Republicans was a victory. Very soon after his nomination, however, a member of the lawmaking body revealed that Sherman had used inflammatory campaign literature. Part of that campaign involved Sherman's endorsement of Hinton R. Helper's book *The Impending Crisis,* which was for a time the talk of Washington. The endorsement, however, did not sit well with Sherman's colleagues.

Congressman John Sherman of Ohio (left), brother of Gen. William Tecumseh Sherman (right), badly wanted to become Speaker of the House. For his part, the general scorned politics.

Sherman withdrew his name from consideration between January 30 and February 1. That left a vacuum, for no other member of the body had so large a following. Members of the House cast forty-three votes before William F. Pennington received the post that would have gone to Sherman had he not been caught up in the tremendous impact of Helper's book.

When Sen. Salmon P. Chase resigned to become Lincoln's secretary of the treasury, John Sherman was elected to succeed him. After having served as secretary of state under President William McKinley, he was twice a candidate for the nation's highest office. His older brother's name, however, will forever be linked with notions about barbarity to civilians as a side effect of his concept of total war. John's name is permanently embedded in America's political heritage because his forty-year national leadership in the field of finance culminated in passage of the Sherman Antitrust Act. Shaped by the brother of the Civil War general, it became law in 1890 and still affects commerce to the present day.

SECESSION AIDED AND ABETTED IN WASHINGTON

PRESERVATION OF the Union, not the abolition of slavery, was the consuming goal of our sixteenth president. Beginning with his first inaugural address, Lincoln repeatedly denied that the South had actually seceded from the Union. In his mind, the seceded states were only in a state of insurrection. Lincoln never wavered from this position, so in 1864 he vetoed an act of Congress because its preamble declared that the seceded states were not in the Union. Paradoxically, Lincoln aided and abetted the secession from Virginia of a section of the Old Dominion.

Agriculture, transportation, and economics shaped the two vastly different regions of Virginia—the Tidewater and the Kanawha Valley—long before secession from the Union became an issue. Initially rejected by a state convention, the concept of severing ties with Washington was endorsed by plantation

As early as the seventeenth century, Tideland Virginia was depicted as an earthly paradise, whose bounty was not shared with settlers west of the mountains.

owners and their peers when Lincoln called for volunteer soldiers to swell the ranks of the Union army to five times its prewar size. War was clearly in the offing, and that would mean invasion of the Old Dominion.

Pro-Union sentiment and opposition to secession surfaced as excuses for long-desired action on the part of the "overmountain men." Led by newspaper publisher Archibald W. Campbell of Wheeling, a convention of self-styled Unionists was held in May 1861. During the following month "delegates" from twenty-six counties denounced the Confederacy to which Tidewater Virginia had become attached. Soon the secession of Virginia was used as an emotionally charged issue by which to struggle for "independence from the old government of the state."

A provisional government was formed, a legislature was established, and Francis H. Pierpont was elected as head of the independent entity initially called Kanawha. That name was soon changed to West Virginia. Meanwhile, Unionists of the Tidewater region formed a "restored government at Alexandria," and so there were three Virginia capitals and three separate governments in Richmond, Wheeling, and Alexandria.

A constitutional convention convened in West Virginia in November 1861. The document framed there was ratified by the voters on April 3, 1862; that is, voters who had taken the oath of allegiance to the Union. When the state legislature met in May 1862, a formal application for statehood was made.

West Virginia was recognized almost immediately as a separate entity in Washington, as evidenced by letters sent from the Northern capital to Pierpont, who was formally addressed as governor by the assistant secretary of war, Thomas A. Scott, on

Residents of Wheeling—then in Virginia—celebrated the prospect of statehood for Kanawha.

Francis H. Pierpont of Kanawha was addressed in correspondence from Washington as "Governor of Virginia" soon after the battle of First Bull Run.

August 8, 1861. Yet the influence of the Alexandria faction was strong enough to exert a greater presence in the Federal capital than did its rival west of the mountains.

In the North, even the most ardent backers of statehood for West Virginia, among whom Lincoln was foremost, realized that they faced significant political obstacles. For one, the state of Virginia was not about to concede that a portion of its territory had a legitimate right to separate as a new state of the

Attorney General Edward Bates (left) and Secretary of the Navy Gideon Welles (right) were not alone among Lincoln's cabinet members in registering strong objections to granting statehood to West Virginia.

Grafton, Virginia (now West Virginia), was occupied in 1861 by troops under the command of Union Gen. George B. McClellan.

Federal Union. Instead, the lawmakers in Washington looked to the provisional state government in Alexandria, which approved the measure.

The representatives of several Northern states, however, expressed reservations over the constitutionality of admitting a new state based on the action of a provisional government. Lincoln responded by submitting the issue to his cabinet.

William H. Seward was enthusiastically in favor of the proposed action and gained the support of Chase and Stanton. Attorney General Edward Bates, who was adamantly opposed to statehood for what had been western Virginia, was supported by Montgomery Blair and Gideon Welles. Radical Republican Thaddeus Stevens, who opposed Lincoln on many issues, thundered, "We know [the admission of West Virginia] is unconstitutional, but it is necessary."

Lincoln settled the matter by elevating expediency above legality. When Congress approved a law admitting West Virginia to the Union—albeit with provisos that required the gradual abolition of slavery—the president did not rush to sign the bill. Instead, he revealed in writing his deepest feelings concerning the secession of western Virginia from the Old Dominion. Lincoln noted: "We can scarcely dispense with the aid of West Virginia in this struggle; much less can we afford to have her

When West Virginia was admitted to the Union on June 20, 1862, Virginia became the only state to lose territory as a result of the Civil War.

against us in Congress and in the field. Her brave and good men regard her admission into the Union as a matter of life and death. We cannot fully retain their confidence and cooperation if we seem to break faith with them."

Finally Lincoln consented to the bill, which became law on December 13, 1862, and West Virginia became the thirty-fifth state. As for "her brave and good men," twenty-five thousand fought for the North and fifteen thousand fought for the South. The brothers' war continued in the state long after Lee and Grant had met at Appomattox.

BIBLIOGRAPHY
AND
INDEX

BIBLIOGRAPHY

Abbott, John S. C. *History of Civil War in America*. 2 vols. Springfield, Mass.: G. Bill, 1863–66.

Abbott, Willis J. *The Naval History of the United States*. 2 vols. New York: Dodd, Mead and Co., 1903.

Adams, James T. *Concise Dictionary of American History*. New York: Scribner, 1962.

Allardice, Bruce S. *More Generals in Gray*. Baton Rouge: Louisiana State University Press, 1995.

The American Annual Cyclopedia and Register, 1861–65. 5 vols. New York: Appleton, 1870–74.

American Heritage magazine.

American History Illustrated magazine.

America's Civil War magazine.

Austin, George Lowell. *The Life and Times of Wendell Phillips*. Boston: B. B. Russell & Co., 1884.

Bailey, Hugh C. *Hinton Rowan Helper*. Southern Historical Publications, no. 7. University: University of Alabama Press, 1965.

Beatty, John. *Memoirs of a Volunteer, 1861–1863*. Edited by Harvey S. Ford. New York: Norton, 1946.

Bentley, George R. *A History of the Freedmen's Bureau*. Philadelphia: University of Pennsylvania, 1955.

Bernard, George S. *War Talks of Confederate Veterans*. Petersburg: Fenn & Owen, 1892.

Bilby, Joseph G. *Civil War Firearms: Their Historical Background and Tactical Use*. Conshohocken, Pa.: Combined, 1996.

Blue & Gray magazine.

Boatner, Mark M., III. *The Civil War Dictionary.* Rev. ed. New York: McKay, 1988.

Botkin, B. A., ed. *A Civil War Treasury of Tales, Legend, and Folklore.* New York: Random House, 1960.

Braden, Waldo W. *Abraham Lincoln, Public Speaker.* Baton Rouge: Louisiana State University Press, 1988.

Britton, Wiley. *Memoirs of the Rebellion on the Border.* Chicago: Cushing, Thomas & Co., 1882.

Carpenter, Frank B. *Six Months at the White House with Abraham Lincoln: The Story of a Picture.* New York: Hurd and Houghton, 1866.

Carse, Robert. *Department of the South: Hilton Head Island in the Civil War.* Columbia, S.C.: State Printing Co., 1961.

Castel, Albert. *Decision in the West: The Atlanta Campaign of 1864.* Lawrence: University Press of Kansas, 1992.

Catton, Bruce. *The American Heritage Picture History of the Civil War.* New York: American Heritage Co., 1960.

———. *The Civil War.* New York: American Heritage Press, 1971.

The Charleston Courier newspaper, 1860–65.

The Charleston Mercury newspaper, 1860–65.

Chesnut, Mary Boykin. *A Diary from Dixie.* Edited by Ben Ames Williams. Boston: Houghton Mifflin, 1949.

Civil War Chronicles magazine.

Civil War magazine.

Civil War Times and *Civil War Times Illustrated* magazines.

Clark, Walter A. *Under the Stars and Bars.* Augusta, Ga.: Chronicle, 1900.

Columbiad magazine.

Commager, Henry Steele. *The Blue and the Gray: The Story of the Civil War As Told by Participants.* 2 vols. Indianapolis: Bobbs-Merrill, 1950.

Cooling, Benjamin F. *Jubal Early's Raid on Washington 1864.* Baltimore: Nautical & Aviation Publishing Co. of America, 1989.

The Confederate Veteran magazine, 1893–1932.

Current, Richard N., ed. *Encyclopedia of the Confederacy.* 4 vols. New York: Simon & Schuster, 1993.

Dana, Charles A. *Recollections of the Civil War.* New York: Appleton, 1902.

Davis, Burke. *Jeb Stuart, The Last Cavalier.* New York: Rinehart, 1957.

———. *They Called Him Stonewall: A Life of Lt. General T. J. Jackson, C.S.A.* New York: Rinehart, 1954.

Davis, Jefferson. *The Rise and Fall of the Confederate Government.* Richmond: Garrett and Massie, 1938.

Davis, William C. *Battle at Bull Run: A History of the First Major Campaign of the Civil War.* Garden City, N.Y.: Doubleday, 1977.

———. *Jefferson Davis: The Man and His Hour.* New York: HarperCollins, 1991.

———, ed. *Great Battles of the Civil War.* New York: Gallery, 1989.

DeGregorio, William A. *The Complete Book of U.S. Presidents.* 4th ed. New York: Wings, 1993.

Denney, Robert E. *Civil War Prisons and Escapes: A Day-by-Day Chronicle.* New York: Sterling, 1993.

Devens, Richard M. *The Pictorial Book of Anecdotes and Incidents of the War of the Rebellion.* Hartford: Hartford Publishing Co., 1866.

Donald, David Herbert. *Lincoln.* New York: Simon & Schuster, 1995.

Dowdey, Clifford, ed. *The Wartime Papers of R. E. Lee.* Boston: Little, Brown, 1961.

Drimmer, Melvin, ed. *Black History: A Reappraisal.* Garden City, N.Y.: Doubleday, 1968.

Dunaway, Wayland F. *Reminiscences of a Rebel.* New York: Neale Publishing Co., 1913.

Dyer, Frederick H. *A Compendium of the War of the Rebellion.* 3 vols. New York: T. Yoseloff, 1959.

The Editors of *Civil War Times Illustrated. Great Battles of the Civil War.* New York: Gallery, 1985.

The Editors of Time-Life Books. *Charleston.* Voices of the Civil War. Alexandria, Va.: Time-Life Books, 1997.

———. *Soldier Life.* Voices of the Civil War. Alexandria, Va.: Time-Life Books, 1996.

———. *Spies, Scouts, and Raiders: Irregular Operations.* Alexandria, Va.: Time-Life Books, 1985.

Elson, Henry W. *The Civil War Through the Camera.* New York: McKinlay, Stone & Mackenzie, 1912.

Erbsen, Wayne. *Rousing Songs and True Tales of the Civil War.* Asheville, N.C.: Native Ground Music, 1999.

Evans, Clement A., ed. *Confederate Military History.* 12 vols. Atlanta: Confederate Publishing Co., 1899.

Faust, Patricia, ed. *Historical Times Illustrated Encyclopedia of the Civil War.* New York: Harper, 1986.

Flandrau, Charles E. *The History of Minnesota and Tales of the Frontier.* St. Paul: E. W. Porter, 1900.

Foote, Shelby. *The Civil War: A Narrative.* 3 vols. New York: Random House, 1958–74.

Forbes, Edwin. *Civil War Etchings.* New York: Dover, 1994.

———. *Thirty Years After: An Artist's Memoir of the Civil War.* New York: Fords, Howard & Hulbert, 1890.

Frank Leslie's Illustrated Weekly Newspaper.

———. *Frank Leslie's Illustrated History of the Civil War.* New York: Leslie's, 1895.

———. *Leslie's Illustrated Civil War.* Jackson: University Press of Mississippi, 1992.

Frazier, Donald S. *Blood and Treasure: Confederate Empire in the Southwest.* College Station: Texas A&M University Press, 1995.

Fuller, Charles A. *Personal Recollections of the War of 1861.* Shirburne, N.Y.: News Job Printing House, 1906.

Furgurson, Ernest B. *Chancellorsville 1863: The Souls of the Brave.* New York: Knopf, 1992.

Gordon, John B. *Reminiscences of the Civil War.* New York: Scribner's, 1903.

Gragg, Rod. *The Civil War Quiz and Fact Book.* New York: Harper & Row, 1985.

Grant, Julia Dent. *The Personal Memoirs of Julia Dent Grant.* Edited by John Y. Simon. 1975. Reprint, Carbondale: Southern Illinois University Press, 1988.

Gutman, Richard J. S., and Kellie O. Gutman. *John Wilkes Booth Himself.* Dover, Mass.: Hired Hand Press, 1979.

Hall, Kermit L., ed. *The Oxford Companion to the Supreme Court of the United States.* New York: Oxford University Press, 1992.

Harper's Weekly magazine.

———. *Harper's Pictorial History of the Civil War.* New York: Harper's, 1866.

Hart, Albert Bushnell. *Salmon P. Chase.* 1899. Reprint, New York: Chelsea House, 1980.

Hay, John. *Lincoln and the Civil War.* New York: Dodd, Meade & Co., 1939.

Hennessy, John J. *Return to Bull Run: The Campaign and Battle of Second Manassas.* New York: Simon & Schuster, 1993.

Herbert, George B. *The Model History of the Civil War.* Springfield, Ohio: Mast, Crowell & Kirkpatrick, 1889.

Hewett, Janet B. et al., eds. *Supplement to the Official Records of the Union and Confederate Armies in the War of the Rebellion*. Wilmington, N.C.: Broadfoot, 1994–98.

Higginson, Thomas W. *Army Life in a Black Regiment*. Boston: Field, Osgood, 1870.

———. *Letters and Journals of Thomas Wentworth Higginson, 1846–1906*. Edited by Mary Thacher Higginson. Boston: Houghton Mifflin, 1921.

Hughes, Langston, and Milton Meltzer. *A Pictorial History of the Negro in America*. Rev. ed. New York: Crown, 1963.

Isham, Asa B., Henry M. Davidson, and Henry B. Furness. *Prisoners of War and Military Prisons*. Cincinnati: Lyman & Cushing, 1890.

Jeffcoat, Francis R. *Confederate Records, Lancaster District, South Carolina*. Columbia, S.C.: F. R. Jeffcoat, 1986.

Johnson, Robert U., and Clarence C. Buel, eds. *Battles and Leaders of the Civil War*. 4 vols. New York: The Century Co., 1887–88.

Joint Committee on the Conduct of the War. *Report*. 3 vols. Washington: Government Printing Office, 1863.

Katz, D. Mark. *Witness to an Era: The Life and Photographs of Alexander Gardner*. New York, Viking, 1991.

Keesy, William A. *War As Viewed from the Ranks*. Norwalk, Ohio: Experiment and News Co., 1898.

Keir, Robert Malcolm. *The Epic of Industry*. New Haven: Yale University Press, 1926.

La Bree, Benjamin. *The Pictorial Battles of the Civil War*. 2 vols. New York: Sherman Publishing Co., 1885.

Leech, Margaret. *Reveille in Washington, 1860–1865*. New York: Harper, 1941.

Leonard, Elizabeth D. *Yankee Women: Gender Battles in the Civil War*. New York: Norton, 1994.

Lincoln, Abraham. *Collected Works*. Edited by Roy P. Basler. 9 vols. New Brunswick: Rutgers University Press, 1953–55.

Long, E. B., and Barbara Long. *The Civil War Day by Day: An Almanac, 1861–1865*. Garden City, N.Y.: Doubleday, 1971.

Longacre, Edward G. *Pickett, Leader of the Charge: A Biography of George E. Pickett, C.S.A.* Shippensburg, Pa.: White Mane, 1995.

Lord, Francis A. *They Fought for the Union*. Harrisburg, Pa.: Stackpole Books, 1960.

Lossing, Benjamin J. *Harper's Encyclopedia of United States History*. 10 vols. New York: Harper & Bros., 1902.

————. *The Pictorial Field Book of the Civil War.* 3 vols. Hartford: T. Belknap, 1874.

Lowry, Don. *No Turning Back: The Beginning of the End of the Civil War, March–June 1864.* New York: Hippocrene, 1992.

McGuire, Alexander K., ed. *The Annals of the Civil War.* 1878. Reprint, New York: Da Capo Press, 1994.

McHenry, Robert, ed. *Liberty's Women.* Springfield, Mass.: Merriam Co., 1980.

McPherson, James M. *Battle Cry of Freedom: The Civil War Era.* The Oxford History of the United States, vol. 6. New York: Oxford University Press, 1988.

Manigault, Edward. *Siege Train: The Journal of a Confederate Artilleryman in the Defense of Charleston.* Edited by Warren Ripley. Columbia: University of South Carolina Press, 1986.

Marrin, Albert. *Unconditional Surrender: U. S. Grant and the Civil War.* New York: Atheneum, 1994.

Marszalek, John F. *Sherman: A Soldier's Passion for Order.* New York: Free Press, 1993.

Martin, Christopher. *Damn the Torpedoes! The Story of America's First Admiral, David Glasgow Farragut.* New York: Abelard-Schuman, 1970.

Mathews, Mitford M., ed. *A Dictionary of Americanisms on Historical Principles.* 2 vols. Chicago: University of Chicago Press, 1951.

Mearns, David C., ed. *The Lincoln Papers: The Story of the Collection.* 2 vols. Garden City, N.Y.: Doubleday, 1948.

Meyer, Howard N. *Colonel of the Black Regiment: The Life of Thomas Wentworth Higginson.* New York: Norton, 1967.

Miers, Earl S. *The Web of Victory: Grant at Vicksburg.* New York: Knopf, 1955.

————, ed. *Lincoln Day by Day: A Chronology.* 3 vols. Washington: Sesquicentennical Commission, 1960.

Military Order of the Loyal Legion of the United States, Iowa Commandery. *War Sketches and Incidents As Related by Companions of the Iowa Commandery.* Des Moines: n.p., 1893– .

————, Minnesota Commandery. *Glimpses of the Nation's Struggle.* 6th ser. Minneapolis: Aug. Davis, 1909.

————, New York Commandery. *Personal Recollections of the War of the Rebellion.* New York: Military Order of the Loyal Legion of the United States, New York Commandery, 1891–97.

Miller, Francis T., ed. *The Photographic History of the Civil War.* 10 vols. New York: The Review of Reviews Co., 1912.

Mitgang, Herbert, ed. *Lincoln As They Saw Him*. New York: Rinehart, 1956.

Mohr, Clarence L. *On the Threshold of Freedom: Masters and Slaves in Civil War Georgia*. Athens: University of Georgia Press, 1986.

Moore, Albert B. *Conscription and Conflict in the Confederacy*. New York: Macmillan, 1924.

Moore, Frank, ed. *The Rebellion Record: A Diary of American Events*. 12 vols. 1861–68. Reprint, New York: Arno Press, 1977.

Mosocco, Ronald A. *The Chronological Tracking of the American Civil War*. Williamsburg, Va.: James River Publications, 1994.

The National Cyclopedia of American Biography. 57 vols. Clifton, N.J.: James T. White, 1977.

Neely, Mark E., Jr. *The Abraham Lincoln Encyclopedia*. New York: McGraw-Hill, 1982.

————. *The Fate of Liberty: Abraham Lincoln and Civil Liberties*. New York: Oxford University Press, 1991.

Nevins, Allan. *The War for the Union*. 4 vols. New York: Scribner, 1959–71.

New York Illustrated News newspaper, 1863–65.

Nicolay, John G., and John Hay. *Abraham Lincoln: A History*. 10 vols. New York: The Century Co., 1917.

Nofi, Albert, comp. *The Civil War Notebook: A Collection of Little-Known Facts and Other Odds-and-Ends About the Civil War*. Conshohocken, Pa.: Combined, 1993.

Oates, Stephen B. *A Woman of Valor: Clara Barton and the Civil War*. New York: Free Press, 1994.

————. *With Malice Toward None: The Life of Abraham Lincoln*. New York: Harper & Row, 1977.

Page, Thomas Nelson. *Works*. 18 vols. New York: Plantation, 1906.

Perkins, Howard C., ed. *Northern Editorials on Secession*. 2 vols. New York: D. Appleton-Century Co., 1942.

Phillips, Wendell. *Speeches, Lectures, and Letters*. Boston: Lee and Shepard, 1884.

Phisterer, Frederick. *Statistical Record of the Armies of the United States*. New York: Scribner's, 1883.

Ploski, Harry A., ed. *The Afro-American*. New York: Wiley, 1983.

Pratt, Fletcher. *Stanton: Lincoln's Secretary of War*. New York: Norton, 1953.

Priest, John M. *Antietam: The Soldier's Battle*. Shippensburg, Pa.: White Mane, 1989.

————. *Before Antietam: The Battle for South Mountain*. Shippensburg, Pa.: White Mane, 1992.

Ray, Frederic E. *Our Special Artist: Alfred R. Waud's Civil War.* 1974. Reprint, Mechanicsburg, Pa.: Stackpole Books, 1994.

Rhode Island Soldiers and Sailors Historical Society. *Personal Narratives of Events in the War of the Rebellion.* 10 vols. Providence: Rhode Island Soldiers and Sailors Historical Society, 1878–1915.

Robertson, James I., Jr. *Soldiers Blue and Gray.* Columbia: University of South Carolina Press, 1988.

———. *Stonewall Jackson: The Man, the Soldier, the Legend.* New York: Macmillan, 1997.

Rodenbough, Theo. F., ed. *The Cavalry.* Vol. 4 of *The Photographic History of the Civil War.* New York: The Review of Reviews Co., 1912.

Roller, David C., and Robert W. Twyman, eds. *The Encyclopedia of Southern History.* Baton Rouge: Louisiana State University Press, 1979.

Roman, Alfred. *The Military Operations of General Beauregard in the War Between the States.* 2 vols. 1884. Reprint, New York: Da Capo Press, 1994.

Rowland, Thomas J. *George B. McClellan and Civil War History: In the Shadow of Grant and Sherman.* Kent, Ohio: Kent State University Press, 1998.

Sandburg, Carl. *Abraham Lincoln: The War Years.* 4 vols. New York: Harcourt, Brace & Co., 1939.

Scharf, John T. *History of the Confederate States Navy.* New York: Rogers & Sherwood, 1887.

Schlesinger, Arthur M., Jr., ed. *The Almanac of American History.* 1983. Reprint, New York: Bramhall House, 1986.

Schwab, John C. *The Confederate States of America, 1861–1865: A Financial and Industrial History of the South During the Civil War.* 1901. Reprint, New York: Burt Franklin, 1968.

Sears, Lorenzo. *Wendell Phillips, Orator and Agitator.* New York: Doubleday, Page & Co., 1909.

Sears, Stephen W. *Chancellorsville.* Boston: Houghton-Mifflin, 1996.

———. *Controversies and Commanders: Dispatches from the Army of the Potomac.* Boston: Houghton Mifflin, 1999.

Shavin, Norman. *The Atlanta Century: March, 1860–May, 1865.* Atlanta: Capricorn Corp., 1975.

Sherman, William T. *Memoirs of General William T. Sherman.* 2 vols. 2d ed. New York: D. A. Appleton and Co., 1886.

Sifakis, Stewart. *Who Was Who in the Civil War.* New York: Facts on File, 1988.

Southern Historical Society. *Southern Historical Society Papers.* 52 vols. 1876–1959. Reprint, Wilmington, N.C.: Broadfoot, 1992.

Speed, Thomas. *Who Fought the Battle: Strength of the Union and Confederate Forces Compared.* Louisville: F. G. Nunemacher, 1904.

Speer, Lonnie R. *Portals to Hell: Military Prisons of the Civil War.* Mechanicsburg, Pa.: Stackpole Books, 1997.

Thomas, Benjamin P. *Abraham Lincoln: A Biography.* New York: Knopf, 1952.

Thomas, Emory M. *Robert E. Lee: A Biography.* New York: Norton, 1995.

Tucker, Glenn. *Chickamauga: Bloody Battle in the West.* Indianapolis: Bobbs-Merrill, 1961.

———. *High Tide at Gettysburg: The Campaign in Pennsylvania.* Indianapolis: Bobbs-Merrill, 1958.

Turner, George E. *Victory Rode the Rails: The Strategic Place of the Railroads in the Civil War.* Indianapolis: Bobbs-Merrill, 1953.

The Union Army, 1861–65: A History of the Military Affairs in the Loyal States. 8 vols. Madison, Wisc.: Federal Publishing Co., 1908.

United States, Naval War Records Office. *Official Records of the Union and Confederate Navies in the War of the Rebellion.* 30 vols. Washington: Government Printing Office, 1894–1922.

United States, War Department. *The War of the Rebellion: A Compilation of the Official Records of the Union and Confederate Armies.* 128 vols. Washington, D.C.: Government Printing Office, 1880–1901.

Vandiver, Frank E. *Mighty Stonewall.* New York: McGraw-Hill, 1957.

Wall, Joseph F. *Andrew Carnegie.* 1970. Reprint, Pittsburgh: University of Pittsburgh Press, 1989.

Walraven, Bill, and Marjorie K. Walraven. *The Magnificent Barbarians: Little-Told Tales of the Texas Revolution.* Austin, Tex.: Eakin Press, 1993.

Warner, Ezra J. *Generals in Blue: Lives of the Union Commanders.* Baton Rouge: Louisiana State University Press, 1964.

———. *Generals in Gray: Lives of the Confederate Commanders.* Baton Rouge: Louisiana State University Press, 1959.

Wilcox, Arthur M., and Warren Ripley. *The Civil War at Charleston.* Charleston: Charleston News and Courier and Charleston Evening Post, 1966.

Wiley, Bell I. *The Common Soldier of the Civil War.* New York: Scribner, 1975.

Williams, T. Harry. *Lincoln and His Generals.* New York: Knopf, 1952.

———. *The History of American Wars from 1745 to 1918.* New York: Knopf, 1981.

Wills, Mary Alice. *The Confederate Blockade of Washington, D.C., 1861–1862.* Parsons, W.Va.: McClain Printing Co., 1975.

Wise, Stephen R. *Gate of Hell: Campaign for Charleston Harbor, 1863.* Columbia: University of South Carolina Press, 1994.

Wish, Harvey, ed. *Ante-Bellum Writings of George Fitzhugh and Hinton Rowan Helper on Slavery.* New York: Capricorn Books: 1960.

INDEX